Troubling Inheritances

Troubling Inheritances

Memory, Music, and Aging

Edited by
Sara Cohen, Line Grenier and Ros Jennings

BLOOMSBURY ACADEMIC
NEW YORK • LONDON • OXFORD • NEW DELHI • SYDNEY

BLOOMSBURY ACADEMIC
Bloomsbury Publishing Inc
1385 Broadway, New York, NY 10018, USA
50 Bedford Square, London, WC1B 3DP, UK
29 Earlsfort Terrace, Dublin 2, Ireland

BLOOMSBURY, BLOOMSBURY ACADEMIC and the Diana logo are trademarks of
Bloomsbury Publishing Plc

First published in the United States of America 2023
Copyright © Sara Cohen, Line Grenier, and Ros Jennings, 2023
Each chapter copyright by the contributor, 2023
This paperback edition published 2024

For legal purposes the Acknowledgments on p. vii constitute an
extension of this copyright page

Cover design: Antonia Hernández
Cover image © Antonia Hernández

All rights reserved. No part of this publication may be reproduced or transmitted in
any form or by any means, electronic or mechanical, including photocopying,
recording, or any information storage or retrieval system, without prior
permission in writing from the publishers.

Bloomsbury Publishing Inc does not have any control over, or responsibility for, any
third-party websites referred to or in this book. All internet addresses given in this
book were correct at the time of going to press. The author and publisher regret any
inconvenience caused if addresses have changed or sites have ceased to exist, but can
accept no responsibility for any such changes.

Library of Congress Cataloging-in-Publication Data
Names: Cohen, Sara, 1961– editor. | Jennings, Ros, editor. | Grenier, Line, editor.
Title: Troubling inheritances / edited by Sara Cohen, Line Grenier, and Ros Jennings.
Description: [1st.] | New York: Bloomsbury Academic, 2022. |
Includes bibliographical references and index. | Summary: "Explores the
relationship between music, memory, and ageing through a focus on
"inheritance tracks," with contributions from leading scholars of
popular music studies"–Provided by publisher.
Identifiers: LCCN 2021059510 (print) | LCCN 2021059511 (ebook) |
ISBN 9781501369506 (hardback) | ISBN 9781501369544 (paperback) |
ISBN 9781501369513 (epub) | ISBN 9781501369520 (pdf) | ISBN 9781501369537
Subjects: LCSH: Music and older people | Memory–Age factors. |
Music and intergenerational communication. | Music–Social aspects.
Classification: LCC ML3838 .T76 2022 (print) | LCC ML3838 (ebook) | DDC 781.1/1–dc23
LC record available at https://lccn.loc.gov/2021059510
LC ebook record available at https://lccn.loc.gov/2021059511

ISBN: HB: 978-1-5013-6950-6
PB: 978-1-5013-6954-4
ePDF: 978-1-5013-6952-0
eBook: 978-1-5013-6951-3

Typeset by Newgen KnowledgeWorks Pvt. Ltd., Chennai, India

To find out more about our authors and books visit www.bloomsbury.com
and sign up for our newsletters.

CONTENTS

Acknowledgments vii

Introduction 1

1 Reflections on Women and Musical Inheritances: Exploring the Musical Threads of Memory and Emotion 17
Ros Jennings

2 Inheritance Tracks, Shared Memories, and Collective Self-Therapy 43
Andy Bennett

3 Bordering Musical Inheritance: Navigating Borderscapes and Belonging through Memories of Finnish Childhoods 61
Helmi Järviluoma, Elina Hytönen-Ng, and Sonja Pöllänen

4 Storytelling and Disrupting Borders: A Sicilian Workshop 81
Abigail Gardner

5 Songs That Matter: Assessing through Trinidadian Storytellings the Power of Music, Memory, Age, and Aging 103
Jocelyne Guilbault

6 Collective Music Listening, Reminiscence, and the Tensions of Aging: Lessons from Two Workshops with Older Adults in Liverpool 129
Sara Cohen, Lisa Shaw, and Jacqueline Waldock

7 Journeys of Attachments, Trajectories of (Mis)fitting: Musicking in Deaf Communities in Montreal 161
Line Grenier and Véro Leduc

8 Sharing and Reflecting on Inheritance Tracks: Some Afterthoughts 197
Murray Forman

Author and Contributor Information 207
Index 211

ACKNOWLEDGMENTS

The editors would like to acknowledge the Social Sciences and Humanities Research, Canada (SSHRC), for supporting Ageing + Communication + Technologies: Experiencing Digital World in Later Life (ACT), an international research and partnership project that all three editors and most of our authors participated in. We would like to thank Kim Sawchuk and Constance Lafontaine of Concordia University, respectively director and associate director of ACT, for their financial and intellectual support, and Wendy Martin, who hosted the ACT conference where the editors and authors first met to discuss this book project.

We are indebted to Naomi Paul for her outstanding and meticulous editing work. Praised by the authors and extending well beyond changes in wording and style, this work undoubtedly helped to strengthen the book. So too has the striking cover design by Antonia Hernández incorporating the book's core themes of music and aging.

We appreciate everyone who participated in the workshops organized by the authors for the purposes of the book. It has been a privilege to work with participants who so willingly shared their songs, their memories, and their emotions with us and each other. Sharing is at the heart of this book, which has been a thoroughly collaborative project throughout, and a powerful emotional and cognitive roller coaster. To the authors who so generously joined us on this journey, we extend our sincere gratitude. We are touched by the confidence you showed in us, the time and energy you invested in the project, your wonderful camaraderie, and your willingness to embrace Inheritance Tracks as a method for exploring music, memory, and aging. We have learned much from your readiness to share ideas, friendship, intellectual curiosity, and peer critique, and the book is far richer for it.

Introduction

This book explores the complex relationships and interconnections between music, memory, and aging. Our work on it has been guided by three main objectives. The first is to provide an interdisciplinary and a much-needed innovative focus on music, memory, and aging, by examining how they intersect outside of a formal therapeutic context and by problematizing the familiar association of aging with decline. The second is to contribute to the development of qualitative research methodologies, by utilizing and reflecting on methods for studying music, memory, and aging across diverse and interconnected contexts. Our third objective is to "trouble" the book's core themes of music, memory, aging, inheritance, and also methodology.

These core aims and objectives, as with any research undertaking, were reexamined and finessed as the project rolled out and came to completion. Looking back, we should have realized that the initial encounters between the editors and contributors that took place at Brunel University, UK, and the University of Liverpool, UK, were portent of what was to come. Our meetings led to whiteboards covered with explosions of color as we used marker pens to share and map out our ideas for the book and how its content would be produced. We scoped out possible theoretical and methodological connections in order to structure the project that was ultimately set out in the book and is explained later. As initial findings were shared, the notion of "troubling," so central to the book's title, emerged as an important lens. It also became clear that what had originally been shared as a method and almost prescriptive set of guidelines to conduct the research for the book led to multiple reconfigurations of the process, depending on how they were interpreted and with whom the research was undertaken. The method morphed as it was rolled out, producing astonishingly different outcomes across the book's chapters, although each was still engaged with music, memory, aging, and inheritances.

Ultimately, this is a book about sharing—the sharing of ideas, friendship, intellectual curiosity, and peer critique between all the authors. It is also about the privilege of working with participants who generously shared their songs, their memories, and their emotions with us. This has been brought about by the ways in which the songs, which form the Inheritance Tracks of this project, bring things affectively into being to share with others. Since sharing is at the core of notions of inheritance or bequeathing, this seems apt for a project that has seen us embark on a powerful emotional and cognitive roller coaster, as we have engaged with our individual as well as shared project.

Inheritance and Inheritance Tracks

Inheritance Tracks as a Research Method

"Inheritance Tracks" is the method we have used to explore the relationship between music, memory, and aging. The inspiration for this method, and later for the book, came from one of the longest standing and most "common" and easily accessible music media, namely, radio. More specifically, it was based on a regular feature broadcast on British radio—BBC Radio 4's *Saturday Live* (2006–) "Inheritance Tracks" format of the prerecorded, five-minute segment of the weekly program. The segment features a special guest invited to talk about and play excerpts from their two Inheritance Tracks: a piece of music—a song or "track" that they have inherited and one that they would like to pass on to others: "Celebrating the music that special guests cherish and would like to bestow to future generations." The prerecorded segments are archived and can be downloaded from BBC online as podcasts and feature a wide range of public figures such as actors, music performers, artists, and also scientists and public intellectuals (https://www.bbc.co.uk/programmes/p02p8zrg/episodes/downloads). For example, three of those who have shared their Inheritance Tracks as part of *Saturday Live* are performer/artist/writer Patti Smith (Saturday, January 9, 2016), who inherited Artie Shaw's track "Nightmare," and wished to pass on Neil Young's "After the Gold Rush"; actor Sir Michael Caine (Saturday, June 22, 2019), who had inherited "My Old Man's a Dustman" by Lonnie Donegan and wished to pass on "Comme d'habitude" by Claude François; and former Miss World and now actress Priyanka Chopra Jonas (Saturday, February 13, 2021), who had inherited "Desi Girl" by Shankar Mahadevan and wished to pass on "The First Time Ever I Saw Your Face" by Roberta Flack. In all of the podcasts, the listener hears the music together with a self-reflexive explanation about the connections to the past that the tracks they chose engendered.

In 2015, Ros Jennings started to explore "Inheritance Tracks" as a method to investigate relationships between music, memory, and aging. Working with members of a small group of the Growing Old Disgracefully network in the UK, and then via workshops that she delivered at the University of Hamburg in Germany and the University of Montreal in Canada, the idea of "Inheritance Tracks" was further developed as a method. It was then shared, rolled out, and further developed by colleagues who had started working together on aging and popular music as part of the Critical Mediations research stream of the Ageing + Communication + Technology (ACT) partnership. Funded by the Social Sciences and Humanities Research Council of Canada (SSHRC)—see actproject.ca—the aim of the partnership was to support research whose goal was to better understand the transformations of the experiences of aging in the digital era and times of intense mediatization.

When the method was first used in 2015, Ros Jennings had conceived of it as a research method located in the mundaneness and everydayness of recognizable media/radio practices that used music to generate narratives drawing on memory for people (usually celebrities) to talk about themselves and their lives. In the British context, there were many well-known and enduring radio formats that used music in this way such as the "Tracks of My Years," a feature on BBC Radio 2's *Ken Bruce Show* since 1998, and BBC Radio 4's *Desert Island Discs*, which has been on air since 1942. The latter has, over its eighty years, embedded itself not only in British popular culture but also in the British imaginary, as a way to think about meaningful musical choices—that is, what songs would you take to a deserted island if you were to be stranded there on your own? The currency of popular radio formats in British culture is evidenced by the fact that, as discussed in Chapter 1, when "Inheritance Tracks" was first repurposed to become a research method by Ros Jennings, with a group of older women who belonged to a regional Growing Old Disgracefully group, the women had actually already used the technique themselves as a means to share and get to know each other better. As a format, it was also manifestly accessible as a research method and was to prove so beyond a UK context, as it was adopted by colleagues working together in the popular music stream of ACT.

Line Grenier was the first member of the ACT partnership to undertake research using the Inheritance Tracks method. She had seen the method in operation firsthand when Ros had run a workshop with a group of Line's undergraduate students at the University of Montreal. As Line began to pursue the method, she was less interested in the biographical or autobiographical lines of questioning in relation to memory work that were integral to Ros's autoethnographic approaches to research. Her interest was more toward exploring "memory work" akin to Annette Kuhn's notion of "call[ing] to mind the collective nature of the activity of remembering" as it connects "public historical events, structures of feeling, family drama, relations of class, national identity, and gender, and 'personal' memory" (2002: 5). This, together with the idea of "memory making" (*faire-mémoire*) (Valois-Nadeau 2014) where music generates a site/space of "ageing together" (Katz 2009; Grenier 2012), shaped Line's approach. Ongoing discussions followed between Ros and Line on their experiences of conducting Inheritance Tracks research. It was evident to both that the method's flexibility in relation to context made it productive. It lent itself to being used in different ways by different people, as a research method employed to examine connections between music, aging, and memory. The method was slowly passed on and tried out by other colleagues in and beyond the ACT partnership, creating a corpus of ideas and data that fed into this book and also into the Critical Mediations stream of ACT research. At the same time, as will be discussed in more detail later in this introduction, several ACT colleagues who were undertaking Inheritance Tracks research (namely, the three editors of this book plus Helmi Järviluoma) were also involved in contributing to *A Senior Moment: Cultural Mediations of Memory and Ageing* (Grenier and Valois-Nadeau 2020), leading to further exchange discussion about methods and the role of music as a powerful cultural mediator of memory and aging.

The first formal stage of bringing this book to fruition was a workshop that took place as part of the annual ACT symposium in 2018 at Brunel University, UK. At this event, the method was shared with the researchers who wished to learn more about it both as a concept and as a set of developing practices. The majority of the people in the workshop were keen to contribute to this publication and eager to carry out their own Inheritance Tracks research in relation to research contexts that were of interest to them. Armed with a set of examples and guidelines, the contributors embarked on projects that were conducted in Australia, Canada, Finland, the United States, Sicily, and the UK. Deployed across these diverse research contexts what at first seems a simple format revealed a combination of different techniques (storytelling, focus group discussion, collective listening and memoryscaping, testimonies, sound/music-elicitation) in a dispositif that through practice and reflection we found was able to orientate and guide but not restrict and constrain. As the chapters that follow will demonstrate in their distinctive ways, its open and performative nature makes Inheritance Tracks a remarkably adaptable method.

This is the spirit in which we have engaged with it: method as improvisation/journey/dialogue. We have tried to be flexible about using it—not only open to different approaches from our fellow researchers but also open to where it might lead us—going along with the flow (bottom up) and adapting accordingly. As the chapters will illustrate, it is a method that works like a sponge, absorbing elements of connection and spitting them out. The method has an agency of its own that engages distinctively with diverse participants in diverse contexts.

Inheritance

As indicated earlier, using "Inheritance Tracks" as a method has opened up various lines of questioning. First and foremost, it has raised questions about understandings and definitions of what Inheritance Tracks might be (especially in terms of the phrase's linguistic meaning across the various languages of the studies featured in this book) and of the term "inheritance" more generally.

For example, when Line started using the Inheritance Tracks method, she had to translate the term "Inheritance Tracks" for French-speaking research participants in Montreal, Canada. Equally, Helmi and her coresearchers, Hytönen-Ng and Sonja Pöllänen, had to translate the concept into Finnish. In French, the word "tracks" was problematic, and the French term *pistes* was both too specialized (relating to the semantic field of sound recording) and too narrowly associated with eight-track cartridges/cassettes. In the same vein, even referring to "songs" proved to be too restrictive for certain participants as for ome of their inherited music consisted of classical music pieces or film soundtracks. Helmi and her research team decided to translate "tracks" into Finnish using the word *musiikkiraita*, meaning literally "music track." *Raita*, which also means "stripe," or "thread," and originated from the notion of "groove" (*ura* in Finnish), is associated with the word *ääniraita*, meaning "soundtrack." The word *musiikkiraita* is not as widely used but nevertheless perfectly understandable for the purposes of the research at hand.

As it quickly became clear in the study overall, notions of "inheritance" can vary, and questions of language are pivotal to the possible understandings of the term. In Finnish, "inheritance" is more easily translated as *peritty*, meaning both material and immaterial things that are inherited from someone or somewhere. The notion of inheritance conveyed by the word *peritty* is rather different from conventional understandings of "inheritance" in Australia, (English) Canada, and England. In the Finnish context, inheritance is associated in everyday discourse with material things that are passed on (more often than not) after someone dies and less often with immaterial concepts. It is also associated with money and legal issues and with things passed on within families and from one generation to the next. In French, there are two words, *héritage* and *patrimoine*, which are used to cover the concepts of inheritance. *Héritage* has etymological roots in Latin ideas of "blood" and places stress on things inherited genetically/through blood from our ancestors such as physical and/or personality traits as well as the passing on of cultural traditions and know-how (Bourdieu and Passeron 1979). Importantly, *héritage* usually signifies a relationship or a link over time through blood. *Patrimoine*, on the other hand, refers to possessions/material things that are usually passed on/bequeathed after the death of a family member, forging a link within families and from one generation to the next and thus explicitly linking *héritage* and *patrimoine*. In Finnish and French, therefore, ideas of inheritance are conveyed with specific words that signify differences and nuances in meaning, while in English, the meanings are collapsed into one word leaving precise meanings open to interpretation. As such, notions of inheritance, as central to the Inheritance Tracks method and the aims of this collection, open up a rich area of debate and discussion related to ideas of culture, materiality, the ephemeral, and passing on. This includes debates and discussions concerning bequeathing, families, and generation, to name but a few of the themes that emerged.

Troubling Inheritance

This book troubles such conventional understandings of inheritance, because the Inheritance Tracks workshop we ran showed that tracks, pieces of music, or songs are not necessarily passed on as material things and that this passing on was not always undertaken by blood relatives and did not necessarily happen within the context of the family or across generations. Moreover, inheritance was not readily associated with death and notions of legally bequeathing money or property.

As the chapters progress, this book explores meanings of inheritance in diverse contexts, each one troubling conventional understandings of inheritance. The chapters consider: Who is inheriting what music, from whom, and why? What music is being passed on, to whom, and why? Is this inheritance positive or negative; is it voluntary or involuntary? What is inherited through music? If inheritance is about the act of passing on (and linking), then what connections (and relationships) does this establish across time and space? In this way, inheritance moves from the singular to the plural, making the purview of the book a matter of troubling inheritances.

Inheritance as Process

The different inheritances discussed in this book imply process. They involve the work of paying attention, sorting, and selecting "the complex and contradictory nature of the stories that we are encouraged to live" (Biggs 2001: 303), including engaging with the mundane, extraordinary, painful, and often "toxic" narratives of inheritance passed down through families (Goodall 2001). It also includes acts of re-storying (Henson 2017) and reconstituting, for as Karine Bellerive (2021: 133) states, inheritances are materials that we work with to "(re)constitute our personal and family histories, to tell each other these stories, to repeat these stories without them ever being the same, exact replicas" (our translation).

Underpinning this is also a process of valorization in that what is transmitted matters and has value, whether for a person, a group, or an organization. This valorization might also be bound up, as is the case in several Inheritance Tracks included in this book, with transmission from people (not necessarily family members) who matter or mattered to those who inherit. Inheritance brings to the fore the tensions between inheritance as becoming and inheritance as social reproduction. From a Derridean perspective, inheritance is task, something that is unfinished and that we need to reopen differently to keep it alive (Derrida and Roudinesco 2001), whereas from a Bourdieusian perspective, inheritance is a form or mechanism of social reproduction (Bourdieu 2006). These tensions play out in the chapters of this book whether it is the music that people liked in their teens that they then pass on in the vein of Bourdieu or in the vein of Derrida, by reworking the past and opening up new futures through the re-storying of the narratives that were shared.

But this book also does more, because what started with an ostensibly simple and accessible method to conduct research proceeded to cascade and multiply like the colors on the whiteboard in our meetings at Brunel and Liverpool universities. What actually happened in our collective examination of the inheritances was that a process or, perhaps more accurately, an unexpected eruption of diffraction, became evident. What is important here, as Donna Haraway (1992: 300) points out, is that a diffraction pattern "does not map where differences appear, but rather map where the effects of difference appear." And it is these differences in the notion and form of inheritance that trouble this book as they intersect with our core themes of aging, music, and memory. Looking across the chapters, therefore, we can ask what is being reproduced and what is being transformed by the notion of inheritances being troubled and pivotal to this is the diffracted nature of what is produced, thus aligning with Karen Barad's (2007: 72) idea of diffraction as "patterns of difference that make a difference."

So far, we have discussed the core theme of "inheritance" and explained our use of "Inheritance Tracks" as a methodology to investigate the intersections of music, memory, and aging. We have also mentioned that much of the groundwork for this book was undertaken for another edited collection, *A Senior Moment* (Grenier and Valois-Nadeau 2020). *A Senior Moment* addresses issues of aging and memory and includes several chapters focusing on music. With *Troubling Inheritances*, however, music becomes more central and is examined alongside, and through its intersection with, memory and aging. Together, music, memory, and aging provide three additional core themes that the book's chapters trouble or at least question and explore. As with inheritance, we approach each of them as a social practice and process.

Aging

In Western societies, human aging is commonly understood as a process that is biological and universal. It is typically associated with the transformation of bodies and minds and with "phases of growth (valued) and decay (denigrated)" (Grenier and Valois-Nadeau 2020: 10). While people "grow older," "aging" has become associated with the deterioration of people's physical health and cognitive abilities. For aging studies scholar Margaret Gullette, in contemporary society, "ageing equals decline" (Gullette 2004: 7). She points to the ageist attitudes that inform this narrative of decline and the demonization of aging-past-youth (8). Old age has become stereotyped as a negative process connected to loss and disease, with older adults increasingly portrayed through negative media images tending to represent them as frail, dependent, and deteriorating (Bugental and Hehman 2007; Ng et al. 2015).

This is not a book about old age, but it does concern aging. It developed from discussions among ACT members who have been involved in research on music across various disciplinary fields (cultural studies, anthropology, communication and media studies, ethnomusicology, age studies) and who share a concern with the narrative of aging as decline. In seeking to counter this narrative, we build on the work of scholars who have studied aging as a process that is social and cultural, as well as biological. Examples include the pioneering work of social anthropologists such as Margaret Clark (1967), Sharon Kaufman (1986), and Barbara Myerhoff (1992) and of the contributors (some of them ACT members) to the interdisciplinary *Routledge Handbook of Cultural Gerontology* (Twigg and Martin 2015). We do not mean to deny or diminish the discomfort and anxiety that can accompany aging; indeed, one of the book's chapters makes these explicit. Rather, we want to move beyond the limitations of scholarship that investigates aging only in relation to issues of health and well-being and that adopts neuroscientific, biomedical, and therapeutic approaches to examine the relationship between music and aging and between music and memory. These issues and approaches are dominant in aging studies, and while we recognize the importance of this work (Edwards 2011; MacDonald, Kreutz, and Mitchell 2012; Creech et al. 2013; Ferreri et al. 2019; Gouk et al. 2019), it leaves other issues and perspectives unstudied, rendering them invisible.

Also countering the decline narrative are notions of "healthy aging," "successful aging," and "active aging" and the interventionist policies that accompany them. In response to the aging of the world's population, for example, the World Health Organization (WHO) launched a global strategy and action plan to promote healthy aging (WHO 2016), and the United Nations and European Commission launched the 2018 Active Ageing Index to understand and monitor national progress in supporting quality of life and active participation of older adults (UNECE/European Commission 2019). As argued by the aging studies scholar Stephen Katz (2000), initiatives like these raise questions about the various power relations informing processes of aging and highlight the ideal of activity in the political context of a neoliberal "active society." Moreover, they render individuals responsible for their own aging, leaving aside the conjunctural elements and structural inequalities that shape life course trajectories.

There are, therefore, two broadly contradictory media images of aging that circulate widely in contemporary Western societies (Marshall 2015). On the one hand, there are the images of aging as decline. On the other hand, there are the more positive images of active seniors, portrayed as increasingly "health-conscious, fit, sexy and adventurous consumers, who take good care of themselves and control a significant proportion of disposable income" (Marshall 2015: 210). These contradictory images illustrate a normative aging that does not do justice to the heterogeneity of aging experiences and of cultures of aging. What emerges from the pages of this book is an alternative view of aging that is not about individuals but about social relations. Through the sharing of Inheritance Tracks and musical memories, aging also appears as a complex, multifarious process that is lived, performed, experienced, and represented differently, according to class, gender, sexuality, ability, race, and ethnicity, among other sites of differences.

Memory

Like aging, memory is a social and temporal process, and by putting memory together with aging, the edited collection *A Senior Moment* provides a better understanding of their complex entanglements. This enables it to challenge the widely held view, inspired by biomedical discourse, that memory is a personal reservoir, whose size, content, and accuracy are dependent on the aging process: "either lost or becoming faulty due to the physiological aging of the body that carries it, or on the contrary thickened and enriched thanks to accumulated lived experiences and the care taken to prolong its proper functioning" (Grenier and Valois-Nadeau 2020: 10). The book's title hijacks the expression "a senior moment," which tends to make fun of older adults' moments of forgetfulness or confusion attributed to age. Memory, the book's editors argue, cannot be reduced to some universal human faculty or to the mere content stored in one's brain (13).

Following on from *A Senior Moment*, this book approaches memory as a multifarious and heterogeneous, situated, and mediated practice. The groups participating in the Inheritance Tracks workshops the book discusses engaged in "memory work," "memory acts," "technè of memory," and "memory making." Some of the chapters illustrate quite starkly the efforts involved with this memory work and how it implies forgetting as much as remembering. Several chapters provide vivid examples of how affective remembering can be, particularly when connected with music, and a reminder that memory is an embodied as well as a cognitive process (van Dijck 2007). Remembering takes people on journeys that traverse through points of connection and encounter that can bring moments of sadness or joy, epiphany or despair. It is embedded not only in the everyday but also in social-cultural frameworks that define what is appropriate to remember and how to remember it. Through its focus on Inheritance Tracks, the book shows that remembering is rife with power relations and that when connected with aging, memory is not only about loss and nostalgia but also about "the value given to the past in the present and for the future" (Grenier and Valois-Nadeau 2020: 12).

Music

Music offers a richly productive focus for examining how aging and memory are made and interconnected in singular ways, for particular people, in particular situations and circumstances. The contributors to this book have an interest in popular music, and the book's Inheritance Tracks theme and methodology were inspired by a popular BBC radio program. Most of us know each other not only through ACT but also through our long-standing involvement with the International Association for the Study of Popular Music. Moreover, popular songs accounted for almost all the Inheritance Tracks chosen by individuals participating in the workshops we ran. Often, they were songs that other workshop participants were also familiar with, encouraging a sharing of memory and experience and even collective singing and dancing. Music is a participatory, everyday practice that a wide range of people engage with, though in many diverse ways and in different contexts. Arguing that music is a practice rather than a thing, the ethnomusicologist Christopher Small (1998) introduced the verb "musicking" and applied it to all aspects of music performance, whether performing live or rehearsing, listening to Muzak in an elevator, selling tickets for a performance, or cleaning up after the audience has gone. The term could likewise be applied to the practices discussed in this book, such as listening to, remembering, and talking about music.

As an everyday practice, music is embedded in experience across the life course, providing so many individuals with a "lifetime soundtrack" (Istvandity 2019). People therefore age with music, albeit in different ways, and music provides a resource for autobiographical remembering. Consequently, life stories can be constructed through music, as illustrated by another well-known BBC Radio 4 program, *Desert Island Discs* (Brown, Cook, and Cottrell 2017). Moreover, music enables people to travel both back and forth in time, providing them with a vehicle not only for remembering but also for expressing their hopes, dreams, and fears for the future. This was clear from the Inheritance Tracks workshops discussed in this book, and the collective listening to music at these workshops made the affective and corporeal nature of music experience strikingly visible. Clearly, music matters to people albeit in different ways, and due to the affective alliances it produces and performs, the cultural studies scholar Lawrence Grossberg refers to music as a "mattering map" (1992: 57). Music offers people a meaningful map through which they can locate themselves in connection with people, times, spaces, places, practices, technologies, etc. Building on Antoine Hennion's sociologically informed notion of "mediation" (2012), the anthropologist and musicologist Georgina Born argues that music is "never singular, but always a multiplicity; it exists only in and through its multiple and changing mediations" (2005: 89). Through its focus on Inheritance Tracks, the book explores the multiplicity of mediations of music and, in their wake, the entangled practices and experiences of memory and aging that they embody, perform, and materialize.

By putting music together with memory and aging, this book shows how difficult it is to separate these three core themes, and how interconnected they are. Moreover, putting them together has both reflected and produced a diversity of experiences and ideas concerning aging, remembering, and musicking. Much of the scholarship that examines music in relation to aging and memory is informed by biomedical approaches and by instrumental, interventionist approaches to music as therapy, memory prompt, or device for regulating movement and behavior. Yet for those participating in the Inheritance Tracks workshops, music does and means many different things, and is lived, experienced, and imagined in many different ways. Music offers, we argue, ways of being and becoming attuned to differences and to "how differences are created in the world and what effects they have on subjects and their bodies" (Geerts and van der Tuin 2016). It maps patterns and effects of differences, refracting differences, making differences visible, and enabling them to be recognized and worked through.

In fact, having begun our collaborative work on this book with a blueprint for a specific methodology that each of the contributing authors adhered to, we became fascinated with the kinds of differences that emerged as this methodology was put into practice and became adapted and repurposed. The method is important, we argue, because of the differences, as well as potential mutualities, that it generates.

Structure and Content

The seven core chapters of the book differ in various respects, although each is based on the Inheritance Tracks research and method, and each engages with the book's core themes of music, memory, and aging. For a start, the chapters explore music, memory, and aging in relation to diverse musical styles, geographical locations, and social groups. Among the latter are Deaf adults in Montreal, Trinidadian immigrants in Miami, university staff and students in Brisbane, and older adults in Eastern Finland and in Liverpool care centers. Moreover, while the Inheritance Tracks selected by members of these groups largely involve popular music, defined in its broadest sense, they include those connected to the diverse worlds of rock, pop, folk, soca, dance, and popular classical music. The chapters are also informed by different disciplines, including musicology, ethnomusicology, sociology and anthropology, media and communication studies, and cultural and aging studies.

Further differences and similarities emerge when considering what happened at the Inheritance Tracks workshops these chapters discuss and as each author examined the intersections between music, memory, and aging.

In Chapter 1, Ros Jennings reflects on the music inheritances of the groups of women she worked with, and deploys the notion of "musical contagion" to make sense of what happened at the workshops in which she was involved. She uses this notion to discuss how music travels across and through time and space, producing instances of affect that engender emotional connectivities. The relationship between music and affect also provides a focus for Chapter 2 by Andy Bennett. This time, the notion of "soothing sociality" is developed to account for the sharing of musical memories that happened as Inheritance Tracks were discussed by a group of colleagues at the University of Brisbane. This sharing, Bennett argues, generated common feelings and emotions, as well as environments of empathy and trust, in ways that potentially work as a form of collective self-therapy.

While affect also plays an important part in the events discussed in Chapters 3 and 4, the focus of these two chapters is on bordering. Helmi Järviluoma, Elina Hytönen-Ng, and Sonja Pöllänen (Chapter 3) examine the various borders and borderscapes that were revealed, through narration, by layers of emotionally laden musical remembering. As a group of older adults discussed their Inheritance Tracks at a town hall library in Eastern Finland, their remembering established, confirmed, and challenged the various social, spatial, and temporal distinctions through which everyday life is negotiated, including those of age and generation. The concept of bordering is used to make sense of the complexities of this musical remembering and how it creates a "belonging-in-between." In Chapter 4, Abigail Gardner shows how the Inheritance Tracks selected by a group of nongovernmental organizations (NGOs) in Palermo prompted a storytelling that revealed the contingency of borders, especially those of the affective self, and of place and time—of what belongs where. The chapter tells a story about the "song worlds" that emerged through this process, a phrase used to refer to the interplay between a song and its role, which occurs at a particular moment in a participant's life (or relationship to a particular person) and the worlds that are shared by a group of people who come together in a particular space and at a particular moment in time.

Chapter 5 by Jocelyne Guilbault is, like the previous chapter, also about "song worlds," in that it describes the distinct worlding that songs conjure up and how this triggers memory. The songs it focuses on are related to soca, a style of party music from Trinidad and Tobago, and were selected as Inheritance Tracks by a group of Afro-Trinidadian professionals living in Miami. Guilbault explains how the entanglements between the personal experiences and "collective frames of listening and appreciation" become "remarkably audible" as the group members share party songs that matter to them.

The two remaining chapters of the book examine interconnections between music, memory, and aging, by discussing Inheritance Tracks workshops that illustrated the participants' complex, challenging, and changeable relationships with music. These workshops trouble taken-for-granted assumptions about how people engage with music and their "natural" and always beneficial connection with it. In Chapter 6, Sara Cohen, Lisa Shaw, and Jacqueline Waldock discuss the Inheritance Tracks selected by older adults at two Liverpool community care centers and the embodied selfhood that surfaces as remembering extends beyond words. They consider tensions this raises between losses and gains, freedoms and constraints, agency and restricted engagements. In Chapter 7, Line Grenier and Véro Leduc use the notion of (mis)fitting to examine the musical remembering of Deaf adults in Montreal. They consider the stories of Deaf aging that emerge through this process and what they reveal about how Deaf adults experience aural and audist understandings of music. Tracing the trajectories of (mis)fitting involved, they build an argument concerning inheritance as orientation.

The final chapter of this book is a contribution by Murray Forman. He had been a part of the initial planning and developmental thinking between the editors and contributors that took place at Brunel University, UK, in 2018. For various reasons Murray did not get the chance to run his own workshop as a basis for his involvement in the book, but all three editors felt strongly that the book would benefit from his research expertise in relation to music and the experiences of older people. In particular, his seminal 2012 study "How We Feel the Music: Popular Music by Elders and for Elders" had been an important influence on all three of us and our own thinking as scholars of music and aging. We were therefore keen to involve him in the book. As someone privy to the backstory of its development and creation, we wanted him to engage with the completed chapters and tease out what he considered to be the most salient themes, thus adding depth to the collection as a whole and an alternative emphasis to the book's main material. Looking across the seven chapters, he has highlighted key issues such as "sharing," "embodiment and location," and "affect" that came to the fore in his own detailed readings of each contributor's work and across the book as a whole.

References

Barad, Karen. 2007. *Meeting the Universe Halfway: Quantum Physics and the Entanglement of Matter and Meaning*. Durham, NC: Duke University Press.

Bellerive, Karine. 2021. "Écrire les vieillissements: une recherche-création." PhD Communication Studies, Université de Montréal.

Biggs, Simon. 2001. "Toward Critical Narrativity: Stories of Aging in Contemporary Social Policy." *Journal of Aging Studies*, 15(4): 303–16.

Born, Georgina. 2005. "On Musical Mediation: Ontology, Technology and Creativity." *Twentieth Century Music*, 2: 7–36.

Bourdieu, Pierre. 2006. "Cultural Reproduction and Social Reproduction." In David B. Grusky and Szonja Szelényi (eds.), *Inequality: Classic Readings in Race, Class, and Gender*, 257–71. Boulder, CO: Westview Press.

Bourdieu, Pierre, and Jean-Claude Passeron. 1979. *The Inheritors: French Students and Their Relation to Culture*. Chicago: University of Chicago Press.

Brown, Julie, Nicholas Cook, and Stephen Cottrell. 2017. *Defining the Discographic Self: Desert Island Discs in Context*. Oxford: Oxford University Press.

Bugental, Daphne B., and Jessica A. Hehman. 2007. "Ageism: A Review of Research and Policy Implications." *Social Issues and Policy Review*, 1(1): 173–216.

Clark, Margaret. 1967. "The Anthropology of Aging: A New Era for Studies of Culture and Personality." *The Gerontologist*, 7: 55–64.

Creech, Andrea, Susan Hallam, Helena McQueen, and Maria Varvarigou. 2013. "The Power of Music in the Lives of Older Adults." *Research Studies in Music Education*, 35(1): 87–102.

Derrida, Jacques, and Elisabeth Roudinesco. 2001. *De quoi demain …: Dialogue*. Fayard: Galilée.

Edwards, Jane. 2011. "A Music and Health Perspective on Music's Perceived 'Goodness.' " *Nordic Journal of Music Therapy*, 20: 90–101.

Ferreri, Laura, Aline Moussard, Emmanuel Bigand, and Barbara Tillmann. 2019. "Music and the Aging Brain." In Michael. H. Thaut and Donald. A. Hodges (eds.), *The Oxford Handbook of Music and the Brain*, 623–44. Oxford: Oxford University Press.

Forman, Murray. 2012. "How We Feel the Music: Popular Music by Elders and for Elders." *Popular Music*, 31(2): 245–60.

Geerts, Evelien, and Iris van der Tuin. 2016. "Diffraction & Reading Diffractively." New Materialism Almanac. July 27. https://newmaterialism.eu/almanac/d/diffraction.html.

Goodall, Harry A., Jr. 2001. "Narrative Inheritance: A Nuclear Family with Toxic Secrets." *Qualitative Inquiry*, 11(4): 492–513.

Gouk, Penelope, James G. Kennaway, Jacomien Prins, and Wiebke Thormahlen (eds.). 2019. *The Routledge Companion to Music, Mind and Well-Being*. New York: Routledge.

Grenier, Line. 2012. "Ageing and/as Enduring : A Discussion with Turtles [That] Do Not Die of Old Age." TEM 2012: First Conference Proceedings of the CCA Technology and Emerging Media Track. http://www.tem.fl.ulaval.ca/www/wp-content/PDF/Waterloo_2012/GRENIER-TEM2012.pdf.

Grenier, Line, and Fannie Valois-Nadeau. 2020. "Introduction." In Line Grenier and Fannie Valois-Nadeau (eds.), *A Senior Moment: Cultural Mediations of Memory and Ageing*, 7–31. Bielefeld, Germany: Transcript Verlag.

Grossberg, Lawrence. 1992. "Is There a Fan in the House? The Affective Sensibility of Fandom." In Lisa A. Lewis (ed.), *The Adoring Audience: Fan Culture and Popular Media*, 50–68. New York: Routledge.

Gullette, Margaret M. 2004. *Aged by Culture*. Chicago: University of Chicago Press.

Haraway, Donna. 1992. "The Promises of Monsters: A Regenerative Politics for Inappropriate/d Others." In *Cultural Studies*, edited by Lawrence Grossberg, Cary Nelson, and Paula Treichler, 295–337. New York: Routledge.

Hennion, Antoine. [2003] 2012. "Music and Mediation: Towards a New Sociology of Music." In M. Clayton, T. Herbert, and R. Middleton (eds.), *The Cultural Study of Music: A Critical Introduction*, 249–60. London: Routledge.
Henson, Donna F. 2017. "Fragments and Fictions: An Autoethnography of Past and Possibility." *Qualitative Inquiry*, 23(3): 222–4.
Istvandity, Lauren. 2019. *The Lifetime Soundtrack: Music and Autobiographical Memory*. Sheffield: Equinox.
Katz, Stephen. 2000. "Busy Bodies: Activity, Aging, and the Management of Everyday Life." *Journal of Aging Studies*, 14(2): 135–52.
Katz, Stephen. 2009. *Cultural Aging: Life Course, Lifestyle, and Senior Worlds*. 2nd ed. Toronto: University of Toronto Press.
Kaufman, Sharon. 1986. *The Ageless Self: Sources of Meaning in Late Life*. Madison: University of Wisconsin Press.
Kuhn, Annette. 2002. *Family Secrets: Acts of Memory and Imagination*. London: Verso.
MacDonald, Raymond, Gunter Kreutz, and Laura Mitchell. 2012. *Music, Health, and Wellbeing*. Oxford: Oxford University Press.
Marshall, Barbara A. 2015. "Anti-Ageing and Identities." In Julia Twigg and Wendy Martin (eds.), *Routledge Handbook of Cultural Gerontology*, 210–17. Abingdon: Routledge.
Myerhoff, Barbara. 1992. *Remembered Lives: The Work of Ritual, Storytelling, and Growing Older*. Ann Arbor: University of Michigan.
Ng, Reuben, Heather G. Allore, Mark Trentalange, Joan K. Monin, and Becca R. Levy. 2015. "Increasing Negativity of Age Stereotypes across 200 Years: Evidence from a Database of 400 Million Words." *PLoS One*, 10(2): e0117086. DOI: 10.1371/journal.pone.0117086. PMID: 25675438; PMCID: PMC4326131. https://pubmed.ncbi.nlm.nih.gov/25675438/.
Small, Christopher. 1998. *Musicking: The Meanings of Performing and Listening*. Middletown, CT: Wesleyan University Press.
Twigg, Julia, and Wendy Martin (eds.). 2015. *Routledge Handbook of Cultural Gerontology*. Abingdon: Routledge.
UNECE/European Commission. 2019. "2018 Active Ageing Index: Analytical Report." Report prepared by Giovanni Lamura and Andrea Principi under contract with the United Nations Economic Commission for Europe (Geneva), co-funded by the European Commission's Directorate General for Employment, Social Affairs and Inclusion (Brussels). https://unece.org/fileadmin/DAM/pau/age/Active_Ageing_Index/Stakeholder_Meeting/ACTIVE_AGEING_INDEX_TRENDS_2008-2016_web_cover_reduced.pdf.
Valois-Nadeau, Fannie. 2014. "Un Centenaire, des Faire Mémoire. Analyse des pratiques de mémoire autour du Canadien de Montréal." Unpublished doctoral dissertation, Université de Montréal.
van Dijck, José. 2007. *Mediated Memories in the Digital Age*. Stanford, CA: Stanford University Press.
World Health Organization. 2016. "Global Strategy and Action Plan on Ageing and Health 2016–2020: Towards a World in Which Everyone Can Live a Long and Healthy Life." https://apps.who.int/iris/handle/10665/252783.

1

Reflections on Women and Musical Inheritances: Exploring the Musical Threads of Memory and Emotion

Ros Jennings

Introduction

In producing this chapter, I am attempting to synthesize some of my ongoing deliberations and reflections on research I have conducted using the method called Inheritance Tracks. These deliberations center on debates I have had in my own head, in my personal research journals, and in conversations with participants and colleagues, especially those collaborating on this book. They have taken place during approximately ten years of pursuing research into understandings of musical inheritances and their relationships with the spatiotemporal intricacies of memory and aging. As a result, I bring a combination of personal, theoretical, and experiential baggage to the endeavor. After a lengthy distillation of thinking, the research story I present here is laced through with theoretical and experiential connectivities developed during a number of projects, including several Inheritance Tracks workshops and a conceptually linked but differently oriented research publication on the "Soundtrack of My Life" (Jennings 2020). This chapter incorporates solicited and unsolicited moments of reminiscence from me and from research participants. Because they are activated in relation to music chosen as an "inherited track" from someone or somewhere, and because they are also discussed in a shared space, these reminiscences are also shot through with Kathleen Woodward's (1997) notion of social companionship where in the act of sharing, the meanings take on heightened significance. Although they do not engage with the concept of inheritance, Carol Krumhansl and Justin Zupnik (2013) use the idea of "reminiscence bumps," arguing that, in the relationship between autobiographical memories and music, there are periods of intense association (childhood and early adulthood) that provide rich musical memory resources to connect with in terms of autobiography. They also suggest that "music-evoked autobiographical memories may be distributed differently over the life span than other kinds of autobiographical memories are" (Krumhansl and Zupnik 2013: 2058). They emphasize memory making related to music that was encountered within familial contexts, though I would argue that other social contexts in early life are also meaningful in facilitating processes of musical cultural transmission. These transmissions take place over time, with the music providing coordinates that intersect with the life course, corresponding with Krumhansl and Zupnik's (2013) notion of "reminiscence bumps." In so doing, they form connections between music and memories that cascade over time and space.

As an academic who specializes in feminist approaches to research, I am particularly oriented toward the experiences of women, and this emerged strongly in the process of deciding on the focus of this chapter. In addition, as someone who frequently draws on autoethnographic methods in their research (Jennings 2012, 2019b), I am acutely aware that I am not a dispassionate observer in the research that I undertake; I am in the research, and that requires me to adopt self-reflexive processes as part of what I do. Underpinned by a process of self-reflexive practices, autoethnography is open to recognizing and engaging with the emotions produced in the research process (Grist and Jennings 2020); these emotions are seen to contribute to the richness and authenticity of what is produced. I have come to learn that research focusing on inheritances that are linked through music, memory, and aging operates in multimodal TimeSpaces,[1] which link and weave, intensify and lessen. TimeSpaces can be deeply suffused by emotions—emotions that, as I will go on to discuss, have "special powers" to "trouble" research processes and meanings. As an autoethnographer, part of my method is to keep ongoing journals about the research I am involved with, in which I reflect on the processes, experiences, and feelings involved. Taking this approach to research positions me in what Ruth Behar (1996) describes as "an intermediate space we can't quite define yet, a borderland between passion and intellect, analysis and subjectivity, ethnography and autobiography, art and life" (174). This is a shifting terrain that has evolved and continues to evolve since I first set out on my journey to conduct research using Inheritance Tracks methods.

What follows is an attempt to pin down some of the key issues and reflections that have emerged by exploring three very different occasions when Inheritance Tracks methods were employed with groups of women. As I looked through my notes and related research artifacts for these three separate occasions (transcripts, playlists, etc.), it became clear that many dimensions involved in the women's relation to culture and music either were not revealed or were not revealed to the same extent in other events I had facilitated (that were not women-only). Differences in the focus and the research practices employed during the three occasions form the terrain of this chapter. Nevertheless, the musical threads that were in each research situation provoked some strong emotional connectivities in the rooms where we were together but created different atmospheres. In particular, issues pertaining to women and cultural agism, generation, and intergenerational relations emerged, as well as a shared feeling that men were dominant in both the domestic and the public spheres in relation to music and the power to "pronounce" musical choices. Moreover, in the last of the three events, I became aware that, because the majority of the experiences I had initiated to share music and memories created a pleasurable atmosphere, I had failed to take the power of affect seriously enough when organizing the session. This realization made me come face-to-face with the ways in which my own investment in the method was shaped by my own perspectives and "baggage" in relation to music and feelings.

I begin with a brief consideration of my development of Inheritance Tracks as a research method (which, as discussed in the introduction to this book, acted as the springboard for the research explored in this collection). This outline underpins the approaches used in the cases that are discussed in this chapter. Following on from this is an analysis of three specific instances where Inheritance Tracks were explored and shared with the women who participated.

Choosing Inheritance Tracks: Selecting the Cases for This Chapter

As indicated earlier, I have undertaken a number of inheritance workshops/research activities over a period of almost ten years, working with diverse groups of people in various locations in Europe and North America. These cases comprise the first-ever research events I carried out using Inheritance Tracks and the two most recent. Together they illustrate a progression in terms of practices, understanding, and reflections in relation to the use of this research method over an extended period of time.

In keeping with the rest of this book, this chapter investigates meanings, associations, and feelings elicited by music and, more especially, popular music as constituted by songs and their connective links to the micro and macro of the histories, geographies, and identities of the participants. In analyzing these micro and macro connections of histories, geographies, and identities generated in this form of memory work, I am attentive to the experiences and manifestations of emotion/affect. These revealed themselves in the interactions between participants and frequently in the questions they provoked about the ways traces and legacies of affect are interwoven in our memories over time (Freedman 2020). As I have intimated earlier, this attentiveness to affect was shaken during the final Inheritance Tracks event. I am committed to evolving and developing my autoethnographic practices, and conducting this research has made me resensitize my approaches and assumptions in a productive way.

In particular, I am now more cognizant of the power of affect inherent in De Chaine's (2002) idea of reawakening feelings when remembering them via music. I have always felt able to choose, play, and talk about music, and as someone who has undergone extensive therapy and counseling, I have become comfortable with sharing both sadness and joy in professional and private contexts, having come to view expressing vulnerability as a form of strength. After conducting Inheritance Tracks-based research over an extended period of time, however, I now know that my own individual comfort and, perhaps more specifically, my deeply rooted devotion to music as an integral part of my life and history, need to be considered and reconsidered when engaging in qualitative music-based research with others. Because of the inclusive group ethos of the events discussed in this chapter, I also participated with my own song choices in each case. The encounters with feelings that were in evidence during each instance of research became pivotal to my reflections on the content and process of the research, and the experiences and impact of affect "troubled" the musical inheritance memories in multiple ways. These included connections between memories and music and their emotional/affective power on the individual choosing the track and also on others taking part in the social setting of a group research situation.

Musical inheritance has been a central feature of my life. Intertwined vertically and horizontally from people, to people, and with people, music circulates and has circulated in my life since I was a baby and has influenced my academic teaching and research (Jennings 2019b, 2020; Jennings and Gardner 2012). From the outset, the potential of the Inheritance Tracks research method was exciting for me, since it resonated with my way of being in the world. What I was to learn as the research process evolved was that my own assumptions as a researcher were to be both unsettled and further developed, thus enriching the method and my future research and also my ability to reflect on the complexities entangled (Grenier, Sawchuk, and Valois-Nadeau 2020) through sound in an "intertwinement of subjectivity and culture" (Nielsen 2017: 1). As the discussion that follows illustrates, it became clear to me during my prolonged engagement with this research method that sharing musical inheritances with others was always interesting and rewarding but not always that straightforward.

Why Women? Deciding on the Focus of This Chapter

In a chapter that aims to interrogate the ways that music and memory disrupt notions of linear chronological time, it might seem rather perverse to structure this chapter along chronological timelines to present my three research case studies. However, I have chosen to do so as a means to integrate a process of self-reflexivity in a research journey that developed over the period between the first event and the last. On balance, and as I have indicated earlier, when reflecting on all the Inheritance Tracks sessions I have engaged with, it was the three women-only sessions that not only stayed with me more than the others but also offered insightful contributions in terms of inheritance and the specificities of women's musical experiences. Moreover, the sessions revealed a type of emotional bravery I did not encounter in the other research events I facilitated.

Although all three cases discussed in this chapter utilize Inheritance Tracks as a method, they do not follow an identical format in the way that they were conducted, and as such, they are not standardized or designed for their replicability. Their form was developed organically over time based on reflection, feedback from participants, and discussions with colleagues who were also using Inheritance Tracks in their research. Most importantly, from a feminist, epistemological position that recognizes that the research process is often messy, I attempted to do what felt right (Hill 2004) for the participants and the research aims.

All three occasions discussed here were group situations, with their inevitable interpersonal power dynamics in play. Above all, each research environment constituted a liminal space or at least liminal-like space of engagement (Skjoldager-Nielsen and Edelman 2014), where the process of doing memory work individually and collectively enabled something akin to a sense of *communitas* (Turner 1969) and, certainly for some of those involved, an encounter with individual moments of affect within the context of affective atmospheres (Lupton 2017).

Part 1: Inheritance Tracks Grow Old Disgracefully

The first Inheritance Tracks session that I conducted happened almost by happenstance. Following a public engagement event in 2014 where I had talked about the work of the Centre for Women, Ageing and Media (WAM 2021), I was contacted to give a talk to a national meeting of the UK network for women, Growing Old Disgracefully (2021). Unfortunately, I was unable to do this talk because of a diary clash, but after further phone conversation, it was agreed that an advertisement could go out in the network's national newsletter to invite expressions of interest from its members to pursue doctoral study with WAM. The advertisement was answered by a coordinator of one of the regional groups (Sue), and in a long and interesting phone conversation, we explored the ways that self-reflexive approaches could be used in research to explore women's identities along the life course.

During this conversation, I was robustly grilled about my own research, and I mentioned that I was planning to conduct some research about aging, popular music, memory, and identity inspired by the BBC Radio 4 (2021) *Saturday Live* "Inheritance Tracks" format at some point in the future. Sue told me that her group of Growing Old Disgracefully members engaged regularly with musical activities and that, coincidentally, one of the members had already run an Inheritance Tracks session at one of their meetings. As a result of this conversation, I subsequently gained a doctoral student and was able to explore Inheritance Tracks with a group of women who were committed to living lives that challenge the dictates and confines of cultural agism for women (Gullette 2004; Jennings and Grist 2017).

In this first of my engagements with the Inheritance Tracks method, I copied the practice that happens each week in the radio program, where two tracks are selected by the featured person: a track that is inherited (from the past) and a track for others to inherit (to pass forward). In the subsequent inheritance research events that I ran, I chose to focus on inherited tracks rather than tracks chosen to pass on to others, as it was the memory work and connections from the past to the present that were driving my research interests.

Sue and I set up two connected Inheritance Tracks events that were organized to both generate maximum participation from the regional group and to afford me the opportunity to "pay back" by contributing to their next general meeting, talking about WAM research and demonstrating it in practice through their co-participation. In some ways the first event was a recreation of an experience that one of their members, Vicky, had conducted before as a group activity so that they could get to know each other better. There were, however, some additional members at this event adding their music and experiences. Also, I was there introducing a different purpose to the gathering and adding my own musical choices, since members insisted I join in so they could learn something about me as I learned about them.

The women in this regional branch of Growing Old Disgracefully were, according to Sue, aged from their mid-fifties to eighty, all White (reflecting the majority demographic of the provincial/rural area), mostly middle-class, and mostly retired. The original Inheritance Tracks group activity had been facilitated by Vicky as a means for members to share, connect, and learn more about each other and, importantly, as she explained, "to have fun." Unlike all other of my Inheritance Tracks research events, the research carried out with Growing Old Disgracefully was conducted in two stages. The first stage consisted of a small-group discussion at the home of the regional coordinator, Sue (where members of the group met regularly and where they were comfortable). Nine women took part who had either been involved in the original event run by Vicky or had missed that opportunity and now wanted the chance to be involved. Unlike the WAM Summer School research events discussed later in this chapter, which were more informal, this discussion was audiotaped and subsequently transcribed, with all participants deciding that they wanted me to use their real first names when referring to them in the research. The discussion revisited music from the original Inheritance Tracks session and also added music from new attendees. In all but one instance, when a hymn was chosen, the music consisted of recorded pop or popular music.

Four months later, the second stage of the research took place. At this point, the findings of the small-group discussion were taken to the larger meeting of the regional group, which took place in a local community center where they held their formal meetings. Thirty-two members were present, with six of them also having been involved in the group interview at Sue's house. At this meeting, in addition to feeding back to members the core themes generated by participants of the small-group discussion (giving them the opportunity to check out whether I had understood their meanings), I also played them many of the musical Inheritance Tracks that had been shared at the smaller-group discussion. To integrate the wider perspective of the whole group, the women were split into five smaller groups to respond to core themes generated in the smaller discussion group, and they wrote their responses on large flip chart sheets. These responses were then shared with the group as a whole. The discussions were not audiotaped, but I took trigger notes during and afterward and later analyzed the written content on the five flip chart sheets that the women created during this session.

From Rupture to Continuum: Transmitting the Politics of Reflective Aging

Barrett, Pai, and Redmond (2012) describe the Red Hat Society as a "gendered subculture of aging." The Growing Old Disgracefully network would also conform closely to their definition. The women involved in both group activities discussed here represent transient nonfamilial and oppositional formations and, in coming together in their groups and networks, respond creatively and oppositionally to the many stereotypes at the intersection of age and gender.

The aims of Growing Old Disgracefully, as expressed on the group's website, are as follows: "To make the most of the rest of our lives; To meet like-minded women and make new friends; To counter stereotypes of older women; To encourage positive attitudes to ageing; To share laughter and a sense of fun; To extend our horizons; [and] To support each other" (Growing Old Disgracefully 2021). The primary difference between the Red Hat Society and Growing Old Disgracefully is that the latter does not adhere to a dress code as a form of expressive visibility. Barrett, Pai, and Redmond (2012) suggest the need to investigate the intersections of gender and other differences when examining subcultures based on age, and indeed, as Margaret Cruikshank (2003) argues, our life experiences bring us to a position where we are possibly the most different from each other the older we are. Membership in Growing Old Disgracefully would suggest a common bond related to the aims of the group as a whole (as stated earlier), but there are of course many differences that suggest a woman's membership is enacted on multiple and, at times, contradictory levels (Haenfler 2004; Halberstam 2005). Through me asking the participants to re-access their musical memory archive (Istvandity 2015) and remember (inherited) music while also asking them to find music that they wanted to pass to future generations (to inherit), the interactional work (Martin 2004) involved in these overlapping sites of past and future came into play in the present.

Resistance Interrupted: Values and Resistance along the Life Course

I have found May and Thrift's (2001) notion of "TimeSpace" a productive way to examine the confluences of time and context in my own work (Gardner and Jennings 2019; Jennings 2020), and particularly so when keeping in mind Halberstam's (2005) argument that queer temporality has the ability to disrupt typical linear heteronormative life course narratives. Both approaches, which interrogate the multiple complexities of time and context, assist with ways to think about *un*thinking stereotypes of older age that underpin linear chronologies of age identity. As Elizabeth Keenan (2008) also explains, "[T]he ideals of femininity are enmeshed with relatively fixed expectations" (396). Subcultural studies of youth groups (Bennett 1999, 2000) have similarly highlighted the energetic space available for resistance in the time before career and family responsibility. The women in the study, however, articulated a sense that a new TimeSpace had opened up for resistance in older age.

> ANNETTE: I've retired before the sort of compulsory age, [since] my job closed down. Growing Old Disgracefully, what attracted me was the disgracefully bit actually, yeah [laughter from rest of group]. I also

want to challenge the stereotype of going gracefully into the night—raging, well, not necessarily raging, but ... SUE: making beautiful music [laughter from the group].

ANNETTE: And similar to Angela I worked in child protection for forty years. It's taken a long time to relax into the freedom. One of the biggest highlights, apart from returning to music and singing and playing like I did when I was younger—some of us have become part of a drumming group—is just the fantastic joy of seeing older women banging away on sets of drums—high hats and ... just makes me want to laugh with joy. Growing Old Disgracefully can give us a political perspective that we have not necessarily explored yet. Doing things that are outside of our comfort zone is right on as far as I'm concerned.

Although the word "feminism" was not mentioned in any of the discussions, the group had organized International Women's Day events together, and the sense of both a renewed reconnection with women and with political activism permeated the conversations in the small-group discussion and also in the formal meeting where I gave feedback on the project.

FRANCES: I've not done paid work since fifty and now sixty-nine, so I have had a lot of freedom—had more freedom when my husband was still working [Frances and group laugh]. I need no help to be disgraceful—singing and doing a conga down the high street. Political work, well, we have the time and while we have health and energy, we are raising awareness in [provincial town where the group is based].

Gendered expectations (Keenan 2008) within their heterosexual relationships still remained for the women, but being able to stop paid work opened up a new TimeSpace for activism, and as Sue explained, "It's also about the connection with women—that sort of heart connection with other women that can be fragmented when you're working—and so it's also about getting back in touch with that."

Cruikshank (2003) suggests that for women, the opportunity to reinvent the self in old age once freed from the same degree of family and work pressures as when younger "may present unanticipated opportunities" (19). The mechanism of Inheritance Tracks, to think back and think forward, also prompted the women to reflect on their identities in the present. In the formal group, a strong sense of their privilege and the improved material conditions of their lives in contrast with previous generations was clear (though, as Sue reflected as we drove to the venue for the second meeting, there were also many differences in wealth among what she had described as a White and mostly middle-class group of women).

For the women involved in the study, there was a sense of entering a TimeSpace where, as older women, they could be resistant to dominant expectations. Sarah suggested, "I think as you get older, you don't worry about what other people think about what you do." Indeed, during a refreshment break in the formal meeting, one of the participants came up to me (unfortunately, I did not get her name) and reflected that when she was younger, her choices of music were influenced by the men around her. She was not sure if they were more forceful in their musical tastes or just more enthusiastic. She stated that she still likes much of the music from when she was younger, as it reminds her of past times, but she is now definitely more sure of what she really likes as an older woman.

Thinking Back and Thinking Forward across the "Generation Gap": Reflexivity in the Context of Inheritance Tracks

In this study, musical choice was a source of both rebellion in taste and values and the sharing of taste and values along the life course. As Halberstam (2005) explains, early formations of subcultural theory from the likes of the Centre for Contemporary Cultural Studies at the University of Birmingham conceived of subcultures as youthful because they rejected their parents' values to create a space where they were able to reshape and reformulate these values on their own terms. With age, the experiences shared by the women suggested that any definitive sense of there being a generation gap between one generation and the next was not necessarily always the case. When using music to mobilize self-reflexive thinking, concepts of generation became blurry, and when placed within a continuum of experiences, generational relationships were multiple and embraced both identifications and connections *and* dis-identifications and differences.

When looking back to her inherited track, Mary explained:

> I chose "Que Sera Sera" because my parents came over here from rural Ireland in the late '40s and for my mum it must have been absolute complete liberation for her, even though it was quite a bad time then, and she was always singing [in] our childhood, there was always something being sung, you know, like "She Wears Red Feathers" [ROS: That's so like my Irish heritage. My grandmother used to sing that too], but she also loved Caruso and all these Irish tenor[y] type people, and we just sopped up all this music. And I would have to choose this as it was also her outlook on life: whatever comes to you, you probably have just to get on with it and just deal with it. And Doris Day must have been quite a romantic person, figure—woman, she seemed quite liberated then back in the '50s, was quite feisty [chorus of "Absolutely" from the group], and

she wore gorgeous clothes. She was just her own woman, and my mum was very much her own woman and quite a strong lady, and I think she passed it on to us all that we could do stuff.

The transmission of values (e.g., "she passed it on to us all that we could do stuff") was central to the discussions of the music chosen. When looking back to choose an inheritance track, Vicky skipped a generation and chose from one of her grandmother's favorite albums, the Rodgers and Hammerstein musical *Carousel*. As mentioned, Vicky had been the facilitator of the original Inheritance Tracks session for the group before the research project began, and for her, music was a core element in how she articulated her identity. "Music has always been a big part of my life," she said. "I taught—you need to know this—for twenty-five years, and I taught music to five- to eleven-year-olds and used different types of music so they got different genres of music." The complexity of the interconnectedness of musical tastes is manifest in the ways that contradictory but also shared contextual positions are held simultaneously within Vicky's family. As she indicated: "My parents tried very hard to get me to like classical music and I suppose, yeah, it's okay. … They would take me to see the CBSO [City of Birmingham Symphony Orchestra] and yeah, it was great, but I never really got into it—it was never really my bag."

Differences in tastes and lifestyles are no longer easily linked to notions of social stratification, but within subcultural studies and popular music studies, musical tastes have tended to signify specific types of, often class-based, cultural, and subcultural capital. Vicky's account suggests that if musical tastes are analyzed over time, there is the potential to take a more flexible view. As she continued:

When we did our inheritance tracks I went back a further generation to my Grandma, who taught me all the words to *Carousel* and *West Side Story* and *The Sound of Music* and *My Fair Lady* and *Oklahoma!*—and I can sing through all of those with no problem, and then I skipped a generation with my parents—I think they, and they will have to forgive me for saying this, I think they were trying to better themselves, they grew up as working-class people and improved themselves … they were trying to make me middle-class.

Despite class-based tensions around popular musical taste, as Vicky recounted, the popular musical *Carousel* created a memory bridge across several generations:

I chose a track from *Carousel* for two reasons. One easy reason, and forgive me those who heard this before, but it became folklore in the family that when something made you tearful you would say, "I'm coming over all *Carousel*." The other one is because on the LP, on the vinyl sleeve, it is written in my grandma's handwriting that "This record sticks at the end of side one," so it's on the track "If I Loved You" when the poor man gets to the word "longing," and we would all sit there and sing "longing, longing, longing" until one of us gets up and punches the machine, and now four generations of the family do that, whenever it comes on the radio we all still go "longing, longing, longing."

The multitemporal interconnectivity of music is apparent in Annette's discussion of her alliance with her mother against her grandparents through their mutual love of the Beatles. As she explained:

The Beatles just blew me away absolutely, and the connection for me really with the Beatles was my mother. She had me very young at twenty and she was a single parent and we lived with my grandparents, and there was definitely an alliance between my mother and I with regard to the sort of music that we listened to and the sort of music on the [BBC] Light Programme that my grandparents listened to. And I always remember that the Beatles came to town when I was fourteen and my mum and I queued up in the pouring rain from 7:00 p.m. at night to 6:00 a.m. the next morning to get tickets, and we had our hair done together to go, and we didn't hear a thing [at the concert for the screaming fans], girls were being carried out on stretchers.

When approaching popular music and cultural identity, academics have focused on discontinuities and musical boundaries at the expense of a more holistic continuum of the lived experiences of music fans (Jennings 2015). In a similar way, there has been an overemphasis on generational conflict or age cohort conflict rather than a more productive approach that, at least in some instances, locates older people within a nexus of social and political connectivities (Kertzer 1983).

At the larger formal meeting of Growing Old Disgracefully, when I shared some of the tracks members of the group wanted to pass forward to future generations, particularly their children and grandchildren—for instance, the Beatles track "Eight Days a Week" (Annette), Leonard Cohen's song "Hey, That's No Way to Say Goodbye" (Mary), or anything by Meat Loaf (Vicky)—it was clear that the women recognized that they both not only shared tastes with their children but also maintained tastes of their own. As Andy Bennett (2013) suggests, there is a spectrum of conflict and continuity when music is shared multigenerationally.

For the postwar generations, who either came of age in the 1960s or felt a strong bond with the period, their formative musical tastes were part of a TimeSpace that gave them "intellectual nourishment that those with a predisposition for radical, counter-hegemonic thought carried forward with them" (Bennett 2013: 161). The largest age cohort within the study group was women in their sixties who came to adulthood in the 1960s. In the small-group discussion, where the majority of the women were in this category, the Beatles emerged as an important horizontal "bridge" between their individual and collective memories and more particularly, in this women-only and feminist-influenced grouping, to notions of resistance and value formation. Approaches from popular history (Marwick 1998) and popular music, aging, and lifestyle (Bennett 2013) suggest that an important element of the 1960s is a narrative of rupture between that period and those that had come before. Improvements in economic and social conditions (including health care and, for women, the arrival of the contraceptive pill) that took place in the 1960s coincided to produce vibrant instances of popular cultural practice (particularly art, music, and cinema) and develop networks of subcultural energy captured under the umbrella term "counterculture" (Marwick 1998; Bennett 2013). Bennett (2013) cites the Beatles album *Sgt. Pepper's Lonely Hearts Club Band* as "anthemic of the countercultural movement" (159) and proposes that for the now aging popular music fans who feel a strong link to the music and values of 1960s counterculture, their wish is not to become more conservative with age.

In addition to the Beatles, a strong link to the "other face of countercultural music" (Bennett 2013: 163)—the acoustic singer-songwriters such as Joni Mitchell, Leonard Cohen, and John Martyn—was evident in the discussions of study participants in their fifties and sixties. The discussion of John Martyn in the smaller group resulted in Annette, Lizzie, Mary, and me singing "May You Never" to the rest of the group, and it was significant that during the second, formal group meeting, where I played to the larger group Inheritance Tracks chosen by some of their members at the small-group meeting, the majority of the group spontaneously sang along with popular hits such as "Que Sera Sera" (Doris Day) and "Eight Days a Week" (Beatles). But once I played tracks ("Suzanne" and "A Case of You," which were written and performed by the countercultural singer-songwriters Leonard Cohen and Joni Mitchell, respectively), the singing from the larger group, comprising mostly women in their late sixties upward, dropped away, leaving only me and the women involved in the small-group meeting who had indicated their attachment to this gentler acoustic music singing. Generally, when discussing the relationship between music, gender, and genre, the masculine genres (such as rock) have been more validated and received more critical attention than genres associated with female audiences (girl groups, mainstream pop). In this women-only study, it is interesting that the "gentler acoustic music" was important to many participants in terms of identity formation along the life course while also pointing to some intergenerational differences among group members as a whole.

Significantly, when the whole Growing Old Disgracefully group was asked what they wanted their choices of music to pass forward to signify, the values they wrote on the flip charts were feelings and emotion, enthusiasm, choice, life is worth living, peace and relaxation, love, enjoyment, sharing, fun, rhythm, song and dance—all strongly associated with 1960s counterculture. It would seem that, despite the group containing a minority of members who came of age either before or after the 1960s, there was consensus among the whole group and across their age-range spectrum that these freedoms were not just the values that they wished to impart or "pay forward" but also the values they wanted to live by as women "growing old disgracefully" and approaching old age in a more expansive and affirmative way.

Part 2: Women, Aging, and Musical Inheritances

The second part of this chapter differs from the first in several respects. With Growing Old Disgracefully, I was invited into a preexisting group as an academic specifically to conduct Inheritance Tracks research. The events under discussion in this part of the chapter focus on Inheritance Tracks events that took place at two WAM International Summer Schools (2017 and 2018) that I facilitated with my WAM codirector, Hannah Grist. The summer schools featured here incorporated Inheritance Tracks in two different and distinctive ways: the 2017 summer school, with a theme of Noisy Women, used Inheritance Tracks as an icebreaker exercise, and the 2018 summer school, with the theme of Performativity and Age, incorporated Inheritance Tracks as a workshop demonstration of "research in action." As women-only events, both occasions provide a strange symmetry between this part and the first part of this chapter. They were not only the most recent occasions where I used the Inheritance Tracks research method (Growing Old Disgracefully being the first) but the summer schools were also underpinned by similar preoccupations about women, aging, and identities to the first time I explored Inheritance Tracks, with the Growing Old Disgracefully group. The two summer schools therefore enable poignant comparisons to be made in terms of the themes, concerns, and issues that were raised.

There were nevertheless some significant differences in the way the summer school events were conceived of and conducted compared with the Growing Old Disgracefully research, and in turn, the two summer school events were also conceived and conducted differently from each other. These differences are apparent in both the tone and the modality of the way I present my consideration of these events in this section of the chapter and reflect the more informal ways that Inheritance Tracks methods were used at the summer schools. In contrast to the research discussed in Part 1, the summer school sessions were not audiotaped and transcribed, and they did not follow the

BBC Radio 4 format of choosing both a track that was inherited and a track to pass on but rather concentrated only on tracks that had been inherited. Importantly, these Inheritance Tracks research events formed a small part of the wider set of academic events over three days centered on giving formal research presentations and were thus integrated into two gatherings of international and intergenerational women academics and practitioners who were all involved in aging studies research and/or related creative and reflective practices. The purpose for the participants at the summer schools, unlike the work undertaken with the Growing Old Disgracefully group, was not primarily about participating in Inheritance Tracks research but to participate in it as part of a schedule of research-led and research-informed sessions. What follow here therefore are my own reflections on the events based on my research diaries, trigger notes, and the Spotify playlists that were compiled. Unless I had consent from a participant to identify them, participants in this second part of the chapter remain anonymous.

Women and the Musical "Noises" of Our Lives

In keeping with the theme of the 2017 summer school, Noisy Women, I wanted to focus specifically on tracks or "noises" inherited from women. I thus asked participants to come with a piece of music that they had inherited from a woman or women in their life. (So many of the Inheritance Tracks that emerged in the workshops I had previously conducted had either been inherited from men or were songs written and performed by men.) At this summer school, fourteen women took part, aged between their late twenties and late sixties. The participants consisted of a mix of doctoral researchers, early career and senior academics, creative artists, and health and social care practitioners, and the location for the event was the University of Gloucestershire, UK.

As indicated earlier, this workshop had not originally been anticipated as part of any published research project. It was developed as an icebreaker to assist with building the rapport we try to establish between participants in each summer school, to foster an ethos of sharing, respectfully challenging ideas, and thinking through issues together. Inheritance Tracks were used as the first event on the first day of the summer school, and for the majority of the participants, this was also the first time they had met each other. The session was never intended to be curated and recorded but rather was intended to form an integrated and spontaneous part of the program. As explained earlier, the participants remain anonymous apart from myself and my Ageing + Communication + Technology (ACT) colleague, Line Grenier, who joined in via Skype to set out some of the principles and history of what Line and I had been doing with Inheritance Tracks across the ACT partnership.

Although there is often a music strand threading through the annual WAM Summer Schools, it is not primarily a meeting of music scholars or necessarily even of music enthusiasts. Music in the form of an annual dance event where the playlist is generated by the participants does mean that there are musical associations with WAM Summer Schools, and through Inheritance Tracks, I wanted to capitalize on the pleasurable musical associations with WAM to attempt to subvert the almost universally loathed conference or workshop icebreaker, to encourage participation and engagement with music's valuable aspects.

To enter into this type of experience, no matter how friendly the intent of the welcome, can still cause some anxiety for many people. There are power differences (this group including PhD researchers, early career academics, professors who write about music, and others), and there are also cultural and academic differences about how much you share and discuss. The fourteen participants came from Austria, Canada, France, Germany, Ireland, and Romania as well as the UK. For me these sorts of situations and discussions are comfortable. Previous training in, and engagement with, psychotherapy has helped me with this. For others taking part, this is perhaps not the case, and this is something I have now come to understand through my autoethnographic journal reflections focused on events when I have used the Inheritance Tracks as a research method. Going forward this is something I would want to think carefully about not only if I were to continue to use the method again in the future but also as something I have learnt as part of autoethnographic reflection to take into consideration regarding my role as a researcher. On this occasion Hannah and I did not know the musical choices, and we did not preload the tracks on to a Spotify playlist in advance but generated them as we went along, with Hannah trying to find the version that was being discussed if at all possible on Spotify, so at least a snatch could be played to everyone in the room.

The WAM Summer School operates within the ethos of being a safe and supportive space. Not everyone present was able to put forward an inherited track, and I made it clear that this was fine. We did however discuss within the group some of the reasons why this might be the case. One of the participants explained that music really did not feature in a memorable way at home until she began to build her own relationship with music through peer friendships during her teenage years. For several others (even if they were able to choose a track to share), they had to dig deep when tracing through their memories to be able to make any connection between themselves and a woman through a piece of music. This was telling in terms of gendered relations to music and resonated with findings from discussions with the women of Growing Old Disgracefully and from my observations of the choices and stories I had heard in all my Inheritance Tracks research: men tended to dominate musical tastes and the choices of track made by the majority of people who engaged with me in Inheritance Tracks exercises.

A key factor in this was not just men's confidence in disseminating personal musical taste but also, and perhaps more significantly, who controlled music technologies in the house and, as frequently reflected on when sharing Inheritance Tracks, in the car.

For some of the participants, their musical inheritances from women were inherited from women friends at different points across the life course. In one case, the Christine and the Queens song "Tilted" (2015) was suggested as a track inherited from WAM. The participant first encountered it at a previous WAM Summer School dance evening, when it featured as one of the dance tracks I had chosen. (I also expressed my Christine and the Queens fan credentials by wearing a Christine and the Queens T-shirt at the event, so my enthusiastic dancing also marked this song in the participant's memory.)

Other Inheritance Tracks put forward that were related to women revealed familial and generational transmissions of music. The three of us who were either Irish or of Irish heritage (as I am on my mother's side of the family), all had strong matrilineal connections to music. Mine was through my grandmother, and for the others, the connection was through their mothers. The memories shared in the session were not only of recorded songs but also of songs that had been sung to us or sung with us. The sharing of the songs (they were all songs) in relation to our Irish heritages manifested an emotionally powerful mix of joyful and sad feelings (our mothers and/or grandmothers had all passed). The songs chosen were "Black Velvet Band" (the Dubliners), "When You Were Sweet Sixteen" (the Fureys), and "You Are My Sunshine," sung by Johnny Cash (a version in which his older voice, vulnerable in its cracks, seems to reinforce the strength of its message). I remember this track leaving me in emotional pieces during the workshop, as my father (also passed) had sung me to sleep with it when I was small.

"Black Velvet Band" sparked a sing-along from the three of us who were well schooled in the song, with some others who did not know it or did not know it very well joining in on the chorus. The experience was uplifting and communal. I had chosen the "When You Were Sweet Sixteen," played by the Fureys, which I love and listen to regularly, but what I really wanted was a recording of my grandmother singing it. My grandmother was a wonderful singer, and when I spent time with my grandparents, uncles, and aunts as a child at our family gatherings in Glasgow, we had a well-established tradition that required us all to do a "musical turn." When I hear the Fureys' version, I cannot help but superimpose my grandmother's voice over the plaintive sound of the banjo that underpins the musical arrangement. To me the banjo is the dominant sound when I hear the song, and the simplicity and beauty of this banjo sound yank at my heartstrings, drowning me in complex feelings of happiness, beauty, and loss brought together in that moment—feelings and memories from the past brought into the present all at the same time. The participant who chose "You Are My Sunshine" also had a strong link to a woman's singing voice. She recounted that while she was growing up, her mother used to be asked "to give us a song, Margaret" as the women in the street hung out their washing to dry on washing day. After the sharing of these three moments of musical inheritance, another of the participants, who had lost her mother relatively recently, was moved to be very open about her sometimes problematic relationship with her hippie rock chick mother.

And here, in what we might conceptualize in terms of a sound encounter, we are in a "constant process of re/membering our experiences, creating new and shifting articulations of time, space, emotion, cognition, consciousness. Our memories are products of an activity in which our adherence to chronology becomes untethered, allowing us to engage in a kind of bricolages" (De Chaine 2002: 92). The musical affect can thus be understood to have engendered emotional connectivities within the room, producing what I have come to think of as musical contagion. As someone who trained in counseling and has engaged in much therapy over the past twenty years, I am aware that losing emotional control is not the "done thing" in Western "civilized societies." Patriarchal ideologies privilege ideas of rationality as the benchmark of behavior. The solidity of rationality is seen as a projection of masculinity and masculine values, while the emotional sphere is perceived to be feminine and by association to be a form of weakness and paradoxically also something to be scared of. I spent time during the rest of the summer school checking in with the women who had felt moved to share grief and loss in the session through being touched by these contagious sound encounters. Although the stories told in relation to each of the inheritance songs in question were not shared specifically to talk about loss, the process of shared listening and talking worked to produce these tangible experiences of loss for many of the participants in the room. Thus, memories excavated deliberately and individually in the context of this Inheritance Tracks exercise to produce songs and stories of memory take on further powerful circulations within the overall group. As we listen to our own and other tracks in the moment of the workshop, we encounter shocks of recognition that have emotional resonance. In addition, notions of aging in relation to understandings of time in these moments are complex, not restricted to dominant within restrictive notions of time (Baars 2012). We age across the musical memory bridges of our life courses (Katz 2005; Andrews and Grenier 2015) and within the musical experiences of our life courses. We take with us knowingly and unknowingly what Karin Bijsterveld and José Van Dijck (2009) have called "sound souvenirs," and it is these souvenirs that collide and converge in the sound encounters produced through sharing Inheritance Tracks.

In addition to aging with music (Bennett 2013), we are also "aged by music." Common articulations of fandom almost demand of us to be able to chronologize our gigs and musical purchases by their dates, and as I listened to the choice of another participant ("Sweet Dreams Are Made of This," by the Eurythmics), I later looked at my trigger notes and wrote the following in my research diary: "I so love that song. It's my karaoke song. My daughter must associate it with me. She grew up with it. She is older than the participant ... how old does that make me?" I was in my twenties when the song came out, and on hearing it in its context as an inheritance from a mother to a daughter, I became aware that in that moment, I had been taken on a memory journey, and memory journeys inevitably involve transaging (Moglen 2008). In that moment and in that space, I was simultaneously the younger woman and the older woman listening and thinking that my own daughter was now much older than the participant but had been a toddler when I first bought the album. In reengaging with the song, my self-reflexive writing process that followed alerted me to the understanding that this transaging held an awareness of a life course of experiences converging on a continuum between my younger and older selves.

Troubling the Method: Cascading Reminiscences

The positive feedback to the use of Inheritance Tracks as a means to facilitate sharing and team building at the 2017 Summer School offered some insights into how Inheritance Tracks could be used in addition to the more formal research process that I had conducted with the Growing Old Disgracefully group. This set me thinking about how I might again modify use of the research method for the 2018 Summer School. Its role in this summer school was to form part of a "research in action" workshop, which updated participants on the ways Inheritance Tracks were being used by colleagues working together in the ACT partnership, while also offering attendees the opportunity to take part in the process of Inheritance Tracks themselves. The Inheritance Tracks event was featured in the information sent out before the summer school, and chosen Inheritance Tracks were requested in advance so they could be added to a Spotify playlist that would be used in the session. As had been the case with the 2017 Summer School, the 2018 event was not audiotaped. My subsequent analysis is again based on trigger notes taken at the time, discussions with some of the participants after the event, plus autoethnographic reflections from my research journal.

In contrast to the previous year, the workshop was scheduled toward the end of the program, when significant rapport among participants had already been established. Taking place once again at the University of Gloucestershire, the theme of the 2018 Summer School, Performativity and Age, influenced the interests of those taking part in the workshop. This time I did not stipulate that the chosen tracks had to be inherited from a woman but rather from someone who was older so that issues of age, generation, and connectivities that had surfaced in the previous year could be further explored. I loaded the tracks from all seventeen participants into a Spotify playlist ready for the session. In terms of method, I also added another dimension. Since everyone had chosen a track, I thought it would add spontaneity and perhaps be fun to put the playlist on shuffle. The idea was that when each track started, the participant who had chosen it would give their explanation as to why they had chosen the track and tell their stories.

The theme of performativity seemed absolutely on point from the first song to be generated from the Spotify shuffle. It was the Irish Eurovision Song Contest entry for 1965, "Walking the Streets in the Rain," by Butch Moore. As soon as the first notes could be heard in the room, the song's chooser was on her feet not just singing along but performing the song complete with hand gestures and a smile, to the admiration of everyone in the room. The song was not well known to most of the others, but the participant's friend and colleague who had come with her jumped up too and joined in. This set the tone, with people singing along with the majority of the songs that were shared and everyone joining in noisily with the clapping on Eve Boswell's song "Sugar Bush" when it came on.

In the session, the sound encounters were of course personal, but also in particular convergences, they were facilitators, as observed in the 2017 Summer School, for others in the room to remember and to feel. This became very clear when one participant suddenly became tearful. When others showed concern, she indicated that she had suddenly been hit by an unbidden memory while listening to someone else's song choice. Greg Seigworth (1995) suggests that

> [a]ffect isn't always about such notable or "significant" events. Affect is more about the slow, but steady, continual accumulation of seeming insignificances: the very stuff that slips underneath your consciousness because it's barely worth noticing, the stuff that registers without any particular emotion getting attached to it. It is these affective insignificances that make up more (much more!) of who you are and how you act than those other bigger events and powerful emotions that are supposed to mean so much. (23)

Traces of music and memory interweave in unpredictable ways in a something akin to a three-dimensional web that connects vertically and horizontally through time. In doing so, they facilitate a way for participants to feel: to feel time and also to feel aging (Kriebernegg, Maierhofer, and Ratzenböck 2014). Indeed, in his autoethnography of embodied understandings of music, DeChaine (2002) reinforces this notion when he says, "I feel the remembering!" (87).

Feeling and remembering in relation to music were, of course, at the heart of the workshop, and the power of this feeling and remembering, as in the moment of unbidden memory highlighted earlier, could be intense. My failure to take this intensity into enough consideration as the facilitator of this session became all too clear to me when it came to my "fun" idea of playing the tracks on shuffle rather than going round the room or asking participants to indicate when they wanted to share their track. Afterward, I wish I had taken more time to reflect and truly register the emotional affect of Inheritance Tracks as a method. It was as if I knew about the power of affect on an intellectual level but failed to truly understand it until I experienced this particular session. For one of the participants, waiting for her chosen track to start (and unfortunately, it came very late in the session) was akin to playing Russian roulette. She explained to the group that each time a track was about to start, she steeled herself, ready to share her particularly emotionally laden story, and the longer she had to wait, the worse she began to feel. When she revealed this, I felt terrible about my lack of sensitivity, and I think for several in the group this moment was poignant as it prompted a discussion about their general lack of comfort in sharing, although they bravely shared nevertheless.

In so many ways, this session was more emotional than the one held the previous year in terms of experiences of fun and pleasure and sadness. There were spontaneous performances of songs and spontaneous demonstrations of empathy in the room. I wondered whether the staging of the session at the end of two days of intense work and play together (including dinner and dancing, as well as academic presentations and creative art making together) built a depth of trust and confidence among participants that I had not encountered in other sessions. These sessions included my work with the Growing Old Disgracefully members, who, although they had ongoing relationships with each other before the two events I was involved in, shared fun but did not share difficult or troubling emotions while I was there. On reflection, however, my status as an academic who had specifically been invited to participate as an academic most likely impacted the dynamic of the group.

The ethos of WAM Summer Schools is to break down academic and academic/practitioner hierarchies to generate a safe space to think together. Since the school is an international event, participants bring different cultural nuances to the process of exploring music, memory, and aging when sharing their Inheritance Tracks. A notable element that emerged in the 2018 workshop was the ability of music to not only travel across, and through, space and time to produce instances of affect. Music also enabled the transmission of regional and national cultures to be exchanged—moving between and beyond the borders of micro and macro geographies (Gardner and Jennings 2019). For participants who came to the event from Australia, the song "The Water of Tyne," performed by Kathryn Tickell, connected her and reconnected her, as an Australian domiciled daughter, with her elderly mother in the north of England. For the participant, the song itself reflects the folk music of the region, with Tickell's Northumbrian pipes sonically woven through the spaces and places of memory over time.

The women in the room were Australian, Canadian, French, German, Irish, and British, with several of the participants able to speak more than one European language. The majority of the chosen tracks, as was the case in all the Inheritance Tracks exercises I have ever conducted (including in Hamburg and Montreal), were nevertheless sung in English, with three exceptions. These were "Non, je ne regrette rien," sung by Édith Piaf in French (chosen by Sally, one of the English participants); "Weisse Rosen aus Athen," sung by Nana Mouskouri in German (chosen by me); and "Je t'aime, moi non plus," sung by Serge Gainsbourg and Jane Birkin in French (chosen by one of the German participants). The latter, with its rather risqué reputation, captured, for the participant who chose it, her connection to her "hippie chick" mother, a mother who, as she explained, did not conform to hegemonic notions of German motherhood. The other two songs linked Sally and me to our immigrant fathers, who had settled in the UK and who (as we teased out in conversation with each other), we now realized (though not at the time), expressed in various ways, including through music, their longing for a cosmopolitan Europe/Europeanness that was not culturally available to them in England in the 1960s.

At the time of the summer school, I had just completed my contributions to a book I coauthored with my WAM colleague Abigail Gardner on Europeanness, aging, and popular music (Gardner and Jennings 2019), and for one of my individual chapters, I had written about the Greek singer Nana Mouskouri's place in my early life as a signifier of my French father's attempts to forge a European life through collecting and playing non-English music, through the food he prepared at home (he was a chef), and by regularly inviting a group of friends (German, Swiss, and Polish) from the hotel where he worked to spend evenings together at our house. They spent their time listening to Mouskouri records sung in German, French, Greek, and occasionally even in English while playing cards and constantly swapping languages between themselves while doing so (they all spoke French and German as well as English). Mouskouri, and my chosen track in particular, took me back to a little bubble of Europeanness inside a Yorkshire living room during my childhood.[2] Since conducting my autoethnographic reflections on this, "Weisse Rosen aus Athen" had become a key inheritance track for me and was firmly in my mind at the time as one to share when an Inheritance Tracks opportunity arose. In a similar way, by choosing the song by Édith Piaf (which could have equally been an inheritance track for me), Sara could now detect a feeling of longing for something that was missing when she thought back to her father and the song—a longing for something that was not part of the "everyday" of 1960s England.

Conclusion

Over the extended period of time between the first Inheritance Tracks workshop I conducted and the two most recent, I have been able to step back and engage in an ongoing process of reflection about them. These considerations have prompted me to review my own assumptions about the role of music and memory and also my practices as a researcher. First and foremost, I have come to realize that using Inheritance Tracks as a method to investigate music, memory, and aging is a powerful tool. In particular, it facilitates a process of memory retrieval and reminiscence that not only generates simultaneous experiences/re-experiences of the past in the present but also, demonstrated in the last two contexts discussed here, has the ability to produce connections of affect (vertically from the past and horizontally among many of the women participating).

The case studies discussed in this chapter suggest that when the women shared music and experiences using Inheritance Tracks, there was multidirectional process in action that flowed between and to and from to connect experiences and memories over space and time. All three of the Inheritance Tracks sessions focused on in this chapter revealed intricate and multifaceted connections that created ties and bonds between, and beyond, borders (geographical, age, self/other, individual, and collective). The women-only contexts also revealed gendered aspects of musical inheritance. Reminiscences evoked through Inheritance Tracks indicated that the power to confidently pronounce musical taste, for the most part, belonged to men, who often controlled the musical technology within the household and in the car.

The music in the three events featured here predominantly, though not exclusively, consisted of songs and mostly recorded songs/tracks, with the music acting as conduits through time and space. The interweaving of music and memories that are accessed and traced by the women participants can be conceptualized, to use De Chaine's (2002) formulation of music experience, as experiences that "seep, exposing the arbitrariness of binary divisions between memory/imagination and subject/object" (81). They provide location points or reminiscence bumps (Krumhansl and Zupnik 2013) on musical memory lines that not just cascade vertically across constructs of time and generation but do so in more complex ways to "transage" us (Moglen 2008), thus articulating musical inheritances as squiggly journeys that trace and retrace, connect and reconnect, value and reevaluate the past in relation to the present and the future.

Notes

1 See May and Thrift (2001) for a detailed exploration of this concept.
2 See Jennings (2019a).

References

Andrews, Gavin, and Amanda Grenier. 2015. "Ageing Movement as Space-Time: Introducing Non-Representational Theory to the Geography of Ageing." *Progress in Geography,* 34(12): 1512–34.

Baars, Jan. 2012. "Critical Turns of Aging, Narrative and Time." *International Journal of Aging and Later Life*, 7(2): 143–65.
Barrett, Anne E., Manacy Pai, and Rebecca Redmond. 2012. "'It's Your Badge of Inclusion': The Red Hat Society as a Gendered Subculture of Aging." *Journal of Aging Studies*, 26(4): 527–38.
BBC Radio 4. 2021. *Saturday Live* "Inheritance Tracks." https://www.bbc.co.uk/programmes/p02pc9my/episodes/downloads.
Behar, Ruth. 1996. *The Vulnerable Observer: Anthropology That Breaks Your Heart*. Boston, MA: Beacon Press.
Bennett, Andy. 1999. "Subcultures or Neo-Tribes? Rethinking the Relationship between Youth, Style and Musical Taste." *Sociology*, 33(3): 599–617.
Bennett, Andy. 2000. *Popular Music and Youth Culture: Music, Identity and Place*. Basingstoke: Palgrave Macmillan.
Bennett, Andy. 2013. *Music, Style and Aging: Growing Old Disgracefully?* Philadelphia: Temple University Press.
Bijsterveld, Karin, and José V. Dijck (eds.). 2009. *Sound Souvenirs: Audio Technologies, Memory and Cultural Practices*. Amsterdam: Amsterdam University Press.
Centre for Women, Ageing and Media (WAM). 2021. "About." https://uniofglos.blog/wam/about/.
Cruikshank, Margaret. 2003. *Learning to Be Old: Gender, Culture, and Aging*. Lanham, MD: Rowman & Littlefield.
De Chaine, Robert. 2002. "Affect and Embodied Understanding in Musical Experience." *Text and Performance Quarterly*, 22(2): 79–98.
Freedman, Jesse. 2020. "Dialoguing with Pieces of My Body Affect, Sound Objects, and the De-Corporealizing Self." *Society for Ethnomusicology*, 15(2) Fall/Winter: 13–15.
Gardner, Abigail, and Ros Jennings. 2019. *Aging and Popular Music in Europe*. New York: Routledge.
Grenier, Line, Kim Sawchuk, and Fannie Valois-Nadeau. 2020. "Resoundingly Entangled: Ageing and Memory in Étoile des aînés in Quebec." In Line Grenier and Fannie Valois-Nadeau (eds.), *A Senior Moment: Cultural Mediations of Memory and Ageing*, 195–220. Bielefeld, Germany: Transcript Verlag.
Grist, Hannah, and Ros Jennings. 2020. *Carers, Care Homes and the British Media: Time to Care*. Basingstoke: Palgrave Pivot.
Growing Old Disgracefully. 2021. "About Us." https://www.growingolddisgracefully.org.uk/about-us.
Gullette, Margaret M. 2004. *Aged by Culture*. Chicago: University of Chicago Press.
Haenfler, Ross. 2004. "Rethinking Subcultural Resistance: Core Values of the Straight Edge Movement." *Journal of Contemporary Ethnography*, 33(4): 406–36.
Halberstam, Jack. 2005. *In a Queer Time and Place: Transgender Bodies, Subcultural Lives*. New York: New York University Press.
Hill, Sarah. 2004. "Doing Collaborative Research: Doing What Feels Right and Makes Sense." *International Journal of Social Research Methodology*, 7(2): 109–26.

Istvandity, Lauren. 2015. "The Lifetime Soundtrack: Music as an Archive for Autobiographical Memory." *Popular Music History*, 9(2): 136–54.

Jennings, Ros. 2012. "It's All Just a Little Bit of History Repeating Pop Stars, Audiences, Performance and Ageing." In Ros Jennings and Abigail Gardner (eds.), *Rock On: Women, Ageing and Popular Music*, 35–52. Farnham: Ashgate.

Jennings, Ros. 2015. "Popular Music and Ageing." In Julia Twigg and Wendy Martin (eds.), *Routledge Handbook of Cultural Gerontology*, 77–84. Abingdon: Routledge.

Jennings, Ros. 2019a. "Pan-European Stardom and Career Longevity in the Mainstream Remembering Nana Mouskouri and Demis Roussos." In Abigail Gardner and Ros Jennings (eds.), *Ageing and Popular Music in Europe*, 119–37. London: Routledge.

Jennings, Ros. 2019b. "Queering Europe: Pop Music, Intergenerationality Liminality." In Abigail Gardner and Ros Jennings (eds.), *Ageing and Popular Music in Europe*, 72–93. London: Routledge.

Jennings, Ros. 2020. "Soundtrack of My Life: Ageing, Autobiography and Remembered Music." In Line Grenier and Fannie Valois-Nadeau (eds.), *A Senior Moment: Cultural Mediations of Memory and Ageing*, 77–100. Bielefeld, Germany: Transcript Verlag.

Jennings, Ros, and Abigail Gardner (eds.). 2012. *Rock On: Women, Ageing and Popular Music*. Farnham: Ashgate.

Jennings, Ros, and Hannah Grist. 2017. "Future and Present Imaginaries: The Politics of the Ageing Female Body in Lena Dunham's Girls (HBO, 2012–Present)." In Cathy McGlynn, Margaret O'Neill, and Michaela Schrage-Frühe (eds.), *Ageing Women in Literature and Visual Culture*, 195–215. New York: Springer International Publishing.

Katz, Stephen. 2005. *Cultural Aging: Life Course, Lifestyle and Senior Worlds*. Peterborough, Ontario: Broadview Press.

Keenan, Elizabeth. 2008. "Who Are You Calling 'Lady': Femininity, Sexuality, and Third-Wave Feminism." *Journal of Popular Music Studies*, 20(4): 378–40.

Kertzer, David I. 1983. "Generation as a Sociological Problem." *Annual Review of Sociology*, 9: 125–49.

Kriebernegg, Ulla, Roberta Maierhofer, and Barbara Ratzenböck (eds.). 2014. *Alive and Kicking at All Ages: Cultural Constructions of Health and Life Course Identity*. Bielefeld, Germany: Transcript Verlag.

Krumhansl, Carol L., and Justin A. Zupnik. 2013. "Cascading Reminiscence Bumps in Popular Music." *Psychological Science*, 24(10): 2057–68.

Lupton, Deborah. 2017. "How Does Health Feel? Towards Research on the Affective Atmospheres of Digital Health." *Digital Health*, 3: 1–11.

Martin, Peter J. 2004. "Culture, Subculture and Social Organization." In Andy Bennett and Keith Kahn-Harris (eds.), *After Subculture*, 21–35. London: Palgrave.

Marwick, Arthur. 1998. *The Sixties: Cultural Revolution in Britain, France, Italy, and the United States, c. 1958–c. 1974*. Oxford: Oxford University Press.

May, Jon, and Nigel Thrift (eds.). 2001. *TimeSpace: Geographies of Temporality*. New York: Routledge.

Moglen, Helene. 2008. "Ageing and Transageing: Transgenerational Hauntings of the Self." *Studies in Gender and Sexuality,* 9(4): 297–311.
Nielsen, Harriet B. 2017. *Feeling Gender: A Generational and Psychosocial Approach.* London: Palgrave Macmillan.
Seigworth, Greg. 1995. "Sound Affects." *73 Magazine* (December): 21–3, 25.
Skjoldager-Nielsen, Kim, and Joshua Edelman. 2014. "Liminality." *Ecumenica,* 7(1–2): 33–40.
Turner, Victor. 1969. *The Ritual Process.* Ringwood: Penguin.
Woodward, Kathleen. 1997. "Telling Stories: Aging, Reminiscence, and the Life Review." *Telling Stories,* 9 (Doreen B Townsend Centre Occasional Papers): 1–17.

2

Inheritance Tracks, Shared Memories, and Collective Self-Therapy

Andy Bennett

Introduction

Tia DeNora's (2000) groundbreaking study *Music and Everyday Life* offers deep insights into how musical memories contribute to what she describes as "technologies of self," this being used to explain how individuals represent themselves over time with reference to key songs and musical pieces in their personalized biographical soundtrack. In the field of music therapy, the value of musical memory has been widely acknowledged as a means through which to work with people in the healing of trauma (Sutton 2002). Little consideration, however, has been given to how individuals draw on their memories of music in mundane, collective, everyday interactions. As Frith (1996) notes, people frequently talk about music in the course of their day-to-day interactions with others, something that we all have perhaps experienced in one way or another. In Frith's view, however, such interactions are typically focused on proving the worth and authenticity of particular genres, artists, albums, or tracks over others. While this is certainly one way in which individuals converse with each other about the value of music in a mundane context, it is certainly by no means the only way that we can understand the meaning of everyday conversations about music. At the most fundamental level, not all music listeners possess or desire the more in-depth level of fan knowledge necessary to engage in the kind of informed discussions about music described by Frith. Thus, the research findings presented in this chapter suggest that there are other ways of understanding the value of music. A critical factor here is the significance of what is referred to in this book as "Inheritance Tracks," which often assume a personal resonance for individuals particularly when talking about their past with reference to music they find meaningful in a personal sense. Indeed, as this chapter illustrates, such everyday uses of music can also assume significant social properties. Through sharing personal and often intimate memories informed by Inheritance Tracks with each other, individuals can foster instances of what I refer to here as "soothing sociality." Thus, shared musical memories can be used as the basis of supportive and explorative conversations whereby members of a group can find instances of commonality—common feelings, common emotions through which to support each other in informal conversations about ways in which music helps them link with their past and understand themselves in the present. Through participating in such exchanges, groups can create environments of empathy and trust, sharing with others, perhaps for the first time, thoughts and feelings that they have kept largely to themselves. Music in this context appears to act as a critical mediator, acting as a means through which individuals feel comfortable in opening up to each other. The purpose of this chapter is to consider in depth how a focus on the meaning and significance of Inheritance Tracks in such contexts can provide alternative understandings of music's therapeutic qualities as these emerge not through formalized situations of professional help but rather through mundane, informal, and spontaneous forms of interactions between individuals. A single focus group involving six participants formed the basis of the data collection for the research underpinning this chapter. Participants were recruited through a call for expressions of interest in taking part in the focus group.

Music, Emotion, and the Mundane

Despite the fact that popular music studies has been an established area of academic research for over four decades, very little attention has been paid to what is undoubtedly a main feature of music's social significance—specifically, ordinary people talking with each other in mundane contexts about music's specific and personal value to them as individuals. Rather, for much of the time, studies of popular music have focused on other more tangible aspects of music consumption, notably (post)subcultural style (Brake 1985; Muggleton 2000), and music scenes (Shank 1994). Ruth Finnegan's (1989) *The Hidden Musicians* broke ranks with such scholarly tropes to focus on more mundane aspects of music-making (in the English town of Milton Keynes), but a main focus of this study was music-making. It remains the case that the vast majority of people who invest in music—economically and emotionally—are not musicians and know little, if anything, about the technical and theoretical aspects of music-making. For this "academically silent" majority, music is frequently experienced as an ubiquitous aspect of the everyday soundscape (Kassabian 2013). In addition to the "piped" music heard in public spaces such as shopping malls and gyms, since the early 2000s, the increasing prevalence of digital technologies provides for individuals to create their own personalized musical soundscapes or, what Nowak (2015) refers to as, sound environments. DeNora's (2000) *Music and Everyday Life* offered an intriguing glimpse into this musical world, through its presentation of in-depth accounts of music and meaning from a number of ordinary, if individually distinctive, individuals. Divest of any obvious music scene membership or advanced musical skills, the people in DeNora's study discuss musical meaning against a backdrop of mundane activities—doing housework, exercising, driving, or simply sitting and listening to music on the radio or vinyl/CD player (this being just prior to the era of full-fledged digital online music technology). A particular salient finding of DeNora's study is the extent to which the people she selected for interview express a deep emotional investment in music as a means of connecting the past with the present, essentially using music as a "technology of the self" and using musical memories to understand and articulate their biographical stories. Thus, DeNora observes:

> Reliving experience through music ... in so far as it is experienced as an identification with or of 'the past', is part of the work of producing oneself as a coherent being over time, part of producing a retrospection that is in turn a projection into the future, a cuing in how to proceed. (2000: 66)

DeNora's observations are supported by more recent work on the theme of music and aging, which demonstrates how music can become a critical part of how individuals perceive themselves as they move through the life course. Music in this sense becomes a pivotal resource for individuals in charting and understanding their biographical development. Moreover, in this context, music is often understood by individuals as something that has actively shaped them as the people they have become in middle age and later life. For example, my own study of aging music fans notes how early investment in music as a teenager (when most individuals begin to listen to music in a more in-depth fashion and garner a sense of identity as expressed through musical taste) can often result in a more long-standing association with a particular musical genre or genres. As I have argued:

> One might reasonably expect ... that where investment in a musical style has been particularly intensive during one's teenage to twenty-something years such investment may well continue well into middle age and beyond.

> The fact that an individual becomes a follower of a style of music as a 'young' person may matter far less than what that music continues to mean to them as they grow older. (Bennett 2013: 20)

As this observation suggests, such ongoing investment in music will often display strong generational traits with songs linked to a particular time in life marked by generation and thus by generational memory. This, in turn, can often prompt a particular response on the part of popular media who seek to replay such memories back to audiences. In the UK, for example, the rush of retrospective television documentaries on key artists from the 1970s, including 10cc, the Electric Light Orchestra, and Kate Bush, is an interesting illustration of this, with each of these documentaries including the "big song" moment of these artists; 10cc's "I'm Not in Love" (1975), the Electric Light Orchestra's "Mr. Blue Sky" (1978), and Kate Bush's "Wuthering Heights" (1978) are all songs that individuals who experienced their teens during the 1970s in Britain remember as key sonic markers of the decade (see Bennett 2020).

Such generational connections are important as they frequently provide a context through which individuals are able to share memories that are couched within a situation of having lived through a particular era of popular culture and thus sharing a stock knowledge of cultural references. At the same time, however, as highlighted in the work of DeNora (2000) and Bennett and Rogers (2016), the stories that are told through this common tapestry of shared generational musical heritage are frequently characterized by highly individual narratives. The medium of music therefore becomes a vehicle for individuals to talk about themselves in often highly personal ways. Having established their common memories of music, place, and time, individuals then feel sufficiently connected with others, in an emotional sense, to begin to situate themselves as individuals with particular stories to tell in the context of this sonically shared past.

The Value of Musical "Inheritance"

As Frith (1988) explains, since the 1950s, music has increasingly been experienced as a mediated form. For most music fans, recorded music is the primary text (Moore 1993). Live performance has continued to punctuate the cultural significance of music, with landmark events such as Woodstock (Bennett 2004) and Live Aid (Garofalo 1992) encapsulating the capacity of live rock and pop music to capture the zeitgeist of a particular moment and with it the emotions and ongoing collective memories of spectators. But even the huge impact of events such as these is sustained through their mediation (thus, e.g., the iconic legacy of Woodstock has largely been generated and sustained through Michael Wadleigh's [1970] documentary film of the event *Woodstock: The Movie*; see Bennett 2004). In this very critical sense, from the very moment that a musical performance is captured, be this in the recording studio or on video or film, it is effectively archived as a document that will remain in circulation indefinitely. Similarly, at this point the technological aspects of the musical artifact are augmented by the aesthetic qualities of its symbolic appropriation. Earlier it was noted how a key aesthetic quality of music is in the way it allows individuals to feel about themselves and to articulate these feelings to others. It was noted how this frequently occurs at a level of generational exchange. But music can also give rise to intergenerational exchange as individuals belonging to different generations create dialogues between themselves through the exchange of musical resources.

Beginning in the early 2000s, a small but steadily growing body of work has engaged with the theme of shared intergenerational music taste (see, e.g., Vroomen 2004; Bennett 2006, 2012; Smith 2012; Hodkinson 2013). As this work illustrates, one of the most strident ways in which this intergenerational exchange takes place is between parents and children. Such exchange can take myriad forms, from conversations about music and music artists, accompanied by listening to particular songs or albums and watching DVD concert films, documentaries, and so forth, to subtler forms, such as music playing in the family home on a sound system or played as background music at family parties and other get-togethers. Through such forms of exchange, music can also become important in the way that memories are formed, in this case between parents and their children, or in some cases between wider family and friendship networks.

Frith (1987) has suggested that one of the defining characteristics of music is its intangible yet highly malleable nature. Through the process of its appropriation, music is often interwoven with highly personalized meanings. This is illustrated, for example, in research on "mix tapes," which involve personal collections of music on cassette, burned DVD, or other sound carrier and are frequently given to another in the form of a gift—a gift that in this case often speaks to the recipient on the part of the giver in specific ways, for example, as a token of love and affection or perhaps something that seeks to help the recipient understand the giver's sense of self and outlook on the world (see, e.g., Jansen 2009). Although not "given" as a tangible object in the same way as a mix tape, the passing of songs from a parent to a child (or indeed between any two individuals) can create a similar bond—and one that becomes more stridently realized with the passing of time. In essence, what emerges as part of this process is a sense of inheritance—through having spent time in the company of their parents (or significant others) listening to music, perhaps while also engaging in other activities such as talking or socializing with others, individuals feel that a specific musical text (or texts) and a particular way of understanding its significance have been passed on to them.

Talking about Inheritance Tracks

A key objective for the research informing this chapter was to discover what happens when individuals are purposely brought together in a situation where they are specifically invited to discuss the process of song inheritance and their individual experiences of this. The remainder of this chapter is dedicated to discussing the results of an experiment, in the form of a focus group, where this idea was put to the test. By way of a brief overview of the discussion that follows in the chapter, it was found that individuals who participated in the focus group quickly bonded, often telling highly personal, often seldom communicated stories to individuals who in most cases they had never met before. Music, in this sense, appeared to act as a form of individual and collective catharsis, a medium through which the focus group participants appeared comfortable in telling stories about themselves and other important people in their lives to relative strangers. Typically, the "Inheritance Tracks" that were chosen were ones that others in the group had at least some familiarity with (although this was not exclusively the case). That said, one of the most insightful aspects of the focus group was how individuals participating in the focus group were given time and space by other participants to fully articulate their personal stories of inheriting particular music tracks. The common bonding that occurred within the focus group rested on the fact that everyone in the room was there because they had personal experience of having inherited a track (or tracks) from a significant other in their lives. The songs themselves became the vehicle for the telling of stories of inheritance, with the stories being impactful whether or not others in the group were directly familiar with the song being discussed at any given point during the focus group. Even in cases, in fact the majority of cases, where a particular song was known by all members of the focus group, a respectful suspending of their own views and interpretations of the songs was displayed by other members of the group in order that the individual describing their inheritance track were given scope to tell their own story about the song. This routinely occurred with everything from easy listening standards through to rock and roll favorites and classic rock from the 1970s. In engaging in this form of interaction, a form of trust was seen to form between the individuals participating in the focus groups as they came to realize that the story being told by any given member of the group was both deeply personal and, in some cases, may have been the first time the story had been told to anyone else.

The focus group used to gather data for this chapter was conducted in September 2018 on the Gold Coast in Queensland, Australia. The specific location for the focus group was the Gold Coast campus of Griffith University where the author is a professor of cultural sociology in the School of Humanities, Languages and Social Science. The author took part in the focus group as a facilitator only. An application for ethical clearance to conduct the focus group was lodged and clearance granted before the focus group took place. Prior to the focus group taking place, a call for expressions of interest was circulated to potential participants. Participation in the focus group was on a voluntary basis. Eight people were originally due to take part in the focus group, but two had to withdraw due to unforeseen circumstances. Of the six remaining people who took part in the focus group, three identified as female and three as male, and they ranged in age from early forties to early sixties. Prior to the focus group taking place, each participant was asked to choose a song or piece of music that they considered to have been inherited from a parent or another "significant other" in their life. Four of the group chose a single song, while two others selected two tracks that for them were closely related through the process of inheritance. In the interests of keeping the focus group to its scheduled time of ninety minutes, the chosen tracks were not played, although, as noted earlier, most of the tracks discussed were known by all participants. Therefore, it is true to say that the bonding between group members occurred through their own memories of the songs rather than through direct listening, something that also demonstrated the embodied dimensions of musical experience. The eight tracks chosen by the individual participants for discussion were as follows:

Participant(s)	Track(s) and Album(s)	Artist(s)
Male (early sixties)	"King of the Road"	Roger Miller
Female (mid-forties)	"The Girl from Ipanema"	Astrud Gilberto and Stan Getz
Female (late forties)	*Tubular Bells*/*War of the Worlds*	Mike Oldfield/Jeff Wayne
Male (mid-forties)	"Have You Ever Seen the Rain"	Creedence Clearwater Revival
Female (early forties)	"Chantilly Lace"	Big Bopper
Male (late fifties)	"CC Rider"[1]/"Ooh Poo Pa Doo"[2]	Billy Thorpe and the Aztecs

The focus group began with me as the facilitator thanking everyone who had agreed to participate in the group for giving up their time to be there. I also briefly recapped the purpose of the focus group (participants having been sent full briefing notes prior to the staging of the focus group; see Appendix) and asked each of the participants to briefly introduce themselves.

During the course of the focus group, participants were asked to explain at the beginning of their particular inheritance track account, the track they would focus on and who they had inherited the track from. As noted previously, the focus group was originally intended to last for one and a half hours. In the end, however, the session ran to nearly two hours as the topic of Inheritance Tracks fueled some highly engaged conversation between the participants. All who had participated in the focus group agreed that the extra time had been well worth the experience of being able to listen to each other's inheritance track stories.

Understanding Inheritance Tracks: Key Findings from the Focus Group

What was perhaps the most significant insight to emerge from the focus group was the way that the Inheritance Tracks theme served as a bonding device between the participants. Apart from the round of introductions from each participant used to begin the focus group session, little in the way of an ice-breaking process or activity was used (or indeed, as it turned out, was required). Clearly, having provided the participants with the brief for the focus group before it took place had given them time to prepare their story to tell to others in the group. That said, the ease with which they related what were in some cases very intimate details of their past via the medium of music and, more specifically, the "inheritance track," was quite telling. What was also striking was the way in which participants supported each other through the questions and discussions that ensued as each participant completed the telling of their story. Frith argues that there is

> something specific to musical experience, namely, its direct emotional intensity. Because of its qualities of abstractness (which "serious" aestheticians have always stressed) music is an individualizing form. We absorb songs into our own lives and rhythms into our own bodies; they have a looseness of reference that makes them immediately accessible. Pop songs are open to appropriation for personal use in a way that other popular cultural forms (television soap operas, for example) are not—the latter are tied into meanings we may reject. (1987: 139)

An interesting dynamic that manifested in the focus group was how individual participants were able to register such emotional intensity, as related through the various "Inheritance Tracks" stories told. The accessibility of songs, identified by Frith in his previous observation, became in the context of the focus group a vehicle for a shared and collective understanding of how a specific song or piece of music served as a means for the individual story teller to understand and make sense of their relationship with the significant other at the center of their inheritance track story. In this sense, using the song as an object of a story about a relationship between the participant and a significant other added another dimension to the performativity of the song and its narrativization as an inheritance track. From the point of view of the listeners, while they were in many (though not all) cases familiar with the specific songs and pieces of music that became the subject of particular Inheritance Tracks stories, they displayed an ease in suspending any personal meanings of their own which they may have already attached to the songs in order to allow for the participant to tell their own story of the song's meaning for them. This suggests a further dimension to the malleability of songs as vessels for the inscription of meaning outlined in the foregoing account by Frith. Thus, the intertextual quality of songs observed by Frith assumes a dual resonance, both as a means through which individuals can understand themselves and as a means of conveying their memories and emotions to others. This provides a new dimension to the social meaning of songs, a point which is returned to and discussed in more detail later in this chapter.

It was also clear from the dynamics displayed within the focus group that participants saw the topic of the inheritance track as an ongoing process of intertextual exchange facilitated through a sharing of tracks and their personalized meanings. Earlier it was noted how DeNora (2000) considers music to be a technology of the self, that is to say, a means by which individuals both understand themselves and their evolution across the life course. In the case of Inheritance Tracks, an integral element of this is sharing the tracks and the memories inscribed in them with significant others, such that the personalized meaning of a song or piece of music is continually passed on. The following three vignettes, drawn from the focus group data, illustrate this point.

"CC Rider"/"Ooh Poo Pa Doo" (Male Australian Participant, Late Fifties)

The tracks named in the foregoing subtitle are emblematic of the 1970s Australian pub rock scene (see Homan 2000). The participant (originally from Melbourne) recalls being introduced to them and to similar tracks when he was twelve by an older female cousin who was fifteen years old at the time. The older cousin was allowed to go to gigs, whereas the participant was deemed too young at the time to accompany her. The older cousin also went to the now-iconic inaugural Sunbury Festival (see Evans 2017) in 1972 (where Billy Thorpe and the Aztecs were headliners) and was introduced to biker culture, running away with a motorcycle gang. She was not seen again for about fourteen years, eventually returning to Melbourne as a single mother. The participant rarely sees his cousin now, but when he does, they reconnect through Australian pub rock classics. In the intervening years, the participant became more increasingly attached to pub rock, and his son (who was in his early twenties at the time of the focus group) also enjoys this music through his father's influence.

Tubular Bells/War of the Worlds (Female Australian Participant, Late Forties)

The album *Tubular Bells*, and particularly the A side, is important for the participant as it was played for her often by her father (who died when she was in her early teens). Growing up in a working-class family in Melbourne, and moving to Brisbane when she was in her teens, she remembers her father as a creative and inventive person, playing the harmonica and building his own stereo system. She remembers that from her perspective as a young child, *Tubular Bells*, the debut and most successful album by eclectic British music artist Mike Oldfield (see Bennett 2020), had a very exotic feel to it. She linked this to the fact that the album was being played through her father's home-built system, as if that somehow had a part to play in the unusual all-embracing sound of the music. In recent years, the participant has played *Tubular Bells* to her young niece and related the story of why the music is of special significance. The participant feels a similar sense of inheritance attachment to Jeff Wayne's musical adaptation of *War of the Worlds*, based on the 1898 novel by British science fiction writer H. G. Wells that depicts a Martian invasion of the earth. For the participant, her attachment to this piece of music is based on her memories of sitting out at night under the stars with Wayne's album being played on her father's stereo system at loud volume.

"Have You Ever Seen the Rain" (Male American Participant, Mid-Forties)

This participant grew up in a working-class neighborhood in the city of Boston in the United States. His father worked in a series of different blue-collar jobs and was a keen motorcyclist. When at home, the participant's father would often play his acoustic guitar and sing current songs of the time, this being in the early 1970s. One of his favorite songs to sing was "Have You Ever Seen the Rain," a worldwide hit for American rock band Creedence Clearwater Revival in 1971. The participant would often sit and listen to his father playing. In 1974, his father was involved in an accident while riding his motorcycle and sustained a traumatic brain injury. In the following years, the participant learned to play the guitar, and one of his favorite songs to sing, because of the connection with his father, is "Have You Ever Seen the Rain." Although the participant hasn't seen his father in over thirty years, the song is a way that he continues to connect with and remember him. The participant's son also now plays guitar, and the participant has taught him how to play "Have You Ever Seen the Rain." The participant hasn't told his son about the significance that the song holds for him, feeling that it is a private thing between him and his father and that his son should make his own meanings and memories around the song.

In talking openly about the value of particular tracks as Inheritance Tracks, the focus group participants were engaged at a significant level in a common pursuit—the use of music as a means of engaging in deep and, in many ways, highly intimate conversations. The participants were self-selecting and thus opted to join the focus group because they considered it meaningful for them. As noted earlier, a bond quickly seemed to develop between the participants, and it appeared as if they were happy, if not grateful, for an opportunity to discuss music in a way that also allowed them an opportunity to open up about themselves to a group of people who, they were confident, shared similar experiences about music. After the focus group had ended, a few participants exchanged phone numbers so that they could keep in touch. One of the participants followed up with me on email relating more musical memories, including about music inherited from her father. All of the participants said that they had enjoyed the focus group experience and wished that there were more opportunities to meet and discuss music and its personal meanings with each other. This was a welcome, but in some ways unexpected, outcome of the workshop, suggestive of the fact that given the opportunity of a structured event such as a focus group to share their experiences of musical inheritance, individuals can see their way toward creating further opportunities to meet and discuss the importance of such musicalized memories in what may amount to a situation (or situations) of "collective self-therapy."

Collective Self-Therapy and Soothing Sociality

Green (2016) has applied the term "peak music experience" to account for the way that tastes in specific music and genres are often acquired through particularly intense experiences—often at live music concerts and festivals—that subsequently fuel potent feelings of belonging and collective memory among music fans. Thus, as Green observes:

> As meaning is mediated by feeling, the meanings mediated by the strongest feelings may be the ones that persist. Peak music experiences can therefore

provide concrete insight into the question of how encounters with music can affect people in enduring ways. (2016: 340)

Green's observations are highly pertinent in the context of the current discussion in that they help frame a particular understanding of music's emotional impact as tied to particularly strong memories and experiences. As an extension of Green's argument, it is also possible to link the significance of Inheritance Tracks with peak music experiences—specifically when such experiences are shared with, or even instigated by, a significant other in one's life. In this sense, a peak music experience is doubly articulated in that it bespeaks a song that has personal relevance and a connection with autobiographical memory *and* consolidates a sense of having inherited a special way of understanding a song or piece of music that could only have derived from an intimate relationship—between father and son/daughter, between cousins, and so forth. Such intimacy is important in that it feeds an ongoing sense of inheritance and a particular form of musical ownership that exists only between two people, or perhaps between a small group of friends, between siblings, and so forth.

Furthermore, when understood by the individual through the lens of the peak music experience, the inheritance track can become an important means of dealing with personal loss and trauma, which can range from a simple drifting apart to the breakup of a relationship or the loss of the significant other from which a track was inherited. In this sense, and as the focus group that informs this chapter illustrated, the opportunity for individuals to share their inheritance track stories with others can serve as an important form of collective therapy. Group therapy has been a recognized approach in dealing with issues of stress and trauma for many decades (see Brabender, Fallon, and Smolar 2004). Typically, however, group therapy approaches involve some kind of formally structured approach run by a person with recognized skills and held in a formalized setting. The value of and need for forms of therapy, however, may exist on a number of different levels, including instances where individuals do not necessarily need professional support but rather simply an opportunity to engage in what could be referred to as "soft therapy"—talking to others in a supportive environment where they can open up and share memories, feelings, and emotions that they have bottled up for many years. Earlier in this chapter, it was noted how Frith (1987) has cited music as a cultural form that can strongly bond people due to a keenly felt, mutually experienced sense of emotional investment in given artists and tracks. This has also been strongly evident for the author over the course of a number of ethnographic studies focusing on music and meaning in contemporary everyday life (see, e.g., Bennett 2000, 2013; Bennett and Rogers 2016). While the experiences that people share through conversations about a particular song or piece of music may not in every case be painful or traumatic, the relation of memories—even if pleasurable—covers at some level aspects of loss. This may be as simple as reflecting on a time when life was less stressful or based around commitments—to work or a partner and so forth—whereby a song and the opportunity to engage with it through providing a personal account of its meaning provide for an opportunity to reconnect with that past moment. This in itself can present as an important therapeutic exercise for the individual and help them to better cope with their current life situation.

Premised on this understanding and experience of music as a resource that bonds, the focus group offered instructive insights as to how, in discussing the importance of Inheritance Tracks in their personal lives, individuals demonstrate a capacity to engage in a type of informal collective self-therapy. This was most clearly punctuated by the atmosphere that quickly established itself in the focus group, which was one of what could be termed "soothing sociality." Sociality has long been understood as a survival response to the pressures of human social evolution. In the context of human society, sociality is often used to describe the desire of individuals for social connection against a backdrop of an increasingly fragmented society characterized by the decline of more traditional forms of community. In his celebrated study of this phenomenon, Maffesoli (1996) suggests that individuals resist the pathology of individualization by joining together in short-lived flashes of sociality that he refers to as *tribus* (tribes). Maffesoli cited examples of such tribes (or as Shields [1992] recast this "neo-tribes") in the form of the crowds that gather in shopping centers or at sporting events. But if sociality in times of social fragmentation can occur in such settings, it seems entirely reasonable to assume that individuals may also seek opportunities for sociality in smaller, more intimate settings where they feel more able to express themselves and feel a sense of connection, support, and reaffirmation.

The focus group conducted for the purposes of writing this chapter provided an interesting snapshot (albeit under curated conditions, itself a necessity given the experimental nature of the focus group) of how music, and specifically Inheritance Tracks, offers individuals a chance to connect in an instance of sociality where they feel quickly able to relax their barriers and participate in intimate exchanges. Put at their ease by the opportunity to talk about music to an empathetic group of people, all of whom were participating in the focus group specifically to share their inheritance track stories, a situation of mutual trust, respect, and support for each other quickly manifested and remained patently evident for the duration of the session. The Inheritance Tracks theme of the focus group was nonconfrontational and allowed individuals a significant amount of agency in talking over issues such as loss and grief, coming of age, separation, and starting over. It was clear that the chosen Inheritance Tracks, and an opportunity to talk about them with others, provided a source of solace. It was also clear that the Inheritance Tracks focus group provided participants with a visible sense of empowerment in talking about issues such as personal loss and estrangement, which they had seldom or perhaps never discussed with others as was evident when participants told their inheritance track stories.

What then do the results of this exercise add to our knowledge of the importance of Inheritance Tracks? Most fundamentally, it is apparent that the theme of Inheritance Tracks touches the lives of individuals in ways that may not necessarily apply to other songs they consider of personal relevance. If, as DeNora (2000) suggests, musical memories significantly serve in the building of a technology of the self, Inheritance Tracks are inscribed with particular memories of significant others and allow individuals to retain a sense of emotional closeness with them, even in cases where they have been separated from a significant other through the death of that person, or some other event. At the end of the focus group, those who had taken part said that they had found the experience very worthwhile, not least because it had revealed that while the value of Inheritance Tracks was always a matter of individual experience, memory, and interpretation, the actual process of inheriting tracks from a significant other was a common experience. Bringing people together more commonly to discuss the importance of heritage tracks in their lives could, we agreed, serve as an important way for people to share and connect—and to realize that their individual stories connected in a general sense and rekindled a sense of collectivity and community.

Epilogue—Soothing Sociality in Challenging Times

The insights gleaned from the focus group in terms of music's value as a medium for collective self-therapy have perhaps taken on a more salient meaning in recent times in the light of the Covid-19 pandemic. Faced with extreme measures such as social distancing and lockdowns, feelings of isolation and meaninglessness have significantly increased since the early months of 2020. Much has been made of the value of music as a morale booster, with online performances by artists such as Neil Diamond and the Rolling Stones during the pandemic being one major aspect of this (Lehman 2020). Similarly, balcony performances and live-streamed living room performances by musicians across the world have also demonstrated the value of music in helping to bring people together in times of shared crisis and hardship (Hebblethwaite, Young, and Martin Rubio 2020; Frennaux and Bennett 2021). In such a context of risk and uncertainty, informal gatherings of individuals, online or face-to-face, to discuss music and its personal meanings for them could be an important factor in helping people stay connected and engender a caring and supportive environment during these unprecedented times of pandemic crisis and whatever forms of socioeconomic upheaval may follow.

Appendix: Notes Circulated to Focus Group Participants

Inheritance Tracks

Why Is the Research Being Conducted?

The research is being conducted to assess if and how the way people describe their attachment to specific (popular) music tracks, be it songs or pieces of music, can be seen as a process of inheritance. More specifically, the research is concerned with examining ways in which the meanings people associate with music tracks they hold special in their lives are actively handed down to them from significant others and subsequently passed on in the same fashion to other family members, partners, close friends, and so on.

What You Will Be Asked to Do

You have been asked to participate in a focus group session of between sixty and ninety minutes, comprising six to ten people. Participants will be asked in turn to identify a music track that they have inherited and one that they would like to bequeath or pass on. Participants are asked to share what motivated them to choose these particular tracks, what the tracks evoke, who they inherited them from or who they might want to pass them on to, and so on. They are expected to participate in the exchanges and discussions that will be inspired by the music tracks and the accompanying stories.

The focus group will be facilitated by the research team and will be recorded subject to the prior consent of the focus group participants. The recordings will be transcribed. As required by Griffith University, all audio recordings will be erased after transcription. However, other research data (focus group transcripts and analyses) will be retained in a password-protected electronic file at Griffith University for a period of five years before being destroyed. Segments of the interviews and transcripts may then be used in a summary report of the findings presented at an academic workshop to be held in the UK and may also be used as the basis of a chapter to be published in an edited book. By participating in the project, you assign the researchers the rights to publish the results, although no information that identifies the participants will be included in the summary report or the potentially resulting publication unless participants provide the research team with written consent that this may occur.

The research will not be contrary to the best interests of participants and will not create undue distress for the participants due to the general nature of the questions asked during interviews. As questions relate to music tracks that may have personal memories for you, this may involve the discussion of personal information. But at no time are you obligated to divulge such information. Your responses to questions can be as detailed or as general as you are comfortable with.

The Expected Benefits of the Research

The purpose of this project will be to provide a better understanding of the cultural significance of (popular) music in the life course and its value as a biographical soundtrack in people's lives.

Notes

1 "CC Rider" was originally written and recorded by Ray Charles. In addition to Billy Thorpe and the Aztecs version, versions of the song were also recorded and performed by artists including Elvis Presley and The Animals.
2 "Ooh Poo Pa Doo" was originally written and recorded by Jessie Hall. In addition to Billy Thorpe and the Aztecs version, versions of the song were also recorded and performed by artists including Wilson Pickett and Ike and Tina Turner.

References

Bennett, Andy. 2000. *Popular Music and Youth Culture: Music, Identity and Place.* Basingstoke: Palgrave Macmillan.

Bennett, Andy. 2004. "'Everybody's Happy, Everybody's Free': Representation and Nostalgia in the Woodstock Film." In Andy Bennett (ed.), *Remembering Woodstock*, 43–54. Aldershot: Ashgate.

Bennett, Andy. 2006. "Punks Not Dead: The Significance of Punk Rock for an Older Generation of Fans." *Sociology*, 40(1): 219–35.

Bennett, Andy. 2012. "Dance Parties, Lifestyle and Strategies for Ageing." In Andy Bennett and Paul Hodkinson (eds.), *Ageing and Youth Cultures: Music, Style and Identity*, 95–104. Oxford: Berg.

Bennett, Andy. 2013. *Music, Style and Aging: Growing Old Disgracefully?* Philadelphia: Temple University Press.

Bennett, Andy. 2020. *British Progressive Pop 1970–1980.* New York: Bloomsbury.

Bennett, Andy, and Ian Rogers. 2016. *Popular Music Scenes and Cultural Memory.* Basingstoke: Palgrave.

Brabender, Virginia A., April E. Fallon, and Andrew I. Smolar. 2004. *Essentials of Group Therapy*. Hoboken, NJ: Wiley.
Brake, Michael. 1985. *Comparative Youth Culture: The Sociology of Youth Cultures and Youth Subcultures in America, Britain and Canada*. London: Routledge and Kegan Paul.
DeNora, Tia. 2000. *Music in Everyday Life*. Cambridge: Cambridge University Press.
Evans, Peter. 2017. *Sunbury: Australia's Greatest Rock Festival*. Melbourne: Melbourne Books.
Finnegan, Ruth. 1989. *The Hidden Musicians: Music-Making in an English Town*. Cambridge: Cambridge University Press.
Frennaux, Richard, and Andy Bennett. 2021. "A New Paradigm of Engagement for the Socially Distanced Artist." *Rock Music Studies*, 8(1): 65–75.
Frith, Simon. 1987. "Towards an Aesthetic of Popular Music." In Richard Leppert and Susan McClary (eds.), *Music and Society: The Politics of Composition, Performance and Reception*, 133–51. Cambridge: Cambridge University Press.
Frith, Simon. 1988. *Music for Pleasure: Essays in the Sociology of Pop*. Oxford: Polity Press.
Frith, Simon. 1996. *Performing Rites: On the Value of Popular Music*. Oxford: Oxford University Press.
Garofalo, Reebee. 1992. "Understanding Mega-Events: If We Are the World, Then How Do We Change It?" in Reebee Garofalo (ed.), *Rockin' the Boat: Mass Music and Mass Movements*, 15–36. Boston, MA: South End Press.
Green, Ben. 2016. "'I Always Remember That Moment': Peak Music Experiences as Epiphanies." *Sociology*, 50(2): 333–48.
Hebblethwaite, Sharon, Laurel Young, and Tristana Martin Rubio. 2020. "Pandemic Precarity: Aging and Social Engagement." *Leisure Sciences*. DOI: 10.1080/01490400.2020.1773998.
Hodkinson, Paul. 2013. "Family and Parenthood in an Ageing 'Youth' Culture: A Collective Embrace of Dominant Adulthood?" *Sociology*, 47(6): 1072–87.
Homan, Shane. 2000. "Losing the Local: Sydney and the Oz Rock Tradition." *Popular Music*, 19(1): 31–49.
Jansen, Bas. 2009. "Tape Cassettes and Former Selves: How Mix Tapes Mediate Memories." In Karin Bijsterveld (ed.), *Sound Souvenirs: Audio Technologies, Memory and Cultural Practices*, 43–54. Amsterdam: Amsterdam University Press.
Kassabian, Anahid. 2013. *Ubiquitous Listening: Affect, Attention, and Distributed Subjectivity*. Los Angeles: University of California Press.
Lehman, Eric T. 2020. "'Washing Hands, Reaching Out'—Popular Music, Digital Leisure and Touch during the COVID-19 Pandemic." *Leisure Sciences*. DOI: 10.1080/01490400.2020.1774013.
Maffesoli, Michel. 1996. *The Time of the Tribes: The Decline of Individualism in Mass Society*. Translated by Don Smith. London: Sage.
Moore, Allan F. 1993. *Rock: The Primary Text—Developing a Musicology of Rock*. Buckingham: Open University Press.
Muggleton, David. 2000. *Inside Subculture: The Postmodern Meaning of Style*. Oxford: Berg.

Nowak, Raphaël. 2015. *Consuming Music in the Digital Age: Technologies, Roles and Everyday Life*. Basingstoke: Palgrave.

Shank, Barry. 1994. *Dissonant Identities: The Rock 'n' Roll Scene in Austin, Texas*. London: Wesleyan University Press.

Shields, Rob. 1992. "The Individual, Consumption Cultures and the Fate of Community." In Rob Shields (ed.), *Lifestyle Shopping: The Subject of Consumption*, 99–114. London: Routledge.

Smith, Nicola. 2012. "Parenthood and the Transfer of Capital in the Northern Soul Scene." In Andy Bennett and Paul Hodkinson (eds.), *Ageing and Youth Cultures: Music, Style and Identity*, 159–72. Oxford: Berg.

Sutton, Julie P. (ed.). 2002. *Music, Music Therapy and Trauma: International Perspectives*. London: Janet Kingsley.

Vroomen, Laura. 2004. "Kate Bush: Teen Pop and Older Female Fans." In Andy Bennett and Richard A. Peterson (eds.), *Music Scenes: Local, Translocal and Virtual*, 238–53. Nashville, TN: Vanderbilt University Press.

Wadleigh, M. 1970. *Woodstock*. New York: Wadleigh-Maurice. https://www.imdb.com/title/tt0066580/.

3

Bordering Musical Inheritance: Navigating Borderscapes and Belonging through Memories of Finnish Childhoods

Helmi Järviluoma, Elina Hytönen-Ng, and Sonja Pöllänen

In October 2018, the three authors and their colleague Sinikka Vakimo organized an Inheritance Tracks workshop in Eastern Finland.[1] Participants were asked to choose in advance two "Inheritance Tracks" available as recordings: a song they have inherited from their past and another that they would pass on; they were also asked to describe how they first encountered their chosen songs. The event took place at the Vesijärvi Library Hall (name disguised)[2] in Eastern Finland, which was a familiar place to the participants. The participants moved between different layers of remembering during the workshop, recalling emotionally laden past places and times and memory objects such as record players. Through listening to the discussion and later to the recordings made during the event, we observed that the participants' narrations revealed their creation and navigation of national, regional, class-related, and religion-related borders.

This chapter analyses what we call "belongingness in-between" (Konrad 2020) working at and across the layers of musical remembering using the concepts of bordering and borderscapes. We understand bordering as implying "non-finalizable processes in which socio-spatial distinction is constantly created, confirmed and challenged" (Scott and Sohn 2019: 297). The complexities of everyday life can be negotiated through bordering. The borderscape concept has recently emerged in multidisciplinary border studies and is used to describe the multisited, relational, cultural, and socio-spatial configuration of borderlands "resulting in and given form by discourses, locational practices, and material outputs" (Stoffelen and Vameste 2019; see also Brambilla et al. 2015; dell'Agnese and Amilhat Szary 2015). We aim to analyze border-making and mediated acts of remembering through an examination of the workshop discussion of older adults born between 1946 and 1957. We focus on the sociocultural remembering that especially pertains to borderscapes, allowing shared interpretations of borders and their significance.

Research Methods

The participants in our 2018 workshop were recruited through an open call that was advertised partly through printed posters and flyers sent to all of Vesijärvi's libraries and attached to notice boards around town. The event was also advertised on the library's Facebook site. Some of the participants were recruited by the four researchers Helmi Järviluoma, Elina Hytönen-Ng, Sonja Pöllänen, and Sinikka Vakimo. Five older adults joined the workshop. The researchers, although they did not share music or stories, were active participants in the workshop, coproducing the knowledge together with the recruited participants. Secondary data was gathered as some of the recruited participants were interviewed a year and a half later, during the summer of 2020, to dig deeper into the borderscapes theme that we found interesting when analyzing the transcript of the original workshop.

Participants at the workshop were a heterogeneous group. Some of their "inherited tracks" traced back to their roots (discussed later), and some did not.[3] Using two types of data (namely, the group discussion and later individual in-depth interviews; see "Primary Sources"), we analyze how understandings of past borderscapes are created in the present. We pay special attention to technology and its role in remembering musical mediations. Processing or (re)producing of past musical experiences is entangled with changes that have occurred throughout the life course of the people who participated in our workshop.

The Logistics and Dynamics of the Workshop

The Vesijärvi Library Hall is used to host small events and lectures. We chose this location for the Inheritance Tracks workshop since it is both accessible and welcoming, whereas the university and its lecture halls can intimidate nonacademic participants. The advertising worked well enough to attract a sufficient number of participants. The group of five consisted of a male and female married couple born in the 1950s, a female widow born in the mid-1940s, and a sister and brother, both born during the latter part of the 1950s.

The married couple, Maija and Pekka, were both born in the mid-1950s in Kainuu, an eastern province of Finland situated a few hundred kilometers north of Vesijärvi. Maija was still working in a leading management position in education, while Pekka had retired from planning work in the construction industry. They had lived their whole adult life about 50 kilometers from Vesijärvi, in an eastern Finland industrial and mining town that has gone through a major restructuring process in the past few decades. Maija was articulate and an active participant in the group. Pekka was quieter but still participated in the discussions and introduced his song with thoughtful reflection.

Raija, the widow, was born near one of the major cities in southeast Finland, where her family had been removed to when areas in Karelia were ceded to the Soviet Union after the Second World War.[4] When Raija was about three years old, her whole family was able to move to northern Helsinki, where Raija spent her childhood years.[5] She represented the first generation of an evacuee family dislocated from family roots. Raija moved away from Helsinki when she started working in and studying health care in her twenties. After some years, she settled in southeast Finland, close to the areas where she had family roots, and she has remained there for over forty years.[6] Despite the close proximity of the border and the war history of the town, Raija did not feel connected to the ceded areas and her roots on the other side of the border. She was the oldest participant in the workshop, a little over seventy years of age.

Asko and Helena, the youngest in the group, were siblings who lived in Vesijärvi. They were avid participants and are a familiar sight in all kinds of public, open cultural events in town. Consequently, it was no surprise to us that they arrived at our workshop. Asko, in particular, played a central role in the workshop as he commented on the songs that others chose and contributed his own memories of the songs he had chosen. Helena was quieter yet still active in the discussion.

Since a large amount of interesting material resulted from the two-hour workshop, we chose to focus on the comments of two workshop participants instead of five—or nine if we include the researchers (as coproducers of knowledge). This means that the comments and narration of Raija and Maija were analyzed most closely. The processes of creating borders were also most strikingly present when they introduced their Inheritance Tracks. It was obvious, however, that we could not exclude comments from the other participants; the workshop had an intensive group atmosphere,

TABLE 3.1 *Inheritance Tracks Chosen by Participants for the Vesijärvi Library Hall Workshop in 2018*

Participant's Pseudonym	Participant's Approximate Age	Inherited Track	Artist	Inherited From
Maija	> 60	"Va, pensiero" from Verdi's *Nabucco* (1842)	Many (e.g., Metropolitan Opera)	Mother
Raija	~ 70	"Isoisän olkihattu" ("Grandfather's Straw Hat") (1951)	Tapio Rautavaara	Grandmother
Asko	> 60	"Siipirikkoinen" (2016)	Cuulas Trio	Friend
Helena	> 60	"Meksikon pikajuna" ("Orient Express") (1949)	Reino Helismaa	Family, radio
Pekka	60–70	"Day-O" ("The Banana Boat Song") (1959)	Harry Belafonte	Grandfather

and the comments of all nine of us intertwined, with speakers constantly shifting. Some of the transcript excerpts reflect this; in some of the longer quotes, omissions are shown with bracketed ellipses. Besides focusing on two participants, in this chapter, we also focus more on songs that were inherited (see Table 3.1) than on songs participants wanted to pass on. The latter seemed to be chosen on different grounds than the songs participants had inherited, and we needed to limit our focus to enable a deeper analysis.

The participants were given an opportunity to bring a recording with them, but none of them did. All of the songs were found on YouTube. The Library Hall had a computer and good speakers. The workshop was mainly led by Helmi Järviluoma, who mediated the speaking turns and helped Sonja Pöllänen in selecting the appropriate version of the selected songs. We often negotiated as a group the alternatives available so that the song that was played matched the version the participant had in mind. First, each participant was given a few minutes to discuss their inheritance track in relation to their life story, and second, their "own" track was played.

Then, afterward, there was a 10–15 minutes long discussion about the track together with others. After this, the song that the participant wished to pass on to someone else was played, and another discussion was held.

As mentioned, the research team of four cultural researchers participated actively in the workshop by sharing their own experiences and memories associated with the songs. Two of the researchers, Helmi and Sinikka, were born at the turn of the 1950s to the 1960s. Even though all participants did not belong to exactly the same age group, Helmi and Sinikka were able to connect with shared memories more extensively than the other two researchers. Elina and Sonja were born in the 1980s and belonged to a different generation, yet they participated by sharing what they had heard in their own life experiences.

In Table 3.1, the tracks are introduced in the order they were listened to in the workshop.

Bordering Inherited Tracks in the Workshop

Our analysis begins with Maija's story. Maija painted an interesting picture of the place where she grew up and what music meant in connection to that place. She was born a decade after the Second World War in a small rural community in the northeastern province of Kainuu, a region that is often portrayed as beautiful but is also one of Finland's poorest areas. The town she was born in suffered greatly during the Second World War. As Finland broke its ties with Germany toward the end of the war, the German army burned not only practically all of Lapland but also parts of northeastern Finland. Maija's hometown was among those burned down completely in September 1944. As she said, "Everything was burned. ... There was not one old house left except the church and one pigsty."

Relics of the war featured prominently in Maija's childhood; she played games in trenches at old battle sites with helmets, rifle cartridges, and "all kinds of war stuff." Maija described her identity in nutshell: "In the '50s, I was a little girl. In the middle of the woods and my sisters." She chose her inherited music track during the workshop, not beforehand. Since she had worked with children throughout her career, she had dealt with a lot of music and songs. Music had also been a very important part of her childhood family life. So she said that it was not easy to pick one particular track. The one she finally chose was the "Chorus of the Hebrew Slaves," in Italian "Va, pensiero," from Giuseppe Verdi's opera *Nabucco* (1842).[7]

In the late 1950s, Maija's maternal uncle moved to Australia to work, and when he returned, he brought a record player with him. Maija explained how and why the song came to mind:

In our family, we had always been interested in music, even if life was incredibly poor there in my childhood. ... But in the last minutes, a memory came to my mind that, when it was so poor at [name of the place], my mother's brother went to Australia for work. It must have been at the end of the 1950s or early '60s, and he was there for four years. And when he came back, he had a record player and a lot of classical records with him.

At some point, Maija's mother asked to borrow her brother's record player,

and our mother, she listened to classical music really a lot, because she was terribly musical, even though she had never gone to school, and she loved music [clears her throat]. The beautiful piece of music has stayed in my mind. I have not listened to it a lot but I recognize it: "Chorus of the Hebrew Slaves."

It is interesting how Maija juxtaposed both her mother's and her uncle's great interest in classical music and the fact that her mother had not been educated and that the uncle was doing hard manual labor in Australia:

It was my uncle, he was terribly interested in all kinds of music and this kind of classical music, even though he never really went to any school. He was doing some kind of hard work there in Australia, then came back regardless.[8]

Her comments relate to the border between the working class and the bourgeoisie. The category feature[9] of "listening to classical music" is not typically linked to the working or uneducated classes. In the next excerpt, Maija continues connecting the sad, poor, literally burnt, and lost history of her own home region to the fresh winds from the big world that listening to "Va, pensiero" brought to her. It is good to bear in mind that here concrete memory objects (i.e., the record player and the records) had been physically brought to her town across the border from the "greater world," from Australia.

Everything was burned, so it was like, somehow like a kind of breeze from there, like from the great world—that this [hometown] is not the only world, there's something more to it. Since when it comes to music, the only thing one could listen to was hymns, and then, well, sometimes you could hear something from the radio, but that didn't happen often.

Maija said that when listening to the song, she saw with her mind's eye how the slaves walked in a long line one after the other. She did not understand the words, though. Her mother was religious, and even if the words were unknown, the title of the song gave a hint that the content of the song dealt with the Old Testament. The lyrics deal with remembering "my country, so lovely and lost":

> Fly, thought, on wings of gold,
> go settle upon the slopes and the hills
> where the sweet airs of our
> native soil smell soft and mild!

We met Maija and Pekka again in June 2020. This time we interviewed the couple in their home in the former mining town in Eastern Finland. Maija mentioned that the record player and classical music album she had mentioned in the workshop were right there in the house, in the attic. After the interview, we received an email from Maija with a picture of the album cover (see Figure 3.1) and an astonished note: yes, there were many tracks on the record that her uncle had brought from Australia, but "Va, pensiero" was not one of them (for more on her "remembering differently," see the section "Relational Technologies and Memory Objects"). An interesting discussion among the workshop participants occurred when Maija said that since the classical songs were performed on vinyl in a foreign language, she

FIGURE 3.1 *The twelve-record album A Gay Festival of Light Classical Music (Reader's Digest) brought from Australia to Finland by Maija's maternal uncle in the early 1960s.*

tried to learn to sing in that language. Helena confirmed: "Exactly," and Maija continued:

> MAIJA: But it was a bit difficult, when there were no words [laughs], and it was kind of a disaster, but one tried hard at it.
> ASKO: Songs in English, if one could figure out nothing else, one could imagine what the lyrics were, and sing along.
> MAIJA: Yeah.
> RAIJA: Yes. Then gradually the English lyrics turned into "Finnish" so ...

A similar discussion took place at several stages during the workshop. Here, a particular borderscape was created between languages. Often the foreign words that children do not understand in a song are turned into their own language, gibberish or double Dutch, which may sound humorous to others. The gibberish lyrics spread, and often the funny gibberish versions of particularly popular refrains are known broadly in the whole language area. The song is made one's own, in invented "Finnish." One concrete example of this is one phrase from Pekka's inheritance track, "Day-O" ("The Banana Boat Song"), sung by Harry Belafonte in 1959. There is a line in the third stanza of the song, "Come Mister tally man, tally me banana," in which banana boat workers ask their foreman to come and count their banana bunches so that they can go home. Finnish children could sing the phrase "kallistakalinaakalinipanaana," which is nonsense but can be interpreted as something like "expensive-clatter-kalini-banana."

Besides Maija's comments about manual labor and classical music, the social classes and borders between them were also apparent in Raija's interview. She had chosen a song by the Finnish singer and actor Tapio Rautavaara, called "Isoisän olkihattu" ("Grandfather's Straw Hat"). The song was also composed by Rautavaara, and the song is about remembering: the protagonist in the song goes to the attic, finds a straw hat, and quietly ponders upon and remembers the love story between his grandfather and grandmother. The song ends:

> The pictures ran in my memory in the balmy attic
> And I thought how beautiful life is after all
> But how little is left of us to remember for the ones who remain
> Like from the story of Grandfather—nothing but the straw hat.[10]

The interview with Raija brought to our attention that the song was played and listened to on the radio when she heard it as a child. As the relocated family was poor, they did not have the money to buy a record player, but the family listened to the radio together. The Karelian grandmother, who came to visit often, was also an avid singer and knew all the songs on the radio, even the new ones. In this way, the radio connected different generations.

The poor economic conditions of Raija's family also linked her with the singer of the song she chose. Rautavaara, even though he later became a famous singer and actor, lived in the same district and was described by Raija as being like "your next-door uncle." Later in the interview, she explained that she did not know him personally; he just lived in the same district. Rautavaara nonetheless grew up with few resources, the son of a single parent, but had made an athletic career throwing the javelin at the Olympics and became a singer and actor through hard work. His significance to Raija seemed to be created by her familiarity with him and the shared living environment, while he also had children who were similar in age to Raija. Rautavaara had managed to achieve higher socioeconomic status becoming perhaps the role model in the neighborhood.

Raija said that the songs played on the radio were learned from Finnish Schlager[11] leaflets, which contained the lyrics and some musical notes to popular music. The leaflets were called *Toivelauluja* (i.e., "wished songs"). Published by the Finnish music publishing company Musiikki-Fazer between 1949 and 1983, they were bought at kiosks. As Raija explained:

> Our grandmother lived with one of her grandchildren. Leila was older than I was, and she always bought these Schlager leaflets. Leila was a really good singer, and she always sang songs from them, and that is also where Grandmother learned the songs. ... There were lyrics at least, maybe also some notes. We didn't have them ourselves, but Leila did have the Schlager leaflets. From these, Grandmother sang the songs with Leila. ... In a notebook, we also copied lyrics from Leila's leaflets, or if someone we knew bought a Schlager leaflet, we copied the lyrics from it.

Raija's family's connection to the areas ceded to the Soviet Union did not come up in the interview held with her in June 2020, and the remembering of the old country that is often associated with the Karelian people did not appear in Raija's descriptions. The waning of the traditional Karelian songs and the language, or Karelian dialect, was derived in part from the Finlandization (see Suutari and Järviluoma 2017) and self-censorship of one's ethnic minority identity. An example of this self-censorship was in trying to avoid being identified with the "Russkies" by the Finnish population. These forms of self-censorship were most likely related to the younger generation's aim to blend in with mainstream society.

It was only when asked in the interview whether her family ever sang songs about the old country, such as "Karjalan Kunnailla" ("On the Hills of Karelia"), that Raija said the following:

> Of course, people always talked about the places there, told stories about the regions across the border. And how everything was so beautiful and good [there]. But I didn't have this [a relationship with it], as I have spent

my childhood in Helsinki and I have not lived near the border myself, but only as an adult when I lived near [the town near the border]. ... Many people sang those songs. They did exist back then but ... I don't remember. My father did sing somewhat at home, but my mother never sang.

Here Raija explains that she did not have a relationship with the border area (i.e., the regions that were ceded to the Soviet Union after the Second World War). Many people felt that Karelia was violently cut into two with the new national border. She did not have any memories of the old Karelia but only heard stories told by others. As Suutari and Järviluoma (2017) point out, the ethnic dialect and the songs related to the dialect were issues too sensitive to be openly discussed. As more than 400,000 people were evacuated from the Karelian areas and were resettled in different parts of Finland (Raninen-Siiskonen 1999), this event, along with the Second World War, was a major trauma in Finnish history.

Karelian revivalism came later, after the period of active Finlandization, but the reverence for the region and its culture by the evacuee generation's stories was distant to Raija and did not resonate with her. More prominent in her life were the opportunities that the capital, Helsinki, offered in the decades after the war. She was building her identity as a citizen of Helsinki, not as a member of an immigrant or evacuated family. This part of her and her siblings' cultural identity was also highlighted by opportunities to attend cultural and sports events, even world-class events, seized by Raija's family even through limited financial funds. This distinguishes Raija's childhood in Helsinki, where such events were taking place, from the childhoods of others attending the workshop, who lived far away from the capital. Raija's family attended, with some relatives from farther away, the 1952 Olympics in Helsinki, where they watched Tapio Rautavaara throw the javelin. Such cultural events also came up in our interview with Raija. The Olympics also illustrate the multiple roles that Rautavaara had in the cultural scene in Helsinki.

In relation to international cultural influences available in Helsinki, Raija also mentioned music from the global youth culture that her older sisters were listening to and that she was perhaps too young to listen to. The older sisters also took Raija to concerts, like Paul Anka's first concert in Linnanmäki amusement park: "Well, he [Anka] was my big sister's idol, really, or for both of the [older] sisters and we did listen to his music. And we even went to his concerts in Linnanmäki. ... Don't remember the year, but I must have been around twelve or something."

We checked the date later, and the concert took place in August 1959 (Yle 2008), when Raija was thirteen. Such concerts were rare, and it seems particularly interesting that the family had the opportunity to attend such events, and such opportunities were considered important for the young girls.

These references to the Olympics and Anka's concert demonstrate Helsinki's position as an international capital city, as distinct from the other, more rural areas of Finland where Raija's family originated. While the Iron Curtain remained along the eastern border of Finland in the 1950s, and the other borders of the country were not easily crossed by the majority of people, Helsinki acted as a national port where influences could enter from the outside world. Otherwise, the significance of Finland's national borders, which is more pronounced in the other participants' stories, receives less attention in Raija's story.

Another kind of bordering is going on when we consider the songs that participants chose to pass on to somebody else. Maija and Pekka both chose a religious song that they wanted to pass on to their children, children's spouses, and grandchildren. Maija's song to be passed on was an originally Russian religious song, "Odnozvutjno gremit kolono," by Aleksandr Lvovich, known in English as "I Have Heard of a City Up Yonder," and in Finnish "Olen kuullut on kaupunki tuolla" ("Song about Heaven"). Maija described her relationship with religion very openly. She said that she had her doubts just as everyone does, but she hoped that when she dies, she will enter a world on the other side of the border that reminds her of a beautiful place—a place that preferably also contained some rural and not only city features as described in this song. She particularly hoped that the first thing she would see on the other side would be her deceased dogs, who would run to meet her, filled with joy. She also liked to think that she will meet her late parents there. In this borderscape, the fond relationship with more-than-humans, in Maija's case dogs and deceased spirits, is created again.

Maija's spouse Pekka was Lutheran but had strong roots in the Eastern Orthodox religion, since his grandfather was born in the ceded area of the Karelian Isthmus, and his grandfather had to be evacuated in 1939, just like Raija's grandmother. Of the 400,000 evacuees, 55,000 belonged to the Orthodox religion (Kupari 2016). Pekka had many warm memories of Orthodox family festivals from his past, and so he chose a typical Orthodox birthday song, "Monia vuosia" ("Many Merciful Years," lyrics unknown, composed by Dimitri Bortnjanski), which is always sung at Orthodox family birthday parties. The song has also been added to the Lutheran Church liturgy as a song for ecclesiastic ceremonies. Maija and Pekka have a son who is a Lutheran priest but who has a strong interest in his Eastern Orthodox past. It was obvious from these open-minded choices and the creation of an open-minded borderscape, with a mutual respect between different branches of religion—and, as Maija called it, her "heretical" idea that dogs can go to heaven—that the couple wished to pass on part of their musico-religious open-mindedness to future generations.

Several layers of border crossing were present in Maija's and Pekka's musical examples. One of the borders was between generations, since the songs had been chosen to be passed on to children and grandchildren.

The music provided a heritage, immaterial at times, that the participants wanted to pass on to the next generation. At the same time, the border between different religious groups was also present in the discussion (i.e., between the Eastern Orthodox Church and the Lutheran Church). The latter is the religion of the majority of Finnish citizens, while the Orthodox Church represents the minority. It must also be remembered that the Orthodox Church in Finland was initially connected to the Russian Orthodox Church until 1923, when the administration of the church was moved from Moscow to Constantinople (ORT 2021). Orthodox families were still closely linked with Russia, especially the Karelian families. The geographical border became more pronounced along with the religious border.

As Tuulikki Kurki (2018: 42) has pointed out, the Finnish–Russian national border "has a long history as being both a porous border" and "an iron curtain that blocks mobility almost entirely." Kurki also notes that the Finnish-Russian border has been a source of trauma for people living in the borderland, and it has split ethnonational and language groups on both sides of the border.

Relational Technologies and Memory Objects

Nearly all of the workshop discussions about the selected songs highlighted listening to the radio and particularly to some very popular music programs, such as *Lauantain toivotut levyt* (in English, *Saturday's Most Wanted Tracks*). The radio program was aired for the first time in November 1935 and is still aired weekly by the Finnish Broadcasting Company (FBC), the publicly owned radio station. The one-hour program's original broadcasting time was on Saturday at 5:00 p.m. Today the show is fifty minutes long and is still broadcast on Saturdays, from 6:10 p.m. to 7:00 p.m. The format has remained the same throughout the eighty-five years of broadcasting. The first half hour consists of Western art music, including operettas, which is in line with the FBC's ideology of trying to "civilize" the general population (Kotirinta 1986), and popular music is aired toward the end. After the first half hour come the Finnish Schlagers, including foxtrots and waltzes, and in the 1950s, for instance, after the impatient moments of waiting, came the "foreign" hits, including songs by Paul Anka or Harry Belafonte. The producer selects the music based on listener requests—the FBC archives has more than 300,000 request letters waiting to be studied[12]—and one program includes ten to twelve songs. Mainly middle-aged and older people send in requests to the program, but different generations listen to it (Luukka 2005). One of the songs the participants heard in the workshop was among the all-time favorites of the program ("Grandfather's Straw Hat"), and some of the other songs played have also often been heard on the program.

The program *Lauantain toivotut levyt* had a lot of relevance in the 1950s and 1960s, since the FBC had a monopoly and there was only one radio station until the year 1963, when the so-called parallel channel was established. *Saturday's Most Wanted Tracks* stayed on the original general channel and maintained its enlightenment-oriented program policies, while the parallel channel slowly started to include other types of entertainment and popular music in its broadcasts. Commercial radio stations were allowed in Finland first after 1985 (Valta 2013). Thus, it is no wonder that before 1963 it was really rare to hear a catchy Schlager or other popular tracks on the radio. Asko reported that he heard from friends that kids were always riveted to the radio to hear Saturday's requested tracks back then. They were of the opinion that if one stared at the radio rigorously and intently enough, the radio would play "Meksikon pikajuna" ("Mexico Express"), one of the radio favorites of both Finnish children and adults in the 1950s and 1960s.[13]

Children especially seemed to have a reciprocal relationship with the radio as a material object. Raija recognized herself in Asko's story of a child who was sure that intensive staring could indeed affect what could be heard from the appliance. There is generational similarity with regard to the thoughts of Maija, Raija, and Asko, who all at some point of their childhoods imagined the radio as a box filled with really small people who were performing music inside. Asko had a similar story about instruments like the mandolin and the violin. He would think as a child: "Where inside this instrument does the music really reside?"

The "Chorus of the Hebrew Slaves" brought up the memory of Saturday nights for many participants, since it was a song heard on the radio show *Lauantain toivotut levyt*:

> ASKO: But this song, that brings Saturday nights to our minds, because this was a very typically requested song during *Lauantain toivotut* [*Saturday's Most Wanted Tracks*].
> RAIJA: Yes, this came to my mind too, I remember.
> ASKO: Yes.
> HELMI: I have the same vision.

The participants' similar perspectives and shared "vision"—as Helmi put it—created a link between the participants and the materiality of the music and the program. As mentioned earlier, music can have an intensity that creates sensations in our bodies that can sometimes be even more meaningful than meaning itself (Shouse 2005).

Earlier in this chapter, we pointed out that only when Maija found the actual twelve-record box of light classical music did she realize that she could not have listened to the "Chorus of the Hebrew Slaves" from the vinyl. The song was not there. She said she must have heard it on the radio.[14] In what follows, Asko has already hinted that he does *not* remember whether he really listened to the piece on the radio, but based on a general recollection of what typically happened on a Finnish Saturday evening, he must have heard the chorus on the radio.

> RAIJA: Yeah, a mental image that one has heard on the radio.
> ASKO: Yes, yes, yes, yeah. Exactly, one thinks that as a child, that people went to the sauna and then listened to the radio, but in fact, I have no recollection if this really was the case, but one easily gets the mental image that yes indeed *Saturday's Most Wanted Tracks* were listened to [breathes]. And nowadays there's *Tune Is Free*, it comes out several times a year, yes.[15]
> HELMI: Hmm. Did you, Helena, get the same [image]?
> HELENA: Yes, on *Saturday's Most Wanted* ... that was the program that ...
> HELMI: Hmm. I got the same [feeling].
> HELENA: Yeah.

A couple of decades ago (and in Asko's case, more than half a century ago), certain routines—or perhaps one might even call them rituals—were part of the Saturday afternoon and evening of many families in Finland. Going to the sauna bath on Saturday evening was, and often still is, a must for Finnish households. When observed anthropologically, *Lauantain toivotut levyt* and the Saturday sauna act as a liminal state (van Gennep 1960) marking the transition from the six-day workweek[16] to the weekend and holy time, as Sunday was thought to begin when the Saturday evening bells rang at 6:00 p.m.—another borderscape: the time between the secular and the sacred.

The journalist Maija Alftan wrote an essay on the history of *Saturday's Most Wanted Tracks* in 1995, when the program turned sixty years, saying that it

> used to belong to the rhythms of life as a similarly self-evident part as the Saturday sauna. It was still for the baby boomers the only program where they could hear in their early teens the newest Schlagers. ... Everything else has changed, but *Saturday's Most Wanted* has not. ... When an enthusiastic innovator has tried to swap the popular music into the beginning of the show, or tried to tell the names of tracks before playing the tune, the phone lines were jammed. It is as simple as that: you must not alter *Saturday's Most Wanted*: first, you must play the arias, Hungarian dances, religious songs and folk songs, and only after that can you play Schlagers. (Alftan 1995: n.p., our translation)

Even now, more than fifty years later, Maija still related to the record player as a memory object (cf. Marschall 2019). This became clear when she described how she still has her uncle's record player and the vinyl records in her attic. "Well, I took them once, since I am always afraid my brother, who takes a lot of stuff to the refuse dump, will throw them out. So, I always try [laughs when talking] to save the things. ... I think, these are some things he might take to the dump." In Maija's story she is portrayed as the "saviour" of memory. Her brother is different—material memories are not important to him. It is not strange at all that in the workshop Maija "remembered differently" how she first heard "Va, pensiero": the record player she saved in her own attic is clearly not only an ordinary memory object, that is, an object that elicits "deliberate or involuntary memories of homeland, home culture, important places, episodes in one's own autobiographical past and significant social relations (kin, friends, colleagues) associated with home or origin" (Marschall 2019: 3; cf. Chaudhury and Rowles 2005; see also Van Dijck 2007; Hyltén-Cavallius 2012). The record player is more than this; it is an evocative object and a "thing-to-think-with," as expressed by Sherry Turkle (2011). The record player for Maija was an object to think and feel with; it carried passions and ideas (Turkle 2011) that went back to Maija's miserably poor and burned hometown after the war. The wind of change came with the object brought from Australia by her uncle. Maija did not seem to worry about "remembering differently." She just said, "Perhaps I heard it ['Chorus of the Hebrew Slaves'] from the radio after all," and then moved to the fact that she has now started to listen to tracks off the vinyl on YouTube. "Perhaps they bring with them a breeze from childhood," she said. But since she found other vinyl records in the attic, she has considered buying what she called an "old fashioned record player."

Conclusion

The Inheritance Tracks workshop method proved effective in producing interesting material for our analysis of mediated acts of remembering, bordering, and borderscapes. Besides the researchers, the participants in our workshop had been born within approximately ten years of each other in the bleak living conditions of postwar Finland. In their childhood and youth, socioeconomic and cultural conditions meant that technologies through which music could be heard were scarce.

The last ten minutes of the workshop were dedicated to an evaluating discussion. This began with Helmi asking, "What did this workshop feel like?" The participants voiced positive comments in response. The atmosphere was considered to be relaxed and conversational; we laughed together, but we were also emotionally moved together. Maija said, "I participated in time travel to my own childhood, so there were points of contact between the others' stories and my own." Raija thought it was interesting to hear other participants' often familiar-sounding experiences: this partly had to do with the fact that in the 1950s and 1960s, "in addition to [the few] record players, there were so few radio stations" (see the section titled "Relational Technologies and Memory Objects"). Raija even used the word *sukupolvikokemus* (generation experience) in her commentary on the workshop. The participants were somewhat surprised by how much "likeness" and confluence the discussions and music listening revealed and created. Music can be considered one of the affective gateways for re-remembering moments, and it also creates new shared moments, as experienced during the workshop. According to communication scholar Eric Shouse, music provides a good example of "how the intensity of the impingement of sensations on the body can 'mean' more to people than meaning itself" (2005: para. 11). Music's affectivity lies in its power to awaken physical bodily sensations.

Listening to each other's tracks and discussing them created affects, feelings of likeness, and confluence between the participants. The common affective attunements and materiality of music as an affective gateway for re-remembering moments created new shared moments for the workshop participants. Examples of bordering and border-crossing possibilities discussed, produced, and imagined in the workshop included lively borderscapes between classes, fantasies, and comfort created by classical music in poor living conditions and links and relations to the "other," more-than-human side of life, or in the hope created through religion.

The music played at the workshop elucidated the generational experience of the participants, especially those born after the Second World War. The workshop also highlighted the importance of the nationally shared rituals within their families by emphasizing the *Lauantain toivotut levyt* program and its importance to participants' families. While the program marked the transition from the working week to holy Sunday, it highlighted the border between the secular and the sacred. The program also demonstrated how much the radio influenced generational experiences by transmitting the older generations' musical tastes to the younger ones, which is also a border crossing. In this sense, the inheritance of music tracks went on in hundreds of thousands of households in Finland as part of a special Saturday evening ritual and atmosphere.

Notes

1 In Finnish: *Perityt musiikkiraidat*. See the introduction to this volume for an explanation of the Inheritance Tracks concept and approach.
2 We have disguised the names of the towns and people to protect the privacy of the workshop participants.

3   For instance, some of the tracks were related to the areas ceded to Russia after the Second World War or other such borderscapes.
4   Finland ceded areas from the southeast and around Lake Ladoga to the Soviet Union in 1940 and 1944. Thus, half a million people living in Karelia were evacuated to other parts of Finland. "In consequence, many people longed to return to their homelands in Karelia" (Suutari and Järviluoma 2017: 111).
5   In Raija's family story it was said that the father was allowed to work in Helsinki as a mechanic, but the family could not move there until later. This might have been to do with the living conditions and availability of accommodation in Helsinki after the war.
6   She was visiting a relative in Vesijärvi at the time of the workshop.
7   This chorus brings to mind the period of Babylonian captivity after the loss of the First Temple in Jerusalem in 586 BCE. The libretto is by Temistocle Solera, inspired by Psalm 137. The full incipit is "Va, pensiero, sull'ali dorate," meaning "Fly, thought, on wings of gold."
8   In an email in the summer 2020, Maija returned to the issue of her uncle. She specified that he worked for four years on a sugarcane plantation and that he often talked about how hard the work was. He listened to classical records in his free time.
9   Here, we refer to the ethnomethodological qualitative analysis of membership categorization (Sacks 1974; see, e.g., Järviluoma and Roivainen 2010). One of the crucial strategies of interaction is to relate ourselves, others, and things to various categories. Our everyday knowledge of people is to a great extent organized into categories and into activities and category features, which characterize these.
10 "Isoisän olkihattu," composer, lyrics and performer Tapio Rautavaara. Original record Decca 1951, 10-inch single (Fono 2021). Listened: https://www.youtube.com/watch?v=4r22AfN_kTg (retrieved January 26, 2021). Lyrics translated by Helmi Järviluoma and Elina Hytönen-Ng from the original song.
11 Often people think that Schlager music as a term only refers to Germany, but in fact, it is used when referring to catchy popular music in many parts of Central, Northern, and Southeast Europe, including Finland.
12 Letters sent to the program during the years 1935 to 1975 have been examined. The data set including the letters offers interesting research material to their further study.
13 The melody of "Mexico Express" (1949) is the famous "Orient Express," composed by Gerhard Mohr and with original lyrics by Eric(h) Plessow. The Finnish lyrics were extremely funny, about a train robbery in the Wild West. In our workshop, Helena chose "Mexico Express" as the track that she had inherited—from no one and everyone—during her childhood's family radio listening moments.
14 This was confirmed by the fact that the "Chorus of the Hebrew Slaves" can be found in a compilation CD containing the most popular tracks from the program *Saturday's Most Wanted* (Lauantain toivotut klassikot 1996).

15 A call-in program in which you can send music requests to the FBC.
16 The six-day workweek ended in Finland in 1966.

References

Primary Sources

Workshop

Inheritance Tracks workshop [*Perityt musiikkiraidat*] at Vesijärvi city library, October 2018. Recorded with Zoom H4, recording held in the home archive of Helmi Järviluoma. 1 hour 56 minutes and 22 seconds.

Interviews

Maija and Pekka, interview by Sonja Pöllänen and Helmi Järviluoma, June 2020. Recorded with Zoom H4, recording held in the home archive of Helmi Järviluoma. 1 hours 20 minutes and 46 seconds.

Raija, phone interview by Elina Hytönen-Ng, June 2020. Recording held in the home archive of Elina Hytönen-Ng. 16 minutes and 54 seconds.

References

Alftan, Maija. 1995. "Ehtookellojen jälkeen soivat 'Lauantain toivotut levyt'— tuttu kuulutus täyttää tänään 60 vuotta." ["After the Evening Bells 'Saturday's Most Wanted'—the Familiar Announcement Turns 60 Years Today. 'You Must Never Change.'"] *Helsingin Sanomat*. November 5. https://www.hs.fi/kulttuuri/art-2000003482581.html.

Brambilla, Chiarra, Jussi Laine, James W. Scott, and Gianluca Bocchi (eds.). 2015. *Borderscaping: Imaginations and Practices of Border Making*. Farnham: Ashgate.

Chaudhury, Habib, and Graham D. Rowles. 2005. "Between the Shores of Recollection and Imagination: Self, Aging, and Home." In Habib Chaudhury and Graham D. Rowles (eds.), *Home and Identity in Late Life: International Perspectives*, 3–17. New York: Springer.

dell'Agnese, Elena, and Anne-Laure Amilhat Szary. 2015. "Borderscapes: From Border Landscapes to Border Aesthetics." *Geopolitics*, 20(1): 4–13. https://doi.org/10.1080/14650045.2015.1014284.

Fono. 2021. "Kappaleen Tiedot." http://www.fono.fi/KappaleenTiedot.aspx?kappale=isois%c3%a4n+olkihattu&kieli=suomi&ID=631aa788-c946-4650-a6f3-ce08a4173678.

Hyltén-Cavallius, Sverker. 2012. "Memoryscapes and Mediascapes: Musical Formations of 'Pensioners' in Late 20th-Century Sweden." *Popular Music*, 31(2): 279–95.

Järviluoma, Helmi, and Irene Roivainen. [2003] 2010. "Gender in Membership Categorization Analysis." In Helmi Järviluoma, Pirkko Moisala, and Anni Vilkko (eds.), *Gender and Qualitative Methods*, 69–83. London: Sage.
Konrad, Victor. 2020. "Belongingness and Borders." In James Scott (ed.), *A Research Agenda for Border Studies*, 109–28. Cheltenham: Edward Elgar.
Kotirinta, Pirkko. 1986. "Suomen Yleisradion musiikkiohjelmat ja musiikkipolitiikka 1926–1946." ["The Music Programs and Politics of Music of Finnish Broadcasting Company between 1926–1946.]. Unpublished Master's Thesis, University of Tampere, Tampere, Finland, Folk tradition, especially folk music.
Kupari, Helena 2016. "Ortodoksiset, karjalaiset ja 'meidän' perinteet—etnisyys konstruktiona." *Embodied Religion* (blog). March 3. https://blogs.helsinki.fi/embodied-religion/2016/03/31/ortodoksiset-karjalaiset-ja-meidan-perinteet-etnisyys-konstruktiona.
Kurki, Tuulikki. 2018. "Border Crossing Trauma Seen through Hyper-Naturalist Prose and Surreal Forms of Narration." *Mobile Culture Studies*, 4: 39–56.
Lauantain toivotut klassikot. 1996. *Verdistä Bernsteiniin*. [Saturday's wanted classics from Verdi to Bernstein.] CD and sleeve notes. Helsinki: Classica.
Luukka, Teemu. 2005. "Miljoonia toiveita." ["Millions of Wishes." *Saturday's Most Wanted Tracks* is the oldest radio program in Finland.] *Helsingin Sanomat*. November 11. https://www.hs.fi/sunnuntai/art-2000004352233.html.
Marschall, Sabine. 2019. "'Memory Objects': Material Objects and Memories of Home in the Context of Intra-African Mobility." *Journal of Material Culture*, 24(3): 253–69. https://doi.org/10.1177/1359183519832630.
ORT 2021. "Finnish Orthodox Church Autonomous for 90 Years." https://ort.fi/uutishuone/2013-07-06/suomen-kirkko-autonomisena-90-vuotta. Accessed March 28, 2022.
Raninen-Siiskonen, Tarja. 1999. *Vieraana omalla maalla. Tutkimus karjalaisen siirtoväen muistelukerronnasta*. [A Foreigner at Home: A Case Study of Reminiscence and Narration of the Evacuated Karelians in Finland.] Helsinki: Suomen Kirjallisuuden Seura.
Sacks, Harvey, Emanuel A. Schegloff, and Gail Jefferson. 1974. "A Simplest Systematics for the Organization of Turn-Taking in Conversation." *Language*, 50(4): 696–735.
Scott, James W., and Christopher Sohn. 2019. "Place-Making and the Bordering of Urban Space: Interpreting the Emergence of New Neighbourhoods in Berlin and Budapest." *European Urban & Regional Studies*, 26(3): 297–313.
Shouse, Eric. 2005. "Feeling, Emotion, Affect." *M/C Journal*, 8(6). https://doi.org/10.5204/mcj.2443.
Stoffelen, Arie, and Dominique Vanneste. 2019. "Contested Mobilities across the Hong Kong–Shenzen Border: The Case of Sheung Shui." In Anssi Paasi, Eeva-Kaisa Prokkola, Jarkko Saarinen, and Kaj Zimmerbauer (eds.), *Borderless Worlds for Whom? Ethics, Moralities and Mobilities*, 154–66. New York: Routledge.
Suutari, Pekka, and Helmi Järviluoma. 2017. "Finlandisation and the Restriction of Karelian Voices at the Height of the Cold War." In Annemette Kirkegaard,

Helmi Järviluoma, Jan S. Knudsen, and Jonas Otterbeck (eds.), *Researching Music Censorship*, 104–21. Newcastle upon Tyne: Cambridge Scholars.

Turkle, Sherry (ed.). 2011. *Evocative Objects: Things We Think With*. Cambridge, MA: MIT Press.

Valta, Reijo 2013. "YLE radioaalloilla 87 vuotta." ["FBC on Radio Waves for 87 Years"].

Van Dijck, José. 2007. *Mediated Memories in the Digital Age*. Stanford, CA: Stanford University Press. https://poistyopoydalta.blogspot.com/2013/09/yle-radioaalloilla-87-vuotta.html.

van Gennep, Arnold. 1960. *The Rites of Passage*. 2nd ed. Translated by Monika Vizedom and Gabrielle L. Caffee. Chicago: University of Chicago Press.

Yle [Yleisradio Oy]. 2008. "Paul Anka Linnanmäellä." [Video]. https://yle.fi/aihe/artikkeli/2008/04/22/paul-anka-linnanmaella.

4

Storytelling and Disrupting Borders: A Sicilian Workshop

Abigail Gardner

Palermo, Sicily, mid-October 2018. For a newcomer to the city, the noise is deafening. Sirens, car horns, people shouting—in Italian, Bengali, Arabic, and Igbo. The walls of this 2018 Cultural Capital of Italy are equally "noisy," covered in anti-Fascist and anti-corruption graffiti and posters. The audiovisual environment is multilingual and politically intent. This context is vital for understanding the Inheritance Tracks workshop that took place after the meeting of a transnational team working on a European-funded media literacy project for refugee, asylum-seeking, and migrant women. This team was meeting in a small non-air-conditioned nongovernmental (NGO) office not far from Palermo's central post office, commissioned in 1934 by Benito Mussolini, and the alleyways of the market area, Ballarò. Long a Mafia stronghold, where *pizzo* (protection money) is still demanded, Ballarò is where new arrivals to the city, largely Nigerians and Bangladeshis, set up stalls and small shops. It is shabby and vibrant, but there remains a sense that it is still somehow dangerous; as tourists walking with NGO colleagues, we were told not to carry credit cards or items of worth.

In a *New York Times* piece on the area, Jason Horowitz (2019) noted how Palermo is "a city with a history dating back to at least the Phoenicians that adapted to conquerors and waves of immigration. And Ballarò market, in the center of town, is where many of those complications are playing out" (para. 9). The mayor of Palermo, Leoluca Orlando (2018), is an advocate for immigration and maintains that Palermo is home to all who live there. There are no migrants in Palermo; everyone is a "Palermitani." Orlando defied Interior Minister Matteo Salvini's Italian government to allow the Doctors without Borders migrant rescue boat *Aquarius* to dock in January 2018 (Wintour, Tondo, and Kirchgaessner 2018). This city, with its political and historical struggles, was the backdrop to our Inheritance Tracks meeting. Arguably, it is one whose own inheritance has troubling elements and that now troubles a broader Italian politics. Featured in Figure 4.1 is the graffiti stating "Death to Fascism" on Via Roma, Palermo.

The office where we met belonged to the host partner of the meeting, CESIE, a European Centre of Studies and Initiatives, a nonprofit and apolitical organization as well as an NGO, established in 2001, and inspired by the works and theories of the pacifist Danilo Dolci (1924–97). Ten participants, comprising two academics, one support staff, and seven NGO workers, took part in the ninety-minute Inheritance Tracks workshop, which, in this chapter, I argue worked to gently disrupt modalities of communication and expression.

I explore the dynamics of those changing modalities by concentrating on the idea of storytelling and borders, using theoretical work from digital storytelling, music and memory, and my own practical experience of working on digital storytelling initiatives. Where the previous chapter

FIGURE 4.1 *Graffiti on Via Roma, Palermo, October 2018. Photo: Abigail Gardner.*

dealt with shared interpretations of borderscapes in an eastern Finnish town library, here, the storytelling that accompanied the songs reveals the contingency of borders, especially those of the affective self and of place and time—of what belongs where. My involvement in the project and in this particular workshop relates to my research in digital storytelling, which I use to position the Palermo workshop as a storytelling event. My focus here is firmly on the storytelling prompted by song choices, on affective selves revealed in confessional "moments" (Lefebvre 2004; Radstone 2007) and on affective "contagion" (Gibbs 2001; Ahmed 2004). José van Dijck, who works on the intersection of music, media studies, and memory, talks about the "inter-generational transfer of personal and collective heritage, not only by sharing music, but also by sharing stories" (2014: 111). And these stories were produced in a specific place, in Palermo. The chapter is therefore a story about the "song worlds" emergent within a Sicilian Inheritance Tracks workshop, which itself involved storytelling prompted by songs chosen by the participants.

I use the phrase "song worlds" to refer to the interplay between a song and its role in one particular moment in a participant's life (or relationship to a particular person) and the worlds that are shared within the space of the workshop. A song therefore acts as a prop or a context for remembering past moments, certain people, and their own selves in that time and place. The use of the song in the workshop as a prop, an object around which to tell a story, was similar to how photographs and prized possessions are used in digital storytelling. I have used the latter method in European and UK projects. In the European project, teenagers' stories were used to promote intercultural awareness (MYSTY 2018). In the UK, research with military veterans, funded by Age UK, flags, medals, and certificates triggered stories (Veterans' Voices 2019). Another project used digital stories to build self-esteem among vulnerable adults (GEM: Going the Extra Mile Project 2017).

The Inheritance Tracks workshop in Palermo shared similar starting points to digital storytelling but differed in one very simple facet: music. Comparable to the artifacts and photographs used to prompt stories in digital storytelling, participants were asked in advance to choose two songs, which acted as memory objects (van Dijck 2007). However, a track by Ennio Morricone does not do the same affective work as an old black-and-white photograph or a veteran's medal precisely *because* it is a piece of music. Playing, listening to, and sharing music change the affective atmosphere. There is a shift in an Inheritance Tracks workshop, and it is like a key change. First, the mood alters (DeNora 2000; Kassabian 2013). And importantly, it alters for different participants according to their own previous exposure to the track playing. Is it something they know? What might their relationship to it be? Music being played not only takes the individual who chose it on a narrative journey but also invites all other group members to travel with them. The resulting stories and conversations demonstrated an iterativity different to the worked-out scripts of digital storytelling. The Palermo workshop had a distinctive character because of this recalibrated, iterative, and shared sonic environment.

Second, the workshop affected the participants' bodies. They were listening to music, and this had not only an emotional effect on the group but also a bodily one; some people started to sway, to move to the music. This meant that the group shared common modes of listening that enabled them to switch register and listen with their bodies (Regev 2013).

As mentioned, the ten workshop participants—nine women and one man—were part of the transnational team working on an Erasmus + Key Action 2–funded project. These projects are funded by the European Commission for work that develops, shares, or transfers best practices and innovative approaches in the fields of education, training, and youth. Ours was called Media Literacy for Refugee, Asylum Seeking and Migrant Women (MedLIT 2018), had been awarded €251,530, and ran from November 1, 2016, to October 31, 2018. The team was made up of six partners: five NGOs (in Italy, Austria, Malta, Ireland, and Greece) and a UK university, which was in charge of the budget and the management of the whole project. The team had built an online toolkit that could be used to develop the digital media literacy of refugee, asylum-seeking, and migrant women, specifically low-skilled women.

Pilot research across the countries involved, in the form of focus groups (some of which had been carried out in refugee camps in northern Greece), had revealed high levels of social media use in parallel with low levels of trust in "media," along with a willingness to learn. Following this preliminary research, the team built an online free-to-access e-learning platform. Uptake of this educational opportunity was driven through peer-to-peer networks. The UK team had worked on the methodology and focus groups, the Greek team had built the platform, and the Italians were charged with the peer-to-peer networking element. The curriculum had been developed by the team in response to demand from the target audience. It offered different access points depending on the skill level of the user. Online modules ranged from how to access health care and education to how to use a computer to how to spot fake news.

Inheritance Tracks in Palermo

The Palermo workshop ran along similar lines as others in the Inheritance Tracks project. All participants were asked to send two tracks: one they had inherited and one that they wanted to pass on. All the tracks that could be were uploaded to a Spotify playlist. Songs that were not on Spotify were sent via YouTube. There were no queries about the initial request; no one questioned what "inheritance" was (as has happened since). Having worked on the MedLIT project, the workshop participants were familiar with each other but not close. Allow me to introduce them, as identified by the initial of their first name. The group included two women in their fifties, D and S(2), from the Inishowen Development Partnership in Buncrana, Ireland; one Spanish woman in her twenties, A(1), who was working in Malta for FSM, a migrant support organization; one woman in her thirties from Athens (E), representing KMOP (a long-established Greek NGO); one woman in her twenties from Austria (B), working for Verein Multikulturell, an NGO in Innsbruck that has since closed down; an American media academic in her forties from the University of York (K), who was the evaluator on the project; two Italian women, one in her twenties and the other in her thirties, S(1) and R, respectively, who worked for the host CESIE (an NGO in Palermo with a broad range of activities related to migrant and youth support); one man in his forties from the University of Gloucestershire (G), the project manager; and myself, A(2), a music and media academic in my fifties. All participants were White. I was the project lead on MedLIT and had introduced the idea of doing the Inheritance Tracks workshop with the team over the previous month.

After our formal project meeting ended, I indicated that we were going to start the workshop. Before we started, I introduced why we were doing the session, explained what it was for, and mentioned what experience I had had of previous workshops. I told the group that at some points in previous workshops, participants had felt very emotional and to bear that in mind as we proceeded. From my laptop, I then played one track from the Spotify playlist to the group. As Ros Jennings had done in the Women, Ageing and Media Summer School 2017 Inheritance Tracks workshop (see the Introduction to this book), this group played a game. After I had chosen and played a track, the group had to guess who had chosen it, while the individual "chooser" could not identify themselves. This added an element of "play" to the proceedings and assumed some interpersonal awareness, which had been built up over the two years of team members working together.

None of the team members, apart from myself, had taken part in such a workshop before, but all had chosen and sent at least one track prior to the meeting. From their selections, it appeared easier for most of the group to select a track they had inherited than to choose one they might pass on—especially for the younger women and the one man who did not have children. "Passing on," for these younger group members, was more about sharing something they appreciated. In Palermo, "inheritance" of tracks came mainly from a parent or an aunt (three each of mothers and fathers; one aunt), and so via a heterosexual family, and from work "family" (colleagues). This may indicate something "troubling" about the notion of inheritance, about how it is inextricably tied up as a cultural imagination to a biological family, which had been questioned in prior workshops. In a previous workshop run by Professor Ros Jennings as part of the Women,

Ageing and Media Summer School (July 2017), queer families and radio families occupied those roles of "family." By radio family, I refer to the idea of a radio presenter acting as a member of the listener's extended family, fulfilling the role of an elder sibling. For me that person was John Peel, Radio 1 deejay, and his late-night shows in the late 1970s and early 1980s.

Table 4.1 illustrates the music choices made by the group, with members identified by their first initials. What the table obscures is how important the group dynamics were in working to sculpt the resulting narratives. The songs were the props for the ensuing stories revealed in that small, hot office in Palermo. The reminiscence that these song props enabled was told to a group; the process was iterative and communal, and stories were commented on, interjected with, added to, and questioned. The stories revealed affective selves and political selves; they engendered empathy and relied on memory. They also troubled the borders of how to belong in this temporary space of working professionals. Nobody knew in advance what they would be sharing; nobody knew in advance how much what they revealed would offer traction for the conversations that followed. And so the workshop was both an act of individual remembrance and a collective sharing and learning.

Affective Selves and Empathetic Listeners

Let us consider what had happened before the Inheritance Tracks workshop, in our team's project meeting. We had followed a formal agenda, had agreed on actions, and had noted what had worked about our project and what we needed to do next. Minutes had been taken. The day before, we had met a group of five Nigerian women from the support network the Associazione Donne di Benin City Palermo (2018). Many of these women are survivors of human trafficking into Sicily, and we heard from them how important it was for them and their community to be media literate, to start rebuilding their lives and recovering their agency. To talk about music after these meetings seemed to me at the time to border on the frivolous. I was wrong. And I had felt this before. When, on September 19, 2018, I had first asked the team to be involved in a workshop, I had had trouble explaining its purpose and why it was important, but the email replies were all positive and indicated the two tracks requested. My reservations about asking something outside the parameters of the professional may have had more to do with my discomfort over shared affectivity than anything else. So yes, the first "trouble" encountered was my own discomfort at the possibility of emotion entering the workshop. This became apparent at the start of the workshop by the first two participants.

I started the session by asking K about her choice. I knew her well and considered that with her background in public speaking, getting her to share her story first would be a "safe bet." But as the song "Dancing Queen" echoed

TABLE 4.1 *Tracks Chosen by Participants in the Palermo Workshop*

Participant (age)	Occupation (nationality)	Inherited Track(s) (artist, nationality)	Inherited From	Track to Pass On (artist)	Passed On to
A(1) (mid-20s)	NGO worker in Malta (Spanish)	"Duerme Negrito" (Mercedes Sosa, Argentinian)	Mother	None	N/A
A(2) (mid-50s)	Media academic (British)	"The Only Living Boy in New York" (Simon and Garfunkel, American)	Father	"Oh! Sweet Nuthin'" (Velvet Underground, American)	Own children
B (late 20s)	NGO worker (Austrian)	"O Leãozinho" (Caetano Veloso, Brazilian)	Colleague who repeatedly played it	"Aïcha" (Khaled, Algerian)	No one in particular
D (mid-50s)	NGO community support (Irish)	"Dead Skunk" (Loudon Wainwright III, American)	Aunts	*Astral Weeks* (Van Morrison, Northern Irish)	No one in particular
E (30s)	NGO worker (Greek)	"Am Thimisis to onirou mou" (Vasilis Legas, Greek)	Parents	"She's a Rainbow" (Rolling Stones, British)	Daughter

(*continued*)

TABLE 4.1 *Tracks Chosen by Participants in the Palermo Workshop* (Continued)

Participant (age)	Occupation (nationality)	Inherited Track(s) (artist, nationality)	Inherited From	Track to Pass On (artist)	Passed On to
G (late 40s)	University funding manager (British)	"The Good, the Bad and the Ugly" (Ennio Morricone, Italian)	Father	None	No one to pass it on to yet
K (late 40s)	Academic (American)	"Dancing Queen" (ABBA, Swedish)	Mother	"Dancing Queen" (ABBA, Swedish)	Her children
R (30s)	NGO manager (Italian)	"Talkin' Bout a Revolution" (Tracy Chapman, American)	Heard as a teenager	"Jamono" (Daara J Family, Senegalese)	No one in particular
S(1) (20s)	NGO worker (Italian)	"Sunrise" (Simply Red, British)	Father	"You're All the World to Me" (Tony Bennett, American)	Someone special
S(2) (50s)	Community worker (Irish)	"Top of the World" (Carpenters, American)	A neighbor	"I Will Survive" (Gloria Gaynor, American)	No one in particular

across the high ceiling of the office, people started swaying and K began to cry. The tears continued with the second participant's story. Immediately, there was an affective change, which I consider later in the chapter with reference to Gibbs's (2001) notion of "contagion."

The second storyteller, S(1), was the young leader for the Italian team. She had a long-established working relationship with the local migrant community, some of whom were using their newfound media literacy skills to produce a recipe book. After I played her inherited track "Sunrise," by Simply Red, she said only that the track "remembers me my father" before choking back tears. Noticing that her work colleague, R, was supporting her with her arm, I went on to the next track, having thanked her for it. Afterward, she told me how her father had died suddenly and unexpectedly when he was in his early forties and she was twelve. A heightened sense of emotional intelligence in the group allowed participants the space to both tell and *not* tell stories. Stories can generate empathy and trust in the audience; at the same time, they demonstrate their usefulness because they have the power to give meaning to human behaviors and to trigger emotions across the group present.

S(1) was involved in a process of "narrating the self" in a way that altered the texture of the meeting. I want to briefly draw on Rebecca Solnit's (2014) work to suggest how important this modulation was. In her book *Men Explain Things to Me: And Other Essays*, Solnit writes of the power of narrating the self. This process, she notes, is crucial for many women, whose histories and stories are hidden, untold, and unmapped. Against a background of domestic and sexual violence, abuse, and erasure, she argues that "the ability to tell your own story, in words or images, is already a victory, already a revolt" (in the essay "Grandmother Spider"). Articulating the self and making audible what has previously been inaudible are for her the work of feminism. For me, in this chapter, her words do much to frame a small moment where a group of people came together to tell each other stories about the music and songs that were important to them. This reference to "revolt" stresses the importance of claiming small moments of "telling" that can be a route to affective moments of connection. And perhaps this telling is also a revolt insofar as it brings into focus the affective self, the emotional self, and the wounded and bereaved self. This revelation is what we saw with K's and S(1)'s stories, which immediately disrupted the atmosphere of the workshop. We all had to shift our emotional antennae. We all started really listening. This required us, as a group, to perform our empathy, which was apparent at later moments in the workshop when there was instant recognition and responsiveness.

For example, for her track to pass on, E told the story of how she heard the Rolling Stones' song "She's a Rainbow." "Two days before I give birth," she said, "I was driving and I was listening to the radio. It is for my daughter." Many in the group were amazed that she was driving that close to having her child. Half of the group were mothers, and this experience and the shared memories of childbirth were apparent in the others' reactions to E when she talked about her song. Stories of dancing around kitchens also provided points of empathy, even when a song was new to the group. Participant D chose Loudon Wainwright III's song "Dead Skunk" as her inherited track because it had been played by her two aunts. She remembered "being in their kitchen and my aunts dancing around." In reference to the American songwriter, she continued, "I always go to see him with my aunts and my cousins. When he comes to Ireland, we all go to Belfast or Dublin to see him." Her reminiscence of shared intergenerational female dancing was something that the other women in the group responded to, showing that D's narrative was one that resonated.

For three younger women in the group—A(1), B, and R—inherited track choices centered on their political identities and morals and their ongoing professional activity, especially in relation to working with migrants. Their stories also demonstrate the importance of passing a song on, and so the inheritance here is a moral or political one. "Duerme Negrito," a song by the Argentinian singer Mercedes Sosa, was sung to A(1) by her mother when she was growing up in Burgos, northern Spain. The song is also, as A(1) herself said, her mother passing on her moral framework to her, given that it sings of injustice and racism. She told how her mother had a social conscience, something she too has inherited. "Duerme Negrito" is about a small boy whose mother tells him not to worry and how she will always return to him and feed him even though she has to go out to work. A(1) went on to say that the song was

> a lullaby I remember as a child. I hadn't realized who it [the singer] was but I really like it. I remember my mum singing this. It is a very sad song. I was always asking for it and we would sing it together. It's a bittersweet kind of memory. ... Recently I am living with a musician and she loves this kind of music, and she sings this song. It is my lullaby.

A(1), the youngest member of the group, reveals intimacies to this group she will never meet again, since she left the Maltese NGO shortly afterward. But the group empathized with and recognized the close relationship she was referring to. The lullaby is a kind of gift, something that is precious.

Participant G, too, referred to this idea when he noted that he did not have a track to pass on as he had "no one to give it to ... yet." Participant S(1) wanted to pass on "You're All the World to Me," by Tony Bennett. "I really love the song," she said, adding that she wanted to dedicate it "to a special person." The song itself comes from the 1951 musical *Royal Wedding*, starring Fred Astaire and Jane Powell (directed by Stanley Donen). The song was clearly a gift from a past, when her father was still alive. Without knowing to whom it will be given, it is a treasure bound up in her relationship with her father, which is still wrapped up in loss. My chosen record too reminded me of my father. As I told the group, he "was really into music, he liked jazz, classical, had catholic taste. He used to sit in the living room in his chair with the headphones on, listening to this. I loved it, as it's a sad song." My father had died not that long before the workshop, and listening to this song brought back the memory of him turning toward the record player in his special swivel chair, which he sat in to listen to his hi-fi system.

As noted earlier, in her work on pop music as a resource for memory, van Dijck argues that when people tell stories about the music they remember, "what we see ... is an inter-generational transfer of personal and collective heritage, not only by sharing music, but also by sharing stories" (2014: 111). Van Dijck's study is primarily concerned with memory and its relationship with various media, including sound technologies. Here, I am less concerned with music and memory, and more with how memory is replayed in the present through storytelling about song, and how that present then offers connections. But what van Dijck has to say about sharing the stories generated by these memories is important for the Inheritance Tracks project, which became clear in the Palermo workshop. To further quote van Dijck:

> [S]tories, like records, are mere resources in the process of reminiscence, a process that often involves imagination as much as retention. In other words, our personal musical repertoire is a *living* memory that stimulates narrative engagement from the first time we hear a song to each time we replay it at later stages in life. It is this vivid process of narrative recall that gives meaning to an album and assigns personal and cultural value to a song. (2014: 111; emphasis in original)

The process of tagging inheritance and passing on asks for a relationship to the past and the future, putting the individual into a perceived, produced lineage. It marks them out as a recipient and a giver of musical pieces entwined with stories of the self. And the fact that the storytelling in our workshop took place with us all sat round in a circle, meant that its process was also similar to digital storytelling. But where van Dijck is using music as a resource for memory, I was using it as a resource for investigating inheritance: what it might mean to inherit music and how music is interwoven with autobiographical narratives and retelling.

This workshop was a process of replaying, where the memory objects were songs chosen specifically for their emotional resonance and perhaps too out of a desire to relay that importance. What happened in the session was a "tagging" process, whereby stories related to song and family were passed on to others in the group. This passing on revealed common and uncommon inheritances, which then became the topic of conversation.

"Used in popular music and memory research, 'autobiographical memory' has come to be typically described in the literature *as memory for events or information concerning the self*" (Istvandity 2016: 232; emphasis in original). This passing on of personal history was apparent when participant D told how she wanted to pass on any of the songs from Van Morrison's album *Astral Weeks*. "It's fifty years old," she said, and added that it was recorded in Boston, where I was living at the time. The group knew nothing about the artist, so D had to situate him as a Northern Irish musician, from Belfast. But they had known of her spending a long time in Boston when she was much younger. This song then invited the group into recollecting her past collectively. The "emotional investment" (van Dijck 2014: 109) D had in the song was essential to the group's understanding of her choice of it.

Two of the participants, R and B, shared songs that were primarily linked to their working lives and professional identity. R chose as her inherited track Tracy Chapman's "Talkin' Bout a Revolution," saying that "as a teenager" it was her "favorite song ever." She said the song chimed with her "attitude and vision of life." She chose to pass on "Jamono," by Daara J Family, a song sung in Wolof, the main language of Senegal. For R, whose job and life revolve around supporting young migrants, and who has adopted migrant children, the song sings about the hopes of young people who want to "cross the Mediterranean," to "cross the sea to change their life," and she said she "make[s] them listen to the song." The track was not on Spotify in October 2018, being only accessible on YouTube. It is now there. The group knew from her work profile that R was engaged with projects that integrated migrants into Italy and perhaps were left with no new knowledge of any life prior to this politically and socially engaged persona. The same was the case for B, who added her comments via Facebook Messenger at a later date (March 2020), since she had to leave the workshop early to catch her flight. The track she inherited—"O Leãozinho," by the Brazilian artist Caetano Veloso—was from a work colleague who used to listen to it all the time. In her words: "At first I did not like it, but then due to the endless repetition of the song, I started to like it." The song she wanted to pass on was "Aïcha," by the Algerian Raï musician Khaled. "The song reminds me of my time that I spent in Mauritania[,] and whenever I listened to it a lot of good memories came up." Both of these women shared stories that were bound up in their professional lives, while B also wanted to pass on a song that she herself had fond memories of.

These several songs were new to the group, but others were supranational, having already crossed borders. Everyone knew ABBA's "Dancing Queen," and everyone knew Gloria Gaynor's disco-era hit "I Will Survive." These songs were part of a musical lingua franca that, due to the dominance of the Anglo-American distribution system, had been heard by all group members. This was not the case for tracks like my track to pass on "Oh! Sweet Nuthin' " by the Velvet Underground, or any of Van Morrison's music from the album *Astral Weeks*. These were songs whose importance to the individual relied on the personal narrative to have the song make sense to the rest of the group; they needed the story as an orientation point. My story about "Oh! Sweet Nuthin'" was that the song took me back to a teenage time when the radio, and one radio deejay in particular, John Peel, was central to my understanding of what music could be and what worlds it conjured up. In turn, I wanted my children to hear songs from other worlds and experience them as doorways to difference. "I heard this on the radio, on the John Peel show," I told the group. "I grew up in a tiny village in the middle of nowhere and as a bit of a weird kid [laughter]. [John Peel] was my window of escape from this boring, rural place. My kids are into music, so I pass this on to them."

Whereas a number of songs crossed borders, some borders remained, the result of language barriers and limits in international record distribution. Participant E played a Greek ballad, "Am Thimisis to onirou mou," sung by Vasilis Lekkas, and although the group recognized that it was being sung in Greek, they had not encountered the song before. "He's the greatest composer in Greece," E remarked. "It's a song my father inherited me. We listened to it on our street and on our holidays." The group needed that personal information to be able to connect to her memories of the song. Van Dijck has noted the importance of understanding the variables that go into making musical memories, which "are shaped through social practices and cultural forms as much as through individual emotions" (2014: 116). So here, E's musical memories were wrapped up in a mix of other life events. Added to this is the potential for what Kenton O'Hara and Barry Brown called "musical occasioning" (2006: 5). This happens when "music is not simply paired with memories but, rather, music is seen as a fundamental part of the thing remembered as well as a fundamental means 'through' which the remembering is done" (5). It is both the means to and a part of the memory. The Palermo participants first encountered their memories when asked to choose a song; they then encountered the memories again in the group workshop and narrated them to the group. And for me now, writing some eighteen months later, my memories of the session, the city, the heat, and those individuals are all associated with the songs we played. What the song stories session did was to act as another iterative moment in that memory, enabling those stories to be witnessed. It included moments of instant "witnessing," wherein other group members related to a song as they knew it, and other moments of delay, where the emotions in the song were clear but the language was not known.

The Inheritance Tracks workshop in Palermo was experiential and embodied; participants shared stories, sang, and moved to the music. Did I mention dancing? When, at the start of the session, K, who had chosen ABBA's "Dancing Queen," started to sway, those sitting next to her—D and S(2)—also swayed and then moved their arms. This immediately changed the nature of the meeting and acted as a point of transition from professionalism to friendship and "fun." Movement happened again at the end of the hour, when S(2)'s second choice came on. Gloria Gaynor's anthem "I Will Survive" (1978) is a disco classic, and when they heard it, everyone in the room started singing and moving to it. The one man in the group expressed discomfort and jokingly said, "I didn't sign up for this." He had joined in the singing for S(2)'s first choice, "Top of the World," by the Carpenters, but the move from singing to dancing was a border he appeared uncomfortable to cross.

This singular discomfort, the unintended dancing at "classics," and the explanation that had to accompany songs that were new to the group illustrate the importance of what I would like to term "shared currency." This refers to how members of the group might share an experience, say, of motherhood or of long road trips and how this shared currency enabled an affective response within the workshop group. The degree to which the workshop had affective impact relied on these shared currencies. It also depended on shared knowledge (of pop songs, of films), and when that commonality was missing (as in the case of E's inheritance track or of R's), extra narrative was required to provide context. Might it be that those stories based on recognized songs were able to provide more texture to the workshop, as other participants brought their own experiences of the song to the discussion, multiplying the narratives? What was going on in that workshop might be conceptualized through theories of affect, notably from Sara Ahmed and Anna Gibbs. The latter's 2001 work on "communicable affect" and "contagion" through an analysis of the Australian prime minister Pauline Hanson's emotional impact referred to the idea that "[b]odies can catch feelings as easily as catch fire: affect leaps from one body to another, evoking tenderness, inciting shame, igniting rage, exciting fear—in short, communicable affect can inflame nerves and muscles in a conflagration of every conceivable kind of passion" (para. 1).

In Gibbs's work, affect is "catching," and this is key to understanding how the conversations worked in Palermo when there was shared "currency." The group was being bound together by emotions that were evoked by the stories and songs. When Ahmed (2004) talks about "affective economies," she mentions how emotions flow between bodies and bind them together. As she wrote, "[W]hile emotions do not positively reside in a subject or figure, they still work to bind subjects together. Indeed, to put it more strongly, the nonresidence of emotions is what makes them 'binding'" (124). It is also worth thinking about how these binds were varied; they were temporary and in respect of the stories people told and/or the songs that were played. They were also binding the participants, albeit fleetingly, to their individual pasts.

The particular block of ninety minutes that had been set aside for the workshop outside the business of the project meeting meant that it was operating in a different modality. In this sense, more borderscapes were at play. In Ricoeur's theory, the borders between past and present collapse as the past returns to the present (Ricoeur in Negus 2012: 483). In Palermo, the borders of propriety and expectation shifted as the focus spotlit the individual and not the meeting agenda. The air changed. This group was a temporary "network," but the music inherited was clearly, in the words of O'Hara and Brown, after DeNora,

> a resource for social "occasioning" in the way it was chosen, listened to and discussed. And so, music became a vehicle through which tastes and values were understood, discussed and evaluated.

When S(2) played "Top of the World" by the Carpenters, a song that many of the group sang along to, her story about how she encountered it illustrates how it is hitched in her memory to a particular person, place, and occasion. "My parents didn't listen to music, just Irish traditional music. This song, I heard it from a neighbor of mine ... she actually sang the song at her wedding." With these words, S(2) set the scene, as did all the participants as they contextualized their songs, with stories whose details resonated with others in the group. These "orientation points," either moments or people recollected, offered the group members some points of contact between each other. That is, their recollection of parental singing, lost fathers, absent fathers, or driving mothers (on road trips in cars) offered a form of "access" where a collective identification was shared through the narration of one song story.

Their recollections also acted as windows into other worlds. D's and S(2)'s stories of Ireland, where dancing happened in kitchens and music came from neighbors' houses, suggested a place of conviviality and sharing. E's talk of listening to Greek singers in the summer evenings and A(1)'s talk of her mother singing her lullabies conjured up pasts that were never mine but enriched the knowledge I had of these people. They were places I would never go, such as road trips across the northern American states in the 1970s, as K narrated. These stories remain vivid to me, and this was unexpected.

In the theory of Roland Barthes (2000), these moments acted as "punctums." Barthes's punctum has an "acute effect ... something in a photograph that pricks the viewer, pierces his/her consciousness and is perceived as poignant" (Ribière 2008: 64). Barthes's use of the term with reference to how photographs might be viewed made play of the word's Latin origin, to "sting" or to "prick" and thereby to jolt the viewer. In that "jolt" comes a realization of something that jumps out at you, which engages you emotionally. This happened in the group a number of times, especially around narratives of childbirth and loss, which many of the group had experienced. One singularly unexpected moment was when the only male member of the group talked about his absent father. This individual was known to the group as the finance and project management officer; he was polite and private. I had talked to him many times about his mother, who is a dual Israeli and British national, having been born before 1948 in

Palestine. I had worked with his mother on a small-scale film documentary about women in the local Orthodox synagogue. In three years of a working relationship, my colleague's father had been entirely missing in conversations, but he became visible when G spoke about his inheritance track:

> I think I picked this because my father's idea of parenting was making us watch westerns [laughter], which I'm not complaining about at all. Not just the track "The Good, the Bad and the Ugly," but all the soundtracks to spaghetti westerns sit with me, because ... I think my moral code ... I learnt from watching westerns—bad cowboys and good cowboys, the good always shoot the bad. The way I behave, a black-and-white sense of morality—[these tracks] left an imprint on me in terms of ways of behaving. ... He used to tell us [G and his brother] stories based on the westerns, 'cause me and my brother shared a room—can't really remember, maybe I made the whole thing up.

The group had never been witness to a personal testimony from G, and it was unexpected. Since his role was as budget coordinator and project manager, his contributions were on financial and administrative matters, and in social settings too, he was reserved. The group was especially silent listening to him; it was novel to hear him speaking about his past and about a father whose emotional involvement was via television. The group dynamic ensured that there was a safety net to the proceedings, that we were all going to leave Sicily later that day or the following day, and that this workshop was not going to be repeated. That G offered a caveat at the end of his story that perhaps his memory was fallible could indicate that he was trying to annul the emotions he had made apparent through the telling of that story. Van Dijck notes how "[a] memory changes each time it is recalled, and its content is determined more by the present than by the past" (2014: 109). The temporary nature of the meeting and the knowledge that the group would never meet together again could have been factors contributing to the *freedom to tell* that this unique workshop enabled.

Stories in Place

Context and place are important for understanding the discussions that happened in this Inheritance Tracks workshop. The group was meeting because of the political context of rapid migration into Europe. Their work was in dealing with those who had crossed borders, who were categorized as "migrants." The word supposes that the subject is always moving, not fixed, always on the border of "citizen" (Cabot 2016; Western 2020). It solidifies the flight from somewhere and maps it onto an ongoing alien subjectivity. The focus on that autumn afternoon was not with migration and migrants but on the team's Inheritance Tracks, their own "sonic agency," in "listening and being heard" (LaBelle 2018: 4, quoted in Western 2020: 296). Work on sound and migration is tangential to the session we had in Sicily, although I am now conducting research in that area. What is useful from those working in the field is the idea that migration is as much a sonic as a physical process. There is, in listening, the potential "to open creative engagements when representing displacement" (Western 2020: 296). And here I found out how that process was key to opening up and shifting the borders of the group's understanding of each other.

How people reacted to each other, how they talked, and what they shared during the workshop (and then privately afterward) indicated that the entire ninety minutes were clearly differentiated in their minds from the previous business. The workshop was not on the official meeting agenda, and so it was placed and contextualized in a novel space. Writing on the very different ways in which "context" has been conceived with regard to music therapy, Even Ruud (2010) addresses the context of musical experience. It is also useful to note that the Inheritance Tracks workshop was not conceived of as a therapeutic tool but rather one that sought to interrogate transference of music across lives and so across individual subjective borders. In that regard, it was interrogating music's place within individual lives and its journey across generations. Here is Ruud on the context of music:

> How we experience music and how music will affect us will depend on our musical background, the influence of the music we have chosen, and the particular situation in which we experience the music. In other words, in such a contextual understanding, the music, the person, and the situation work together in a relational or mutual relation where changes in any of these components will change the meaning produced. (2010: 57)

The idea that meanings are reliant on the relationship between all these different variables illustrates how the conversations that emerged from the Palermo workshop were unique. There were layers of experience at work. First, there was the individual's song story, one that meant something important to them, one whose narration sometimes came with emotion, even tears. When K heard her chosen inherited track of ABBA's "Dancing Queen," which had been played on long car trips to a holiday cabin in North America, her comments of "I heard it from my mum. I want to pass it on to my children ... It just makes me happy" resounded with others, who recalled similar types of car journeys listening to parental music choices. In the recollection of that track, it came into the present, was heard by the group on a laptop, and had a shared meaning through the responses to it. At the beginning of this chapter, I referred to the idea that these song stories were exchanged in "confessional" moments (Radstone 2007). Susannah Radstone's focus is feminist literary confession and memoir. She details the history of the term "confession" and its prevalence in contemporary popular media culture and reality TV. Something of the person is needed by an audience, and there is an exchange: from the confessor there is information, and from the confessor (or TV audience) there is acceptance (or disapproval). Confession can be a pouring out of the heart, truth, or emotions in order to be forgiven, to move forward, and to indicate to the rest of a group that one has atoned, all in line with the Judeo-Christian origin and practice of the term. Here what is useful to keep of it is the idea of an individual revealing something new of themselves to an audience.

In Summary

After the meeting ended, two project team members, D and E, had to leave to get to the airport. The rest of us walked across the town to eat lunch together at Moltivolti. This nonprofit restaurant, meeting place, and social hub was set up in 2014 by eight friends from across Africa, the Middle East, and Europe. The CESIE team is well known at Moltivolti, where the food is a mixture of African, Asian, and Italian cuisine. At our lunch, it was as if the Inheritance Tracks workshop had not happened. We were back in the sunlight of the Sicilian capital, which as I said at the outset is very noisy, and we were in our assigned roles: project lead, hosts, and project members. Whatever "trouble" was engendered in that one hour was now smoothed over, unspoken. I want to think again then about place, for it is important to consider the locational and temporal contexts of these song stories (Forman 2002; Lefebvre 2004). They took "place" in geographically and temporally contextualized bodies. The stories that emerged illuminate shared and shifting musical affiliations and affections, where popular music is handed down and across ages, sometimes where the lines of inheritance are not only familial but also contextualized within a broader complex "traffic." The "inheritances" here were the library of potential pasts that were gifted or chosen, acknowledged, negotiated, and shared in a small hot room in those ninety minutes in the autumn of 2018. There was also a series of small "displacements" happening in that time, notably, in the shift in emotion that had been enabled by the recollection and sharing of the songs and the stories that accompanied them. A change had taken place.

Solnit's idea of storytelling as a revolt is of use to understand what happened in Palermo, because small moments of listening and telling have the potential to blur borders. Her work is about feminist recoveries of forgotten histories and erased subject worlds. But there is something I would like to take from it. *Troubling Inheritance*, as indicated in the introduction to this book, is about the complexities around inheritance in relation to music: how we remember it and with whom. My reading of Solnit's assertion was that storytelling might be disruptive; what we tell and where we tell it, how we listen and how we react to the story, may disturb some kind of stasis or status quo. The disruptions noted here are modal, small, and nuanced, but they reveal the potential for song stories to be instrumental in those changes.

In Palermo, the professionalism of the meeting was disrupted, as was the veneer of "appropriate" (unemotional) business behavior. I myself had been troubled by this possibility at the very start, not wanting to "waste people's time" with the original request in September 2018. Borders of behavior were shifted. Borders of time were crossed together and shared, as people shared the song stories. Toward the end of the session, people were dancing and singing along to the songs. They were united for a short time by the emotional bindings that emerged through the process. There was an atmospheric change in the room caused by the dedicated time of shared listening and telling. Differences and commonalities were revealed, and temporary affective alliances and sympathies emerged. There was a generosity at play in both the ninety-minute workshop and its forgetting. The participants knew how to listen and then how to forget. Modalities of behavior and perception were reconfigured as the group moved from being a group of NGO workers and academics on a media research project to a group of storytellers and listeners. All of these disruptions were afforded by the choice of one or two songs that were important to them and part of their own "lifetime soundtrack" (Istvandity 2016). This song story workshop offered a space for telling and listening; it offered agency and bore witness. It was so much more than just the hour and a half it took. Writing this more than two years later has been instructive. Listening again to the songs on the Spotify playlist and to the recorded audio of the meeting itself does what those songs did in the meeting. It crosses borders and affects me, takes me back to the hot little room in Sicily, and is treasured.

Discography

ABBA. "Dancing Queen." Recorded August 4–5, 1975, as lead single on fourth studio album, *Arrivals*, released 1976. Written by Benny Andersson, Björn Ulvaeus, and Stig Anderson. Produced by B. Andersson and B. Ulvaeus, Polar Music.

Bennett, Tony. "You're All the World to Me." Composed in 1950 by Burton Lane, lyrics by Alan J. Lerner, for the MGM musical *Royal Wedding* (film) (1951), directed by Stanley Donen.

The Carpenters. "'On Top of the World." Recorded 1972 on album *A Song for You* and released as a single in 1973. Written and composed by Richard Carpenter and John Bettis. Produced by Karen Carpenter and R. Carpenter, A&M.

Chapman, Tracy. "Talkin' Bout a Revolution." Recorded 1988 as second single on eponymous album *Tracy Chapman*. Produced by D. Kerschenbaum, Elektra Records.

Daara J Family. "Jamono." Produced in Senegal.

Gaynor, Gloria. "I Will Survive." Released 1978. Written by Freddie Peren and Dino Fekaris. Produced by D. Fekaris, Polydor Records.
Khaled. "Aïcha." 1996. Produced by Goldman and Khaled, EMI.
Lekkas, Vasilis. "Am Thimisis to onirou mou." Remember My Dream.
Morricone, Ennio. "The Good, the Bad and the Ugly." Theme song for same-named movie, 1966, directed by Sergio Leone and starring Clint Eastwood. Written by E. Morricone. Produced by P. Santomarino, Parade.
Morrison, Van. *Astral Weeks*. Released 1968 as second studio album. Recorded at Century Sound Studios, New York. Produced by Lewis. Merenstein, Warner Bros. Records.
Rolling Stones. "She's a Rainbow." Song on 1967 album *Their Satanic Majesties Request*. Written by Mick Jagger and Keith Richards. Produced by the Rolling Stones.
Simon and Garfunkel. "The Only Living Boy in New York." Song on 1970 album *Bridge over Troubled Water*. Written by Paul Simon. Produced by P. Simon and Art Garfunkel, Columbia Records.
Simply Red. "Sunrise." Chart-topping song on the soul band's 2003 album *Home*. Produced by A. Wright, Warner Music.
Sosa, Mercedes. "Duerme Negrito." Third track on Spanish singer's 1971 album *Gracias a la vida*. Produced by Fonogram S.A.
Veloso, Caetano. "O Leãozinho" (Little lion). Eighth track on Brazilian singer-songwriter's 1977 album *Bicho*.
The Velvet Underground. "Oh! Sweet Nuthin'." Released 1970 on American rock group's fourth studio album, *Loaded*. Produced by Geoff Haslam, Shel Kagan, and the Velvet Underground, Cotillion Records.
Wainwright III, Loudon. "Dead Skunk." Novelty song released as single in 1972. Produced by Kaye and Kramer, Columbia Records.

References

Ahmed, Sara. 2004. "Affective Economies." *Social Text*, 22(2): 117–39.
Associazione Donne di Benin City Palermo. 2018. https://donnedibenincitypalermo.wordpress.com/.
Barthes, Roland. 2000. *Camera Lucida: Reflections on Photography*. Translated by Richard Howard. London: Vintage.
Cabot, Heath. 2016. "'Refugee Voices': Tragedy, Ghosts, and the Anthropology of Not Knowing." *Journal of Contemporary Ethnography*, 45(6): 645–72.
DeNora, Tia. 2000. *Music in Everyday Life*. Cambridge: Cambridge University Press.
Forman, Murray. 2002. *The 'Hood Comes First: Race, Space, and Place in Rap and Hip-Hop*. Middletown, CT: Wesleyan University Press.
GEM: Going the Extra Mile Project. 2017. http://www.glosgem.org/.
Gibbs, Anna. 2001. "Contagious Feelings: Pauline Hanson and the Epidemiology of Affect." *Australian Humanities Review*, 24(December). http://australianhumanitiesreview.org/2001/12/01/contagious-feelings-pauline-hanson-and-the-epidemiology-of-affect/.

Horowitz, Jason. 2019. "Palermo Is Again a Migrant City, Shaped Now by Bangladeshis and Nigerians." *New York Times*. May 22. https://www.nytimes.com/2019/05/22/world/europe/italy-palermo-immigrants-salvino.html.
Istvandity, Laura. 2016. "'If I Ever Hear It, It Takes Me Straight Back There': Music, Autobiographical Memory, Space and Place." In Joy Damousi and Paula Hamilton (eds.), *A Cultural History of Sound, Memory, and the Senses*, 231–44. Routledge Studies in Cultural History. New York: Routledge.
Kassabian, Anahid. 2013. *Ubiquitous Listening: Affect, Attention, and Distributed Subjectivity*. Berkeley: University of California Press.
LaBelle, Brandon. 2018. *Sonic Agency: Sound and Emergent Forms of Resistance*. London: Goldsmiths Press.
Lefebvre, Henri. 2004. *Rhythmanalysis: Space, Time and Everyday Life*. London: Bloomsbury.
MedLIT: Media Literacy for Refugee, Asylum Seeking and Migrant Women. 2018. https://www.medlitproj.eu.
MYSTY. 2018. MyStory: Digital Storytelling. https://mysty.eu/.
Negus, Keith. 2012. "Narrative Time and the Popular Song." *Popular Music & Society*, 35(4): 483–500.
O'Hara, Kenton, and Barry Brown. 2006. *Consuming Music Together: Social and Collaborative Aspects of Music Consumption Technologies*. Dordrecht, The Netherlands: Springer.
Orlando, Leoluca. 2018. "On Migration: Palermo's Perspective." *Climate 2020*. November 9. https://www.climate2020.org.uk/on-migration-palermos-perspective/.
Radstone, Susannah. 2007. *The Sexual Politics of Time: Confession, Nostalgia, Memory*. New York: Routledge.
Regev, Motti. 2013. *Pop-Rock Music: Aesthetic Cosmopolitanism in Late Modernity*. London: Polity.
Ribière, Mireille. 2008. *Barthes: Philosophy Insights*. Carlisle, Australia: Humanities Ebooks.
Ruud, Even. 2010. *Music Therapy: A Perspective from the Humanities*. Gilsum, NH: Barcelona.
Solnit, Rebecca. 2014. *Men Explain Things to Me: And Other Essays*. Chicago: Haymarket Books.
van Dijck, José. 2007. *Mediated Memories in the Digital Age: Cultural Memory in the Present*. Stanford, CA: Stanford University Press.
van Dijck, José. 2014. "Remembering Songs through Telling Stories: Pop Music as a Resource for Memory." In Karin Bijsterveld and José van Dijck (eds.), *Sound Souvenirs: Audio Technologies, Memory and Cultural Practices*, 107–20. Amsterdam: Amsterdam University Press.
Veterans' Voices. 2019. http://www.veteransvoicesglos.co.uk.
Western, Tom. 2020. "Listening with Displacement: Sound, Citizenship and Disruptive Representations of Migration." *Migration and Society*, 3(1). https://doi.org/10.3167/arms.2020.030128.
Wintour, Patrick, Lorenzo Tondo, and Stephanie Kirchgaessner. 2018. "Southern Mayors Defy Italian Coalition to Offer Safe Port to Migrants." *Guardian*. June 11. https://www.theguardian.com/world/2018/jun/10/italy-shuts-ports-to-rescue-boat-with-629-migrants-on-board.

5

Songs That Matter: Assessing through Trinidadian Storytellings the Power of Music, Memory, Age, and Aging

Jocelyne Guilbault

Miami, Florida, September 29, 2018, 2:45 p.m. Alvin arrived first. A longtime friend of mine from Trinidad, I had not seen him for three years. He moved to Miami in 2016. An engineer who specialized in air-conditioning, he found work soon after his arrival. However, Alvin's lifelong passion is music. As a lyricist, producer, artist manager, and calypso and steel band adjudicator for national and regional competitions, Alvin has developed an intimate knowledge of the dominant music scenes in Trinidad and Tobago. Joan, a Trinidadian who has been living in the United States for thirty-five years, came with me to the door to welcome Alvin in her house where the workshop was being held. A former social worker in Northern California, she now returns to Trinidad more regularly since she and her husband, Percy, moved to Miami eight years ago.

Percy, a professor emeritus from the University of California, Berkeley, currently teaches at Florida International University. He arrived at the house a few minutes later with his niece, Blossom. As I was greeting Percy and indicating for the record that, among the participants he was the only one born in Guyana, his wife, Joan, quickly added, "It is important to mention that he has been married to a Trinidadian for thirty-three years!" She clapped her hands and laughed. Blossom was born in Trinidad but, at the age of nine, moved with her family to the United States. Living with Percy and Joan over the past few years, she finished her bachelor's degree in psychology and now works part-time at a holistic-approach medical clinic. Also joining our group was Maliqua, a friend of both Blossom and Joan. Born in New York but raised in Trinidad, she works as a communication officer in a city near Miami. Soon after her arrival at the house, she began chatting with Alvin, who, it turned out, had grown up on the same street in Trinidad several years before she did. Such encounters with people from the same neighborhood or with people who know someone that you know unmistakably draw islanders together in diaspora.

The goal in bringing these people together was to conduct a workshop to explore the extent to which music, memory, age, and aging interact together and mediate the selection of songs that people find worth passing on to younger generations and friends. Ahead of time, everyone had been asked to identify a song from the past and one from the present that matter to them and to indicate the technologies of communication and the circumstances through which they had first encountered their selected songs. They had all been asked to share the memories these songs conjure up for them and to explain how these songs came to signify things worth sharing with others. Although this seems on its face to be a simple exercise, sharing the songs that are most meaningful or imbued with particular affective resonances can be a particularly daunting task. As ethnomusicologist Helmi Järviluoma aptly remarks, "Through these acts of remembering, we present ourselves both to ourselves and [to] the others" (2020: 173). Intuitively bearing this in mind, I chose to conduct the workshop with a group of people who know each other well and whom I know well, and who share some affinities by being all from the same ethnicity/race[1] and social class, that is, Afro-Trinidadians, from the professional class, who are all living in diaspora (at this point, all in Miami). While these affinities might contribute to an overlapping of cultural memories despite the participants' different ages (ranging from twenty-five to seventy-four years), as media studies scholar José Van Dijck puts it, "[O]f course, there is no unified collective memory; instead, there are numerous networks, platforms, and sites for constructing versions of a communal past" (2006: 370). Nonetheless, my hope was that the participants' overlapping experiences would provide an environment where everyone would feel comfortable to share the intimate stories attached to the songs that have been significant in their lives.[2]

Some psychologists view asking participants to select autobiographical stories ahead of time as problematic, because "a memory of the act of recalling the original memory ahead of time is likely to be intertwined with the original memory" (Janata, Tomic, and Rakowski 2007: 847). However, the "commission" of autobiographical material can only be viewed as a problem if it is assumed that a first recall is closer to the reality of what is remembered. If we agree that memory is constantly in flux in relation to people's current preoccupations, desires, material conditions, or interactions with others, then the "commissioned" autobiographies are not less close or any closer to a given "reality"; they are all part of a constantly (re)membering process. Significantly, as anthropologist Sara Cohen, drawing on Michel-Rolph Trouillot (1995) and Andreas Huyssen (1995), notes, "[R]emembering is a selective practice, and understanding it demands attention not only to what is remembered, but also to what is not" (2020: 42).

The selective process of remembering was central to my interest. The goal of this workshop was not only to assess how music, memory, age, and aging mutually inform each other but also to identify the "mattering maps" (Grossberg 2010: 316), that is, to map what for these Trinidadians deeply matters to remember and to bequeath to other generations.[3] This project was not meant to take the form of a comparative study of what is remembered about the selected songs in relation to the age of the participants. Rather, it aimed to develop an aggregate knowledge and a better understanding of the different mediations at play in remembering particular songs of the past, valuing them in the present moment, and selecting them as worthy of inclusion in the musical archive of friends and younger generations.[4] What can be learned from the songs that matter to people to the point of wanting to share them with younger generations and friends? What kinds of values do these songs enact for them? And conversely, what kinds of knowledge does the selection of songs reveal about the people who chose them, the mediations that inform their past and current life experiences, and the culture with which they associate themselves?

Before addressing these questions, I mobilize this study to reflect on the highly varying understandings of music, memory, age, and aging and their implications for the study of their interrelations. I then explore the mutual influence of the agency of music and of age and aging on the remembering process and "the doing of memory."[5]

Theoretically Speaking: Music, Memory, Age, and Aging

The terms "music," "memory," "age," and "aging," while mutually informing each other, need to be separately analyzed and to be theoretically clarified. Instead of resorting to universalizing definitions, I address each of these notions by thinking about the varying mediations that inform their meanings in situated personal and social experiences.

Music

This study emphasizes how the specificity of a given music mediates its relative importance over the course of one's life and the extent to which (how much of it and how often) the music is evoked and remembered. This study takes into account how the "specificity of music"—whether through the particularities of genre, the contexts and the kinds of performance to which it is typically associated, the repertoire it is known for, or the specific age group or occasions for which the music is composed—is agentive.[6] This means examining how a given music triggers memory by conjuring up a distinct worlding, to use Martin Heidegger's ([1927] 2010) notion—a distinct assemblage of sounds, sights, people, ages, bodily movements, sensations, emotions, and social relations. It means exploring how the music acts on age and aging, at times in ways that emphasize biological aging or "cultural aging" and at other times in ways that make people forget about age altogether.[7] Viewing as foundational the ways in which a particular musical practice informs memory, age, and aging, I chose methodologically to focus on only one genre of music and one that I am familiar with (that I have studied and experienced over many years), to grasp the many connections the workshop participants would establish during our exchange.[8]

This study focuses on the particular worlding of what in Trinidad is called "party music," a stand-in for soca music, which after twenty-five-plus years of research in Trinidad I know particularly well.[9] As is the case for all musical genres, party songs as concept, experience, and event do not come alone. They come with an associational cluster of soundings, sites, activities, people, behaviors, attitudes, and more that, I argue, is agentive over memory and thus over the stories people recount about songs. Echoing the narratives about party songs on radio and television, in print and online media, and in the interviews I conducted over the years in Trinidad, the participants' stories about their selected songs foregrounded a series of themes that have now become synonymous with party songs. Put another way, party songs act as a trope "[whose] function," sociologist Eleanor Townsley explains, "is to compress and inscribe historically developed collective understandings in a very short space; it reduces complexity and represses contentious detail[s] in favor of 'what everyone knows'" (2001: 99).[10] As such, party songs are invariably associated with carnival during which new soca songs are released, performed, and defended during the annual Soca Monarch competitions. During carnival, they are inextricably linked with parties (home parties and public fetes), and since the 1990s, with all-inclusive parties (paid-in-advance events that include live performances, food, and drinks),[11] cooler parties (entrance fee events that include live performances and that allow attendees to bring their own coolers filled with drinks), and many other parties organized by various associations, institutions, and fete promoters. Party songs also stand for a constellation of activities ranging from Soca Monarch competitions to masquerades, *Jouvè* (also spelled *J'ouvert*, which refers to Carnival Monday revelry in the streets starting at around 3:00 or 4:00 a.m. until daylight), and for some people, going to the gym to look good before all of these events take place.[12] Party songs conjure up masquerade (mas' in Trinidadian talk) bands and steel bands. Outside carnival, they denote the soundtrack for any event taking the form of a party, such as a birthday party, baptism party, wedding reception, gathering of friends, and more. In all cases, party songs come with specific bodily movements like *wining* and dance gestures like *djouk*.[13] They imply sociality, conviviality, and drinking. Promoting particular attitudes like "to free up" and "to let go," they are also connected with rapture and joy, with heightened emotions over several hours—all of which, it could be suggested, afford the mind and body sharper focus and thus greater possibilities to be remembered. For many, soca songs mark their identities, their ways of being, sensing, and acting in the world.

The trope that party songs stand for, however, is not fixed and changes over time. Let me provide one example. Until the 1980s in Trinidad, pan (steel drum) was the premier instrument at parties and was highly reputed for its performance of calypso and soca. However, today pan is relegated to concerts, competitions, and community playing for holidays or particular occasions. Pan is still part of Trinidadian communities in some diasporic locations, but it does not occupy the same importance it used to have. Hence, not surprisingly, while the Trinidadian workshop participants over forty years old all referred to pan at one point or another in discussing their selected songs, the youngest of the group, Blossom, did not refer to it at all during our exchange. It seemingly has not played a major role in her experience of party songs. Overall, however, despite the fact that the party songs trope is not fixed, it nonetheless encompasses a normalized series of associations and, in so doing, encourages a normalized way of speaking about party songs—a way of speaking that, as is the case for most tropes, "tends to efface the power relations that are in place" (Khalili 2014: 25).[14] For instance, it tends to efface the sexual harassment that some women suffer when attending carnival, parties, or fetes; the discrimination against the LGBTQ community; and the heavy presence of police and private security forces at these events. What other types of connection is party music channeling, constructing, or silencing? Is the common local perception of party music as "happy" music, in and of itself, orienting particular "dispositions" toward it and toward ways of (re)membering it? To what extent for Trinidadians is party music mediating the conception of age and aging? I will address these questions at length in the next sections.

Memory

Similar to music, the notion of memory needs to be qualified here. Drawing on several scholars' insights, I explore Trinidadian party music in relation to what I call "emplaced" memory to emphasize how place highly mediates how and what one remembers.[15] As Percy pointed out during the workshop, "Many Trinidadians living in diaspora make an extra effort to remember music from Trinidad. For them, remembering Trinidadian music is a matter of identity and nostalgia." It is a way to feel, and to demonstrate to themselves and to others, that they are emotionally attached to their mother country.

For people living in diaspora, geographic factors can make it harder to stay updated with party songs and thus to remember them. It is not so much a problem of access to the songs (the internet is accessible) as a problem of a small-size community, the lack of opportunities to get "connected," and, after several years of living in diaspora, the *relative* personal desire to stay connected. To explain why the song she selected from her past is in historical terms quite recent ("Black Man Feeling to Party" by Black Stalin released in 1991), Joan remarks, "I could have chosen a song further back, but that's the song I listened to in Berkeley, California. The Caribbean Trinidadian community there is very small. There were Caribbean clubs in Oakland, but they played mostly reggae. The Caribbean people in the Bay Area are mostly Jamaicans. [I selected 'Black Man Feeling to Party' because at that time] I wanted that feeling of being able to party." Echoing Joan's remarks about the Bay Area, Blossom takes the example of her brother who is currently living in Oakland who, she suspects, cannot easily remember party songs from the past but even less so those from the present. He is not exposed to or in contact with Trinidadians living in the Bay Area, she explained. Over the years, he has lost touch with Trinidadian party music.

As a way to emphasize further the link between memory and place, Maliqua pointed out how memory in Trinidad is continually reinforced by the fact that music is played at high volume at people's homes, at the next-door neighbor's home, and down the road during the whole day and until late at night during the week and weekend. During carnival or other festivities, party songs can be heard (like it or not) all night long. The repeated audition of songs in Trinidad, Maliqua suggested, mediates and marks people's memory and simultaneously creates a widely shared repertoire of songs or collective musical archive. Conversely, as Percy noted, for most Trinidadians living in diaspora, memory is cultivated by attending events organized by Trinidadian communities where they now live.

In addition to being "emplaced," memory is gendered. Joan, Maliqua, and Blossom all emphasized their experience of the songs they selected in sensual and affective terms. They spoke about their songs as follows: "It [that song] is sensual, you feel sexy; I like the moves"; "I was feeling good about myself, [with this song] I was feeling extra good about myself; I was feeling so good about myself that every now and then I took pictures of myself"; "I don't remember the lyrics, just the vibe; it's like the music vibrate through your body and we were just on a high of just soca." In contrast, both Percy and Alvin spoke about what their selected songs compelled them to do or they recounted the stories of the songs. They did not communicate their sensual or affective experiences of the songs. Alvin recalled, "I could sing the chorus by the following morning; I went straight to Silver Stars panyard [the location where steelbands rehearse]"; "We *wined* to that tune all night." After declaring that he is not into party songs (more on this later), Percy referred to what one *does* during carnival: "You go every night to the panyard and you drink the beer, and you may go from one panyard to the other, or you may go to your own panyard [the one you most associate with] ... And we go to the savannah [a term used to refer to the Queen's Park, the largest open space in the capital of Port of Spain where many large-scale events take place] and we stand outside in the drags [where the steel bands wait and rehearse their tune just before entering the stage], we drink the beers, and we hang out with the band. That's my idea of carnival." The question is, would these ways of speaking about one's experience of party songs have been challenged and reconfigured if there had been more participants and more diversity in terms of class, sexual orientation, and ethnicity/race among participants (e.g., Indo-Trinidadians or White Trinidadians)? This is a question that could only be answered by conducting other workshops with people from various constituencies.

Age and Aging

In this study, like music and memory, age as well as aging cannot be taken for granted. As has been widely recognized,[16] the two terms cannot simply refer to biological or chronological time. As Maliqua put it, "Some people are only thirty, and they feel too old to party." Furthermore, even if it is a truism, it still needs to be stressed: age and aging are valued and experienced differently in different cultures. Both are associated with highly varied conventions of what is permissible and what is not, and even within the same culture, these conventions usually change over time. Age and aging thus need to be culturally situated. In Trinidad, particularly for Afro-Trinidadians, people from different age groups do mix and often blur age distinctions by adopting similar dancing styles, outfits, or partying habits. As Andy Bennett pithily observes, "While the biological process of aging is ultimately universal and unavoidable, cultural aging presents the individual [and I would add, the collective] with a series of options as to how to construct and represent the aging self" (2010: 259). For many Afro-Trinidadians, this "cultural aging" comes with pride and often with an attitude of defiance against (post)colonial conventions.

In Blossom's experience in Miami, there is no difference among people of different age groups at a party.

> When I have been out at parties, the crowd is mixed and everybody is dancing. There might be people standing on the side, but everybody is dancing. I used to go to fetes with my friends' parents! Even when you go to *Jouvè* in carnival, *you don't see age*. People are just there to enjoy themselves. There does not seem to be a distinct separation. (emphasis added)

Percy agreed that "[i]n diaspora, there isn't [a separation of ages]," but he added, "in Trinidad, there is." Alvin concurred. According to them, two mediations make the relation of age to partying in the country more complicated: the cautious attitude of older people and what counts as vintage music in parties concentrating on this repertoire. Percy explained, "During carnival [in Trinidad], the older people really party, [so] it's not a question that older people don't party; it's just that older people don't want to party where it is unsafe ... [They] are more concerned by crime than young people."[17] Alvin in turn described how life experience mediated by age also influences some of the parties people go to:

> There are certain shows [in Trinidad] that all ages go to. But for certain types of vintage parties, you'll tend to see older people—middle-aged and older people. With other types of vintage parties, you'll see young people partying where they have "a special kind of way" [distinct choice of musical eras, of musical genres, of songs, or of dressing the part? Alvin did not explain]. You would not see the mixture of ages at these kinds of parties. But generally, the other parties would be open to everybody, and you would see all ages without seeing any discrimination.

That people of all ages can come together and do so without discrimination in most party music scenes are two significant phenomena that are highly recognized and appreciated in Trinidad. However, the age of the workshop participants to some degree was revealed not only by the selection of songs that marked a particular time in their life histories. It was also revealed by the musical elements they chose to emphasize when speaking about the songs—elements that in and of themselves also marked how the genre, in our case soca, has aged and changed at different moments in its trajectory.[18] The implications of taking into account the age of both the participants and the musical genre itself are important for at least two reasons. Doing so helps to recognize that, in Van Dijck's words, "[m]emories attached to songs are hardly individual responses per se; recorded music [or live music, it should be added] gets perceived and evaluated through collective frameworks for listening and appreciation" (2006: 367). Furthermore, taking into account the age of both the participants and the musical genre helps to discern how these collective frameworks for appreciating and listening to songs within a particular genre of music change over time and mediate memories.

Significantly, except for Joan, the participants' musical aesthetics were closely tied to the musical eras during which they grew up. I say "significantly" because the learning and experience process at a young age has been widely acknowledged as formative of people's musical tastes and competencies as well as of their cultural politics of identities and notions of musical heritage. For instance, Alvin, seventy-four years old, referred to the sociopolitical content of the lyrics, their historical significance, the melodic quality of the tune, the arrangements, and the tempo as the meaningful criteria for his two selected songs—criteria that echo those used to judge calypso competitions during Alvin's youth and up to this day. In contrast, Blossom, twenty-five years old, emphasized the high energy of her two song selections, the ways in which "when you hear it, it just energizes you"— which is how, tellingly, power soca songs (songs performed at top volume, featuring punchy melodic phrases and action-based lyrics propelled by a bouncy tempo) have been evaluated in the soca competitions since they began in 1993, the year Blossom was born. As was the case for Maliqua (more on her song selections later), the features that attracted Alvin and Blossom to select a song from the past were the same ones that led them to select their songs from the present. Aging seemingly did not change the types of songs they love, nor the criteria they use to select songs deemed worth passing on to younger generations.

If the age of the participants could be detected through the aesthetic criteria used to select their songs, age and aging could not be easily guessed by "how much" of the songs was remembered or by how detailed were the stories attached to the songs. In some cases, as mentioned, memory about music may be less determined by age than by how often individuals have heard the songs.[19] In other cases, memory about music is greatly influenced by individual aesthetic preferences. Some people know a great deal about the music of the past and hardly anything about that of the present. In Alvin's words, "A lot of people are living in the past. They want to hear only the vintage music. There are a lot like that. For them, Machel [Montano, a chief exponent of soca nationally and internationally] is wicked. 'I cannot understand anything he says and it is the same tune over and over.' When you hear them, you wonder, what's wrong with them?" In contrast, aging can sometimes help a person further appreciate a song and remember it better by now being able to grasp the meaning of a song lyric they could not understand at a younger age. At the age of six, Maliqua just enjoyed the vibe and dancing to the song "Doh Back Back," by the Mighty Sparrow. Later on, she felt even more strongly about the song through understanding the lyrics and realizing how the song addresses aspects of steel band's history—a history, she feels, that should be known by younger Trinidadian generations.

The mediations that deeply informed not only which songs my interlocutors remembered but also the value they assigned to them could thus far be summarized as follows. Long-term personal investments in a particular genre lead participants to privilege songs from the distant and recent past. Defining personal experiences associated with particular songs also deeply intervened in the process of remembering and in the nostalgic and archival values my interlocutors attached to them. Distinct Trinidadian collective frames of listening cultivated by the canonical definitions of winning songs during national competitions in one's life and in the life (age) of the genre further informed which songs the participants deemed worth remembering. More generally, I was reminded in the workshop how the relative frequency of a song airplay, the personal attraction to musical aesthetics of a particular historical period, as well as aging in relation to song lyrics comprehension, all influenced one's musical memory and affective investments in particular songs.

Keeping in mind these localized notions and experiences of age and aging, situated mediations of memory in Trinidad and in diaspora, and this aperçu of Trinidadian party music, I now turn to the "doing of memory" in relation to the participants' storytellings in the workshop.[20]

The "Doing of Memory" on Storytelling

We all sat at the dining table. Everyone looked at each other, excited to see what songs would be selected as worthy of being passed on to the next generation. This autobiographical memory implied the sharing of intimate memories. However, to paraphrase anthropologist Rivke Jaffe (2012: 82), although the songs each participant would recall stem from individual experiences, they are socially produced and, it must be added, part of vast networks. Indeed, everyone around the table knew well every song that was mentioned during our three-hour exchange. Party songs widely circulate in and out of Trinidad through various events and media: carnival masquerade, soca competitions, radio, television, public parties, home parties, birthday parties, wedding receptions, YouTube videos, Facebook, WhatsApp, and more.[21] Over the past few years, the circulation of party songs has been accelerated by what is referred to as a "blast." As Alvin explains, "There is a guy in Trinidad who you take your song to and say, 'Blast this for me.' He has a couple thousand key people that he sends this to, the deejays in the Caribbean, Miami, New York, London, everywhere. Within twenty-four hours, your song will be in their hands and they in turn will distribute it to their friends and other people if he likes it. So your song can become popular overnight because of a blast." The worlding, to again use Heidegger's ([1927] 2010) expression, that the selected party songs created during the workshop was thus (re)membered not only by the participants who selected the songs but also by all the participants sitting at the table. They spontaneously filled in the gaps in stories recounted by another participant, often interrupting them to situate the song in its historical context, to provide additional information about the performer or composer, or to share their own lived experiences of that song. The resulting composite story produced a rich texture of the worlding the selected party songs conjured up. It also helped to confirm the importance that such a worlding holds not only for the person speaking but also for the other participants and why for them it is important to pass on these party songs to younger generations.

I listened to the stories, sometimes joining the conversation with my own experience of the songs in question. Immediately after the participants named their chosen songs, I played them on my computer from YouTube's vast musical audiovisual collection. I wished I could have played the participants' songs of choice on better sound equipment. Regardless of the thin sounds coming out of my computer's speakers, listening to the songs together proved to be the perfect prompt to elicit storytelling. I was most curious to see the work that memory does in (re)constituting or (re)defining the trope that party songs stand for each and every time people talk about some of these songs.

Storytelling 1

Alvin selected "Jean and Dinah," a classic calypso by the Mighty Sparrow released in 1956, when he was just twelve years old and living in Trinidad. He first heard it on the "big" radio his father owned in their new home in Woodbrook, one year after his mother had died. Age did matter here in terms of his access to the song. As Alvin explained, he listened to "Jean and Dinah" on radio because he was too young to go to the savannah where the calypso competitions were going to be held on Dimanche Gras and also too young to hear the calypsos in the calypso tents. Radio enabled him to listen to songs and to develop his critical listening skills—skills that would serve him well in his artistic and music business activities later in life. In Alvin's own words, "After listening to the first verse [of 'Jean and Dinah'], I said, 'He wins' [and] even though I had listened to the song once, the melody has stuck in my mind right away. In fact, I could sing the chorus by the following morning. And everybody else was singing it too. It was the most amazing thing. He [the Mighty Sparrow] won the road march [that year]."[22] This song "stuck in my mind as a significant starting point musically for me." This song also matters to Alvin in historical and musical terms. The song lyrics address prostitution during the time the US Navy was stationed in Trinidad, a part of Trinidadian history that for Alvin is important to remember. In Alvin's view, "Jean and Dinah" is also a song that "changed [calypso] from [being based on] predictable melodies. Sparrow came and he changed the format, experimented with chords." This song matters so much to Alvin that he made sure all his children learned it after repeatedly listening to him playing his cuatro (an instrument with four [or five] strings in the form of a small guitar) and singing along with it. Alvin's memory of this selected song from the past is mediated by defining moments in his personal life: he heard it only one year after his mother had died, it was the first time he immediately guessed the winning road march of that carnival season, and it was the first time also that he could memorize the tune after only one hearing. His memory of the song is also deeply embedded in and marked by the social events recounted in the song—the surge of prostitution during the occupation of the US Navy in Trinidad during the Second World War and the song's winning of the road march of the year. The affective resonance that this song has had for Alvin thus comes not only from a personal but also from a collective experience of the song.

Using his musical skills, Alvin determined the first time he heard "Full Extreme" by the group Ultimate Rejects that this song was "a mashup! [meaning, a winning song]." It indeed won the road march in the 2017 carnival. From Miami, Alvin heard the song through the special channel mentioned previously called a "blast." At seventy-four years old, Alvin keeps himself informed about new sound technologies as well as about the new dominating musical aesthetics of soca music today. Nonetheless, it is significant that he selected his two songs based on the same criteria: lyrics that cleverly address social commentaries,[23] music that produces good "vibes," and "tempo" that irresistibly makes you dance all night—criteria that have been and remain the hallmarks of winning calypsos, the dominating musical genre of Alvin's younger years. As his stories make clear, Alvin places great value onto the fact that powerful social commentaries do not have to be antithetical to party mood and dancing. On the contrary, to him, songs that cater to both the mind and the body are what make them powerful and their aesthetics important to pass on to younger generations.

Storytelling 2

Joan chose "Black Man Feeling to Party" (1991) by the reputed calypsonian named Black Stalin. She explained, "I may have heard the song ['Black Man Feeling to Party'] with the Trini guy on KPFA [radio], David McBurnie [when I was living] in Berkeley. But most likely, my sister [who still lives in Trinidad] sent them [the songs] to me"—highlighting how, up to the early 1990s, people living in diaspora listened to the latest song releases as much through family connections sending CDs through regular mail as through the usual media channels such as radio. (Calypso songs then were not yet easily available on the internet.)[24]

Joan chose "Black Man Feeling to Party" not only because, as she put it, "I wanted that feeling of being able to party"[25]—alluding to the fact that in Berkeley, there were not many occasions to do so. She also chose that song because "it was about Blackness and being Black." One riff of the song furthermore reminded her of the typical rhythm played by the iron, a percussion instrument in Trinidadian steel bands,[26] and of *Jouvè* when "you're under cover and can party and free up"—a musical tradition she highly values. Maliqua jumped in to explain why *Jouvè* also greatly matters to her: "I like to party. But you have to fix up that, get this, and you have ... you know? At *Jouvè*, you're going to get dirty. You can go by the truck [equipped with big speakers diffusing the music] and not worry. You can be yourself, and you don't have to sweat under the hot sun. No fuss." She went on to further qualify the music such as "Black Man Feeling to Party" that reminded Joan of *Jouvè*. "Usually it's more [in the style of] groovy music you could chip [on]. Back then, you had the steelbands, and you would push the pans."[27] Joan values this song because it generated a party mood and brought a sense of identity through both the lyrics (Blackness) and the sound (reminding her of the Trinidadian traditions of *Jouvè* and of the steel band evoked by the rhythmic pattern usually played on the iron). As Van Dijck (2006: 358) would put it, the memory of this song was mediated in at least three ways: it was *embodied* (physically experienced; she listened to the song and probably danced to it), *enabled* (made accessible through media, in this case mail), and *embedded* (situated in relation to Trinidad's musical and carnival traditions, but listened to in diaspora, in an environment where Joan felt isolated). Van Dijck's concept of human memory as being "simultaneously embodied, enabled, and embedded" is most useful to trace the mediations at play in storytellings about songs.

Twenty years later, Joan was struck by "Hello" by Kes, a 2017 soca song she first heard through Facebook, very soon after it was released. Whereas "Black Man Feeling to Party" evoked Black pride and tradition for her, "Hello" reinforced the importance she places on "feeling good" about oneself, independently of anyone else. This time, the "sweet" melody and soft vocal delivery of Kes spoke to her dancing body. As she put it, "[This song] is sensual, you feel sexy, you don't really need a man to make you feel nice." Alvin quipped, "It's not like the old days when women used to wait for a man to pick them up." Joan answered, "I'm done with that. The flirty, you know. I love it [the song]. I don't know all the lyrics, [only] some of the lyrics. I like the moves. ... This song makes you feel alive." In her two song selections, Joan values party songs that address self-pride, freeing up (emancipation), and self-love not simply through the song lyrics but also through the soundings of the tune—the tone of voice, the melody, the arrangement, the tempo—which, for Joan, all contribute to a feeling of wellness.

At this point in her story, Joan is no longer addressing where she lives (in 2018 she was living in Miami). She is no longer experiencing isolation since Miami is populated by many people of Caribbean descent. And she continues to be strongly connected to Trinidadian music with the instantaneous availability of Trinidadian party songs on Facebook. This is all taken for granted even though, it could be argued, her current situation greatly contributes to her remembering process. What matters for Joan is how the song "Hello" makes her feel, the affective resonance it creates for her, significantly, without the help of anyone else (men in particular). In so doing, Kes's song for Joan has become an "object" of attachment worth passing on to the people she cares about.

Storytelling 3

Maliqua selected the song from her past that marked her introduction to calypso in 1994. Attending her first wedding reception as a flower girl at the age of six, only two years after moving from New York to Trinidad with her family, she recalled with a smile on her face how she loved "Doh Back Back" by the Mighty Sparrow. As she put it, "This was a hot song," not because of the lyrics—she could not understand them at the time—but because it compelled her to dance. Even though she later came to appreciate the song lyrics, which, according to her, attest to women's love of pan men,[28] the connection of calypso/soca with dancing has remained for her what this music first and foremost stands for. Could it be that the memory of this song through dancing has become a defining moment for her by being accompanied by several first-time experiences (mediations?), such as the first time she was a flower girl, the first time she attended a wedding in Trinidad, the first time she may have danced publicly in Trinidad, and in the midst of all this, another first, in her own words, "when that song played, it was my introduction to calypso/soca"?

I was struck by Maliqua's story. It evinced that to think about a song is to think about an event—a song as an event, a song as a happening occurring in a place at a particular time with people talking, listening to music, dancing, singing, drinking, eating, and more.[29] As mentioned earlier, the (re)membering of a song powerfully demonstrates how a musical experience is never only personal; it is socially and materially produced. The (re)membering of a song is also remarkably telling of how the memories of songs selectively highlight some mediations and not others that are constitutive of an event—for instance, whether after the song "Doh Back Back" Maliqua continued to dance, whether she joined other children dancing, or whether that song was played at a key moment in the wedding reception. In this sense, the (consciously or not) selected details in remembering a song event map what, at the moment of relating the story, matters to tell about this past experience—for Maliqua, an unforgettable, embodied, and deeply affective experience of that song at a young age and later on in life.

Nineteen years after her introduction to calypso at the wedding reception, Maliqua is still attracted by "hot" songs, songs that she finds energizing and mentally and physically liberating, as her second selection attests. "Leh Go" by Blaxx, released in 2013, amplified the celebratory mood she was in at the time, following a surgery that to her delight had led her to lose weight. She felt good about herself. It was not the lyrics, she explained, "just the vibe" of the song—a "vibe" that in her story seemed to have been heightened by being able to listen and to dance to the song in a panyard where sociality and conviviality are intensely cultivated.

But before we were told all of this about her second song selection, Joan and Alvin chipped in to add more details about this song event. Joan recalled that Blaxx was the featured performer of Brian MacFarlane's big masquerade band on Carnival Tuesday. Alvin referred to the contenders, soca artists Iwer and Superblue, for the road march competition that year. Maliqua added, "He [Blaxx] is good, but somehow he can never pull it up." (She was referring to the fact that Blaxx has never won a soca or road march competition, even though he is a very appreciated soca artist.) She then commented on the fact that soca singers no longer perform on the trucks (equipped with large speakers going down the streets, followed by the masquerade bands during carnival). "Now, everything is recording." Only then did we learn that for her, the song event of "Leh Go" by Blaxx, she remembers, was not during the carnival. It was during Independence Day in Trinidad. After going to other panyards to listen to different steel bands, she went to Playboyz panyard and arrived when the song was playing. This is why, she remarked, "When I think about this song, I always think about Independence Day and Playboyz panyard." Her remembering of the song is, not surprisingly, not linked to the lyrics—since steel bands only play the tune; they don't have lead singers. It seems that Blaxx's performance of the song—his vocal expression, or tone of voice, or bodily movements—may have served only as a template for what she was hearing on Independence Day that year. Most significantly, it is the combination of the sound of the steel band, the collective panyard atmosphere, and her personal experience of that song and of her own body that marked her memory.

Storytelling 4

The song Blossom remembers as a defining moment in her experience of soca is "Big Truck" by Machel Montano, released in 1997. At the time five years old and still living in Trinidad, she first came into contact with this song through music video, which in the second half of the mid-1990s was still a medium in its infancy for soca. She recalls this song in relation to the situations and activities that are common during the carnival—as a young child, staying at home with a babysitter while her mother and brothers went to a fete and participating in the kiddies' carnival jump up (local expression referring to a fete) organized by the school where she heard the song over and over again. "This was a big song. I would sing it, and you would go to school and I would hear the song." Significantly, even though she mentioned knowing the lyrics back then, she did not mention anything about what they say or what they mean. Instead, she stressed the high energy of this song. She remembers "Big Truck" also as signaling the moment when Machel Montano "came on the scene"[30] and how thereafter, for her and for many other Trinidadians, he became a chief leader of soca and synonymous with what is referred to locally as "power soca"—fast-tempo and high-energy party songs. Alvin pitched in: "'Big Truck' was soca in full force. People started to understand the difference between calypso and soca when Machel [did that song]." To confirm how much that song was circulating at the time, Maliqua added, "That was the song when I played [mas'] with Barbarossa [a famous masquerade band in Trinidad]." These pieces of information were all welcome, but Blossom's remembering of this song by Machel Montano when she was five years old (here age unquestionably mediated her memory) was about something else. Her story focused on her visceral experience of a song and how this song brought Machel Montano "on the scene." It was as much about defining the time of her personal entry into soca culture (at school through the kiddies' carnival) as about defining a historical moment of that musical culture. What her story emphasizes is how for Blossom it was the energy of the song (and by extension, that of Machel Montano's performance) that was transformative and that continues to matter in soca, as her next selection suggests.

For Blossom, Machel Montano stands so much for what soca is about that the second song she chose was a power soca song also by Machel Montano called "Like Ah Boss," released in 2015. Then in her twenties, Blossom's description of the song was more elaborate than that concerning the song from her childhood. This time she referred to her friends who, by word of mouth and through the recording, introduced the song to her. She referred to not only the occasion, *Jouvè*, during which she heard the song played repeatedly, but also the mood to fete that this song created for her.

Blossom: "That year [2015], I did not play mas', but I went to *Jouvè* in Miami and it's just one of those songs, *when you hear it, it just energizes you* [emphasis mine]. I remember, we played *Jouvè*. Maliqua was here. We were just on a high of just soca. And the song gets you in the mood to fete."
Maliqua: "Like Ah Boss" [echoing the title of the song].
Blossom: Yeah.

As a way to explain Maliqua's interjection, Blossom then referred to the song's lyrics, which boast about how Trinidadians know how to party better and longer than anyone else in and out of the Caribbean. In her own words, "We 'out-fete' anyone else, we're Trinis." She spoke these words with pride and more loudly than before during her narrative, to emphasize not only how party songs and partying matter for Trinidadians' senses of identity and senses of belonging but also how she feels part of that "we" Trinidadians. This, I realized, was a particularly sensitive issue for her as a young woman living in diaspora in the United States and also perhaps more importantly because of her status referred to as Deferred Action for Childhood Arrivals (DACA). She entered the United States with her mother and brothers when she was nine years old, and following her family, she stayed unlawfully as an undocumented minor—which put her in a highly precarious position under the Trump administration.[31] Blossom's story about "Like Ah Boss" says a great deal about what she values about soca and, in particular, about Montano's soca songs (they put you in the mood to fete; they energize you) and, by being the party soundtrack, how soca songs assemble people. It also highlights how the remembering of this particular song creates a particular affective resonance and meaning for someone living in diaspora, most particularly for someone in Blossom's position. The issues of place, citizenship, and an uncertain future have undoubtedly contributed to make this song memorable for Blossom in the recent past as much as in the present.

Storytelling 5

Percy provided a two-part story in this workshop. In the first part, he presented his position regarding party songs. Even after thirty-three years of living with Joan, who would certainly qualify herself as, to use David Rudder's song title, "Trini to De Bone," to my surprise Percy declared that he does not like the party scene. "The music is too loud, and people are just jumping up around the place," he said. His understanding of "party," he explained, is based on what the term refers to in Guyana where he was born. "You have birthday party, you have christening, you have all these things, and there is no music. ... You eat and you sit around and drink and play dominoes, and the women eat and chitchat. That's what a party is." There are dances for couples and for boys and girls to meet, but, he added, "party songs" in Guyana do not refer to any particular category of music, as is the case in Trinidad. Based on this definition, Percy spoke of his experience of carnival as centered not on listening to party songs but rather on participating in many of the activities that the trope of party songs and carnival evokes: going to calypso tents (which implies a sitting rather than a dancing audience), listening to calypsos (meaning calypso based on sociopolitical commentaries), applauding, laughing, going to panyard, drinking beer, and hanging out with your favorite steel band before it goes onstage for the panorama competition (an annual carnival competition in Trinidad in which steel bands perform elaborate arrangements of calypsos composed that year).

In the second part of his story, Percy shifted the focus to speak about Trinidadian party songs but through the experience of someone else, his grandson—which enabled him to share memories and at the same time to acknowledge his relative distance (emotional or intellectual investment?) from the topic. Cayden was born in the United States and, according to Percy, did not like West Indian food or music until, at the age of five, he went to Trinidad and heard the song "We Ready for De Road" (officially titled "Differentology" by soca artist Bunji Garlin). Percy remembers how this song transformed Cayden's relation with music from Trinidad. He loved this soca song and remembered the lyrics. He started singing it regularly, however, as Percy recounted with a touch of humor, not to be energized by it but instead to scold his grandmother who was constantly late to drive him to school in the morning. Listening to this unexpected and funny story, I wondered, did Cayden's young age play a role in his unabashed use of the song? Did his minimal understanding of the party songs trope free him from thinking about this song only in relation to Trinidad's party scene?

Percy's second example of Cayden's experience of party songs, at the age of seven, concerns a 2015 song titled "Party Done" by Angela Hunte and Machel Montano. This case illustrates how not only age but also fluency in Trinidadian dialect can contribute to mishearing (and thus, misremembering) lyrics. After another visit to Trinidad, Cayden came back to the United States singing from morning to night this song, "Party Done." Intrigued, Percy asked him what "party done" means, only to learn that Cayden had understood the song to refer to a big party, a party of "dons" (short for "mastodons," referring in his mind to big dinosaurs).[32] Mishearing is certainly not only a matter of young age, but this example serves as a reminder that the relation of memory to music and aging can be affected as much by linguistic skills as by different hearing capacities.

Concluding Remarks

This study explored the various mediations that inform the stories people tell about the songs they view as significant not only in their personal lives but also to the musical archive of younger generations. In particular, it interrogated how the distinct phenomena of music, memory, age, and aging interact and the extent to which they lead people to select some songs and not others as memorable and worth passing on. To investigate these interrelations, I chose to focus on a specific music, Trinidadian soca, to understand how the associational cluster to which this music belongs and simultaneously helps to create has a pulling effect on memory. As is the case for other music and as the stories well demonstrated, soca (party songs) acts as a trope. Focusing on this particular music made it possible to recognize in the stories the affective lexicon it provides ("free up," "leh we go"). It showed how this lexicon in turn helped articulate feelings in ways that make them accessible to memory discourses (as was the case when Joan spoke about the "feeling to be able to party," echoing the title of her selected song). This study also demonstrated how Trinidadian party music channels ways of speaking about songs that reproduce gendered behavior (e.g., the greater use of affective vocabulary by women compared to men). As a trope familiar to all Afro-Trinidadians, party music furthermore stimulated the making (the remembering) of connections that are part of its associational cluster (Blossom remembered her mother and brother going to a fete), which then triggered the remembering of other things (the kiddies' carnival at school). The stories in this workshop further emphasized how the selected songs were themselves agentive by literally and figuratively having "touched" the participants and "impressed" their memories. What this study evinces is that not only as a trope (what party songs stand for in terms of activities, occasions, people, etc.) but also through their soundings, lyrics, tempo, and dance movements, party songs shape, as much as they are shaped by, people's memories.

This study considered the notion of "cultural aging" crucial to understand how the age of the participants did not always dictate their choice of songs or their connections with party music as a whole. However, as the stories exemplified, while the storytellings at times made age hard to guess (Cayden's love of the song "We Ready for De Road"), at other times age mediated life experiences and thus was agentive over the memories of the song events themselves (think of how Maliqua at six years old could not understand the lyrics of the song that introduced her to party music or how Cayden misunderstood the lyrics he attributed to his favorite song). That both cultural and biological age and aging factor into the "doing of memories" has been widely acknowledged. But how the age of the selected songs itself greatly contributes to orient people's memories has been less emphasized. As this study shows, the age of songs brings collective history into focus and thus marks memories in distinct ways (think about how Alvin's memory of "Jean and Dinah" was closely connected to the fact that this song by the Mighty Sparrow was heralding new types of melodies in calypso). In its turn, biological age (the participants' longevity), albeit not always the case, proved in the stories reported here to count as "memory capital" (Bennett 2018: 3), as affording a kind of historical knowledge of party music (of calypso as much as of soca) not matched by younger people. In the workshop, Alvin (age seventy-four), Joan (sixty-three), and Maliqua (forty) intervened to fill out stories far more often than did Blossom (twenty-five). However, as is widely and painfully recognized, long life experiences provide no guarantee of long-term memories. But particular experiences in life, such as Alvin's continued role of adjudicator in calypso and pan competitions, may help to trump age and aging by affording him the opportunity to constantly cultivate and resort to many musical memories as part of his job's mandate.

A focus on the "doing of memory" in this study made remarkably audible the entanglements between the personal experiences of the participants, the cluster of associations with the music, and Trinidadians' collective frames of listening.[33] While the selected songs invariably referred to personal experiences, the stories the participants recounted were all deeply entangled with the production and circulation of songs (the relative frequency of their performances onstage, of their playing on radio, and of their appearances in music videos, on Facebook, and in other social media). They were also deeply entangled with the collective and selective activities and people who mediated their experience of particular songs (the annual soca competitions, selection of tunes in fetes, and dancing to the sound of particular artists with particular people). My request to the participants to select party songs they view as heritage material also played a role in triggering their memories. It led them to highlight what they value in the party songs they selected. I learned how for some participants, the shrewdness and bravado nature of the lyrics (such as those of "Jean and Dinah" or "Black Man Feeling to Party" or "Like Ah Boss") are what wooed them. In other instances, it is the energy of the songs they valued most. In still other cases, some participants indicated that what was most appealing for their bodies and minds were the sensual soundings of the songs. But their stories did not stop there. The participants went on to acknowledge how some of the songs they selected have been constitutive of defining moments in their personal journeys or, in some cases, defining moments of the musical genre itself (think of Maliqua's "Doh Back Back," at her first wedding reception, and Blossom's "Big Truck," which, for many people, is the song that launched Montano's career as a soca artist and launched a particular style of soca). Although most participants chose songs central to first-time experiences, some of them also chose songs that marked particular moments of self-consciousness or achievements in their lives (remember Joan's focus on songs such as "Black Man Feeling to Party" and "Hello," both of which she experienced as reinforcing a sense of identity and self-emancipation, and Maliqua's focus on "Leh Go," which after surgery amplified her celebration of life and the recovery of her younger body shape).

While the storytellings revealed much about what the participants valued in party songs, this study also demonstrated that songs viewed as worth remembering cannot be understood simply in relation to age or memory or the music itself—even after attempting to situate their respective agencies over people—but must be related to a much wider range of affecting domains of experience. A study about songs that matter to people is about, to paraphrase Hennion ([2003] 2012), grasping what constantly changes people's ideas about the value of particular songs and, correspondingly, which ones deserve to be shared.[34] In the final analysis, I agree with novelist and art theorist André Malraux (1996): Culture—in our case, musical culture—is not something that people "inherit" or "bequeath" or simply receive or pass on. It is something that people make their own.[35]

Acknowledgments

I am most grateful to Line Grenier for inviting me to participate in the initial seminar held in London and for our brainstorming on the project. Special thanks also to the editors of this volume for the series of exchanges that followed. To Percy and Joan Hintzen, my deep appreciation for their generous hospitality and for hosting the workshop at their home. My warmest thanks also go to all the participants who took the time to share their song stories with me.

Notes

1 As I have explained elsewhere, in Trinidad, the term "race" is rarely used in popular parlance. Instead, people refer to ethnicity when they speak of Afro-Trinidadians, East Indians, Chinese Trinidadians, or White Trinidadians. For further information on the subject, see Hintzen (2002), Allahar (2005), and Guilbault (2007).
2 In this chapter, I used the term "story" to refer to the result of memory work and to storytelling as what goes on in the process of telling.
3 Grossberg coined the expression "mattering maps" in relation to affective alliances produced through music. For an elaboration of this concept, see Grossberg (1992: 57).
4 The notion of mediation is key here. I refer to mediation not as an intermediary between two different people or objects. Drawing on sociologist Antoine Hennion, I take mediations as what informs the emergence of notions such as age or of practices such as Trinidadian party music. In this study, mediations thus refer as much to cultural politics, materialities, or activities as to musical tempo, sound technologies, or the vocal quality of a singer. They refer to whatever aspects contribute to the formations or meaning production of, in our case, music or memory or age and aging. In this sense, as Grenier and Valois-Nadeau (2020: 19) remark, mediations are performative. Following Bardini (2016), they add that mediations "are the milieus, the means, the operators" (ibid.). See Hennion ([2003] 2012, 2007) for an elaboration on the subject.
5 I owe this expression to Cohen (2020: 41).
6 See also Cohen (2020) and Bennett (2009) for a similar argument.
7 For an elaboration of the notion of "cultural aging," see Katz (2005).

8   I am mindful here of the unavoidable question of the "knowability and legibility" of what is said during an exchange (Khalili 2014: 25).

9   For older Trinidadians, party music refers to calypso. One reason is that soca is a musical offshoot of calypso and thus viewed as being encompassed by the generic label of calypso. The other reason is that, even though it is often discussed and defined in terms of its sociopolitical commentaries, calypso was never limited to this one lyrical and musical expression. Calypso has also been reputed for its party songs as well as for its humoristic song lyrics and what is known as the oratorical, "sans humanité" calypso (an improvisatory style based on only one melody that Gordon Rholehr describes lyrically as having converted "the traditional rivalry and violent confrontation [between two singers] into a struggle for verbal mastery in the backyard tents of Port of Spain" [quoted in Guilbault 2007: 31]).

10 For more information on trope, see the classic study of anthropologist Hayden White, *Tropics of Discourse: Essays in Cultural Criticism* (1978).

11 I thank Trinidadian sociologist and feminist scholar Rhoda Reddock for reminding me when the all-inclusive parties emerged in the country. As she explained, by the 2000s some all-inclusive parties began creating a division of spaces between what is referred to as the "general" and the "VIP" sections in fetes. The VIP section refers to a protected space for people who pay a higher entrance fee and who wish to enjoy the fete at a distance from the "commoners" or the masses attending the event. In some fetes, the VIP section offers free drinks and food to the attendees. It should be noted that this VIP section cannot be reduced to a social class category. It provides a space not only for the wealthy and professionals but also for anyone who has been able to save money to afford the entrance fee and partake in the privileges or meeting opportunities this space offers. Reddock associates this development of the VIP (and now even the VVIP) sections in the new millennium to the impact of neoliberalism, with "its bling and brands and focus on visible wealth and social difference."

12 The term *Jouvè* is the French Creole term for *jour ouvert*, which in French is an expression no longer used (if it was ever used) to refer to dawn.

13 To "wine" or "wining" refers here to a dance movement typical of many African-derived musical traditions in the Caribbean that involves winding or gyrating the hips. The term *djouk* is also a dance movement that involves a pelvic thrust.

14 Here I draw on Khalili's study of the use of affective language used by counterinsurgencies as a way to "flatten the difference between occupier and the occupied" (2014: 25). While party music is far removed from the "calculus of warfighting," it is nonetheless a site of unequal degrees of safety and permissible actions and behaviors for cis men and women and the LGBTQ community. This example substantiates Townsley's definition of trope quoted earlier: "it [trope] reduces complexity and represses contentious detail[s] in favor of 'what everyone knows'" (2001: 99).

15 For an elaboration of memory and place, see anthropologist Wachtel (1986), philosopher Casey (1987, 1996), and more recently, cultural geographers

Hoelscher and Alderman (2006) and psychologist Stevenson (2014), to name only a few.

16 See Gardner and Jennings (2020), Grenier and Valois-Nadeau (2020), Bennett (2010, 2018), and Katz (2005).

17 On the issue of crime in Trinidad, see Seepersad and Williams (2016) and Guilbault (2017).

18 See Gardner and Jennings (2020: 5) for an elaboration of this point.

19 It should be noted that I am referring here to people who have not experienced severe traumas or cognitive challenges commonly associated with Alzheimer's disease and senility, which would impact memory to varying degrees.

20 I draw this expression from Cohen (2020: 41) and Järviluoma (2020: 173), whose emphasis on the agentive power of memory I find most insightful.

21 That party music (carnival music) has traveled far and wide is not new. Alvin pointed out how "by the time carnival is over, you had all the tapes at the airport," to which Maliqua added, "I used to get them from St. James, [from] a man who worked from his living room and who had piles of tapes."

22 A road march refers to a song played to accompany revelers on the road during carnival. The winning title of a road march competition is based on the greatest number of times a song is heard during the masquerade on Mardi Gras.

23 As Alvin explained, "Full Extreme" refers to "the current financial chaos; the change of government; [the fact that] people [are] not happy with the government not fulfilling its promises; and people are complaining, marching in the streets, for more money, for more this, and for more that. And here this man [the leader singer, Maximus Dan who renamed himself MX Prime] saying, the ministry could burn down, we're jamming still."

24 I use the term "calypso" here because this song was composed and recorded by Black Stalin, a highly reputed calypsonian in Trinidad and throughout the Caribbean and its diasporas. Although many of his songs would qualify as "party songs," because of Black Stalin's stature in the field of calypso, all of his songs are usually referred to as calypsos. In all cases, for many Trinidadians what is referred to as soca or party music is simply a variant of calypso.

25 It should be noted that "to be able to party" in terms of both possibility and capacity is strongly associated with people from Trinidad who brag about being the best at it, as is emphasized in Blossom's storytelling.

26 The iron is a metal idiophone, usually a brake drum from a car or truck, greatly appreciated for its propelling ring.

27 Groovy music refers to songs using a slower tempo than those associated with what is locally called "power soca." The term "chip" refers to a dance-like shuffle.

28 This study is not about judging the accuracy of what the participants said about a song. There are various understandings of this song. For some Trinidadians, "Doh Back Back" is less about pan men than about the fact that

at times, women go unsolicited to wine (teasingly? provocatively?) against men (not necessarily pan men) in party crowds.

29 I am paraphrasing here Edouard Casey (1996: 26–7), who thinks about place as an event and as a happening.

30 While "Big Truck" was for Machel Montano and his group Xtatik a defining moment in their career, it should be noted that Montano came on the calypso scene much earlier with his live performance of "Too Young to Soca," at Dimanche Gras in 1986.

31 From September 2017, the Trump administration attempted to dismantle the DACA program created under the Obama government, which, as defined in Dictionary.com, aims "to allow undocumented immigrants who were brought to the U.S. as minors to legally remain in the country to study or work." As Vanessa Romo (2020) reported, it was only on December 4, 2020—months after my interview with Blossom—that a "[j]udge order[ed the] Trump administration to restore DACA as it existed under Obama."

32 Mastodons in reality refers to extinct animals distantly related to elephants.

33 For an elaboration of the notion of "audible entanglements," see Guilbault (2005).

34 About the notion of artistic creation in relation to the work of mediations, Hennion's original sentence reads as follows: "It is less a question of understanding everything (a formula whose epistemological terrorism is readily apparent) than of grasping something at work, from which a constantly changing interpretation can be presented" ([2003] 2012: 259).

35 In Malraux's words, "la culture ne s'hérite pas, elle se conquiert" (1996: 258).

References

Allahar, Anton L. 2005. "Class, 'Race,' and Ethnic Nationalism in Trinidad." In Anton L. Allahar and Shona N. Jackson (eds.), *Ethnicity, Class, and Nationalism: Caribbean and Extra-Caribbean Dimensions*, 227–58. Oxford: Lexington Books.

Bardini, Thierry. 2016. "Entre l'archéologie et l'écologie médiatiques: Une perspective sur la théorie médiatique." *Multitudes*, 62(1): 159–69. https://doi.org/10.3917/mult.062.0159.

Bennett, Andy. 2009. "'Heritage Rock': Rock Music, Representation and Heritage Discourse." *Poetics*, 37(5–6): 474–89.

Bennett, Andy. 2010. "Popular Music, Cultural Memory and Everyday Aesthetics." In Eduardo de la Fuente and Peter Murphey (eds.), *Philosophical and Cultural Theories of Music*, 243–62. Leiden: Brill.

Bennett, Andy. 2018. "Popular Music Scenes and Aging Bodies." *Journal of Aging Bodies*, 45: 49–53. https://doi.org/10.1016/j.jaging.2018.01.007.

Casey, Edward S. 1987. *Remembering: A Phenomenological Study*. Bloomington: Indiana University Press.

Casey, Edward S. 1996. "How to Get from Space to Place in a Fairly Short Stretch of Time: Phenomenological Prolegomena." In Steven Feld and Keith H. Basso (eds.), *Senses of Place*, 13–52. Santa Fe, NM: School of American Research Press.

Cohen, Sara. 2020. "Remembering, Ageing and Musicking: Stories from the Archive." In Line Grenier and Fanny Valois-Nadeau (eds.), *A Senior Moment: Cultural Mediations of Memory and Ageing*, 33–76. Bielefeld, Germany: Transcript Verlag.

Gardner, Abigail, and Ros Jennings. 2020. *Aging and Popular Music in Europe*. New York: Routledge.

Grenier, Line, and Fanny Valois-Nadeau. 2020. "Introduction." In Line Grenier and Fanny Valois-Nadeau (eds.), *A Senior Moment: Cultural Mediations of Memory and Ageing*, 1–31. Bielefeld, Germany: Transcript Verlag.

Grossberg, Lawrence. 1992. "Is There a Fan in the House? The Affective Sensibility of Fandom." In Lisa A. Lewis (ed.), *The Adoring Audience: Fan Culture and Popular Media*, 50–68. New York: Routledge.

Grossberg, Lawrence. 2010. "Affect's Future: Rediscovering the Virtual in the Actual" (interviewed by Gregory J. Seigworth and Melissa Gregg). In Melissa Gregg and Gregory J. Seigworth (eds.), *The Affect Theory Reader*, 309–38. Durham, NC: Duke University Press.

Guilbault, Jocelyne. 2005. "Audible Entanglements: Nation and Diasporas in Trinidad's Calypso Music Scene." *Small Axe*, 9(1): 40–63.

Guilbault, Jocelyne. 2007. *Governing Sound: The Cultural Politics of Trinidad's Carnival Musics*. Chicago: University of Chicago Press.

Guilbault, Jocelyne. 2017. "Music and Militarization: Soca, Space, and Security." In Shalini Puri and Lara Putnam (eds.), *Caribbean Military Encounters: A Multidisciplinary Anthology from the Humanities*, 331–44. London: Palgrave.

Heidegger, Martin. [1927] 2010. *Being and Time*. Translated by Joan Stambaugh. Revised and with a foreword by Dennis J. Schmidt. Albany: State University of New York Press.

Hennion, Antoine. [2003] 2012. "Music and Mediation: Towards a New Sociology of Music." In Martin Clayton, Trevor Herbert, and Richard Middleton (eds.), *The Cultural Study of Music: A Critical Introduction*, 249–60. London: Routledge.

Hennion, Antoine. 2007. *La Passion musicale: une sociologie de la mediation*. Rev. ed. Paris: Editions Métailié.

Hintzen, Percy. 2002. "Race and Creole Ethnicity in the Caribbean." In Verene A. Shepherd and Glen L. Richards (eds.), *Questioning Creole: Creolisation Discourses in Caribbean Culture*, 92–109. Kingston: Ian Randle Publications.

Hoelscher, Steven, and Dereck H. Alderman. 2006. "Memory and Place: Geographies of a Critical Relationship." *Social and Cultural Geography*, 5(3): 347–55.

Huyssen, Andreas. 1995. *Twilight Memories: Marking Time in a Culture of Amnesia*. New York: Routledge.

Jaffe, Rivke. 2012. "The Popular Culture of Illegality: Crime and the Politics of Aesthetics in Urban Jamaica." *Anthropological Quarterly*, 85(1): 79–102.

Janata, Petr, Stefan T. Tomic, and Sonja K. Rakowski. 2007. "Characterization of Music-Evoked Autobiographical Memories." *Memory*, 15(8): 845–60.

Järviluoma, Helmi. 2020. "'Dis-Placement,' Ageing and Remembering: Case Study of a Transnational Family." In Line Grenier and Fanny Valois-Nadeau (eds.), *A Senior Moment: Cultural Mediations of Memory and Ageing*, 165–94. Bielefeld, Germany: Transcript Verlag.

Katz, Stephen. 2005. *Cultural Aging: Life Course, Lifestyle, and Senior Worlds*. 2nd ed. Toronto: University of Toronto Press.

Khalili, Laleh. 2014. "The Uses of Happiness in Counterinsurgencies." *Social Text*, 32(1[118]): 23–43.

Malraux, André. 1996. "Hommage à la Grèce" lecture, le 28 mai 1959." In Janine Mossuz-Lavaux (ed.), *La Politique, la culture. Discours, articles, entretiens (1925–1975)*. Folio essais, no. 298. Paris: Gallimard.

Romo, Vanessa. 2020. "Judge Orders Trump Restore Administration to Restore DACA as It Existed under Obama." NPR (law section). December 4. https://www.npr.org/2020/12/04/943355234/judge-orders-trump-administration-to-restore-daca-as-it-existed-under-obama.

Seepersad, Randy, and Dianne Williams. 2016. *Crime and Security in Trinidad and Tobago*. Miami: Ian Randle.

Stevenson, Andrew. 2014. "We Came Here to Remember: Using Participatory Sensory Ethnography to Explore Memory as Emplaced, Embodied Practice." *Qualitative Research in Psychology*, 11(4): 335–49.

Townsley, Eleanor. 2001. "'The Sixties' Trope." *Theory, Culture & Society*, 18(6): 99–123. https://doi.org/10.1177/02632760122052066.

Trouillot, Michel-Rolph. 1995. *Silencing the Past: Power and the Production of History*. Boston: Beacon Press.

Van Dijck, José. 2006. "Record and Hold: Popular Music between Personal and Collective Memory." *Critical Studies in Media Communication*, 23(5): 357–74.

Wachtel, Nancy. 1986. "Memory and History: Introduction." *History and Anthropology*, 12: 207–24.

White, Hayden. 1978. *Tropics of Discourse: Essays in Cultural Criticism*. Baltimore, MD: Johns Hopkins University Press.

6

Collective Music Listening, Reminiscence, and the Tensions of Aging: Lessons from Two Workshops with Older Adults in Liverpool

Sara Cohen, Lisa Shaw, and Jacqueline Waldock

This chapter uses two Inheritance Tracks workshops as a starting point for investigating the relationship between music and aging. Both workshops were run in Liverpool in 2018 with groups of older adults over sixty years of age and with some of the people who cared for and supported these adults. They were part of a wider project conducted by the research team in the UK and Brazil. The chapter begins by explaining our approach to the workshops and how they came about; the second part of the chapter describes the workshops and what happened. The third and final part of the chapter considers what the workshops reveal about the relationship between music and aging. It does so by discussing the songs the workshop participants chose as their Inheritance Tracks and how they engaged with these songs. In particular, it considers how the songs enabled participants to remember the musical past, a remembering that was evident in their embodied responses to the music as well as in the tales they shared about it. The chapter examines the ideas about and experiences of aging that emerged through this process and the contexts that informed them. This analysis enables a concluding argument about the unique ways in which age and aging are performed, lived, and understood through music, and through music inheritance in particular, and the fundamental tensions involved. Where relevant, the chapter draws on the findings of the wider study conducted by the team, particularly the Brazilian workshops, to highlight cross-cultural similarities and/or differences.

Part 1. Background: Music Listening and Reminiscing with Older Adults

The two workshops in Liverpool were conducted during 2018 as part of a pilot study the three of us worked on. Led by Lisa Shaw, a professor of Brazilian Studies with research expertise in Brazilian popular music and cinema, and supported by the University of Liverpool's 2018 Industrial Strategy Pump Priming Fund, the study was linked to the Industrial Strategy of the UK government, which includes "healthy aging" as one of its strategic priorities. Published in *The Lancet*, the findings of Guzman-Castillo et al. (2017: 307) indicated that between 2015 and 2025, the number of people aged sixty-five and older would increase by 19.4 percent, and the number of older adults with care needs would increase by 25 percent. The government was keen to support the development of products and initiatives designed to serve this aging population and "market." The main aim of our study was to investigate, through collaboration with older adults and their caregivers, the feasibility of digital multimedia reminiscence products designed for people living with early-stage dementia and age-related memory loss. As part of the study, we ran workshops with older adults and their caregivers in both Liverpool and the Brazilian city of Petrópolis in Rio de Janeiro state, which has a similar sized population to Liverpool and is a popular retirement destination. In Brazil, Lisa ran the Memory Film Club, a series of weekly workshops exploring the use of musical film for group reminiscence. The workshop participants were residents of a nursing home and/or people living with dementia along with and staff from the nursing home. Together, these participants watched a selection of short clips from musical films and were then prompted to share any memories or reactions that the clips generated.

The workshops in Petrópolis drew on Lisa's long-standing research on popular culture and musical film (Shaw 1999, 2013; Dennison and Shaw 2004), which she had been using to engage older audiences in care settings for several years as part of an outreach project. In the Liverpool city region, she and media studies scholar Julia Hallam had been visiting care homes and other venues to screen short clips of musical films featuring the singer Carmen Miranda, and of archival footage of Liverpool in past decades, and use them as a prompt for group reminiscence (Shaw and Hallam 2020). Sara Cohen's interest in research on music, memory, and the listening practices of older audiences had begun in the early 1990s (Cohen 1995), but prior to the pilot study conducted with Lisa, she had been investigating how listeners of all ages remembered the musical past. This latter investigation was conducted for Popular Music Heritage, Cultural Memory and Cultural Identity (POPID), a three-year research project on popular music heritage, cultural memory, and cultural identity in Europe, involving a team of researchers based in four European countries.[1] In each country, including the UK, researchers interviewed representatives from cultural, media, and heritage sectors to examine their role in the construction of national popular music histories and heritages, through films, books, exhibitions, and so on. These interviews were followed by research on audiences and *their* music memories and histories. In England, 700 people responded to the invitation to share their music memories, and in-depth interviews were conducted with 30 of them. Their responses show how music accompanies people throughout their lives, inspiring narratives of time and remembering, and its ability to prompt a remembering that can be intensely emotional and visceral (Cohen 2020). Following the POPID project, Sara began using music-based reminiscence as a way of examining people's experiences of aging and led a series of archive-based reminiscence projects. Jacqueline Waldock worked with her on one of these projects. Jacqueline had become increasingly interested in engagement with the arts throughout the life course, and she wanted to investigate this in relation to music listening, having conducted doctoral research on listening and urban soundscapes.

Our shared interest in research on music, memory, and aging led to an ongoing collaboration that began with the aforementioned pilot study. For the purposes of this study, we wanted to not only invite older adults to participate in music and film-based reminiscence activities but also to see firsthand how they engaged with digital multimedia reminiscence products designed for people living with early-stage dementia and age-related memory loss, whether they had a dementia diagnosis or not. Our plan was to begin by testing a museum-based app designed to enable users living with dementia and their caregivers to "explore objects from the past and share memories together."[2] We would do so with the help of groups of older adults and caregivers in Liverpool recruited through Lisa's earlier work with Julia Hallam. The groups attended a couple of daycare centers for older adults run by a small social care organization. Visits to these daycare centers were arranged, but an unexpected problem arose that made it impossible for us to use the museum app, forcing a last-minute change of plan. Since the groups at the daycare centers were expecting us, we decided we would instead test the Playlist for Life digital music initiative that we were investigating for our study. A music and dementia charity founded in 2013, Playlist for Life was established to enable people with dementia "to have a unique, personal playlist and everyone who loves or cares for them to know how to use it" (Playlist for Life 2019: para. 1). The organization, which had attracted UK media coverage and government endorsement over the previous two years, encouraged the creation of personalized Spotify playlists by and for people living with dementia and their relatives, by providing resources to support their use in care settings. These resources included a list of questions designed to help users populate the playlist and labeled "conversation starters."

One of the problems we faced, however, was that Playlist for Life was targeted at individual listening via headphones. This was not ideal for group work and discussion, and in any case, there was no time or budget to secure the headphones, so we urgently needed to devise a new plan for the workshop. As part of her work for the international partnership Ageing + Communication + Technologies (ACT) and the Inheritance Tracks project that this volume is based on (see the book's introduction), Sara had been planning an Inheritance Tracks workshop with musicians that had not yet been organized. Consequently, we decided to run Inheritance Tracks workshops at the adult daycare centers instead, keeping the Playlist for Life questions at hand to use as conversation prompts if, and when, the necessity arose.

While each of us brought different disciplinary perspectives and approaches to the pilot study and its workshops, our shared concern was with the *practices* of music, remembering, age, and aging. The ethnomusicologist Christopher Small (1998) introduced the verb "musicking" to argue that music is a practice rather than a thing. He applied the term to all aspects of music performance, whether performing live or rehearsing, listening to Muzak in an elevator, selling tickets for a performance, or cleaning up after the audience has gone. The practices of remembering through which people engage with music can likewise be described as musicking. Memory is a broad concept defined in various ways and encompassing discourses that are multiple and diverse. Social anthropologists typically conceptualize it as social practice through which people engage with historical events and experiences. The anthropologists Paul Antze and Michael Lambek (1996), for example, make a strong case for moving away from theoretical and political discourses on memory, in order to adopt a more grounded approach that focuses on memory as a lived, an embodied, and an everyday practice. Through ethnographic research on symbols, myths, rituals, and narratives, they and other anthropologists have also drawn attention to the "work" involved in making the past present and meaningful and/or strategically or unwittingly forgotten (Cohen 2020).

For the Liverpool workshops, our aim was to encourage and participate in this work of remembering, by asking the participants to identify songs or pieces of music that could be collectively discussed and listened to during the workshops. To start with, we would ask them to identify a song or piece of music that they had inherited from the musical past and one they would like to pass on to others. We hoped that these questions, and the playing of the chosen "Inheritance Tracks," would prompt participants to share their music-related memories, but if necessary, we would supplement the tracks with the Playlist for Life questions. In the UK, "inheritance" tends to be commonly and narrowly discussed in relation to money or material things that are considered to be assets—property or possessions that can be passed on to others. Less common are discussions of intangible inheritance, beyond familiar references to genetic inheritance, such as a physical trait or health condition passed on from parent to child.[3] Interviewed as part of the POPID research with music audiences in England, Stuart and Ellie explained that because they associated heritage and inheritance with physical things, they found it difficult to relate these terms to music. Referring to "all the music that is out there," Stuart explained, "Nobody's giving you bits of it; it is just there. In terms of passing on, I would hope that what I play and liked might stick, but don't feel as though there would be anything coherent there to give."

In contrast, while the England-based audiences who participated in the POPID research were generally happy to refer to and share their "memories" of the musical past, they were not averse to discussing music as "inheritance," a term they generally found more relevant than "heritage." Music might be authorized as "heritage" by individuals and communities, or by official and commercial organizations, but these audiences had no need to authorize it as such, and for some of those interviewed, the notion of "inheritance" seemed better suited to their experiences of music. When asked to what extent their musical history and memories could be described as part of an "inheritance," they pointed to music that had been passed on to them or that they had passed on to others. They described this process in terms of "tastes" and "influences" that were recognized or traced through music and the connections this establishes (Cohen 2016; Roberts 2018; Roberts and Cohen 2014). David, for example, stated that this inheritance enabled him to "find out more about the building blocks of the records that I really like."

For these interviewees, therefore, music inheritance was a practice. Moreover, as a practice of passing music on or tracing music influences, it clearly made the music involved particularly meaningful and valuable for them. This was most evident when it involved music inherited from a parent or partner. Some explained how they used YouTube, Spotify, or other online resources to follow and map the musical influences of the musicians they were listening to at the time or that their friends or parents had once listened to. Ian, for example, talked to the POPID researchers about his love of music and the music influences he was handing down to his son, while Adam explained that "listening to music from my dad's time" provides "a means of reconnecting with him … like I'm catching up with him." Susan explained how conscious she was of passing on music now that she had become a parent, adding that while her daughter would discover music for herself, she might also remember it being played in the family home. The POPID interviewees also referred to music influences passed between peers as well as across generations, one of them referring to the "mix tapes" that he and his friends used to exchange as "a kind of horizontal inheritance."

One of the main aims of the Liverpool Inheritance Tracks workshops was to consider the ideas about and experiences of aging that emerged as the participants discussed their music inheritances. As with music and memory, the emphasis was again on aging as a social as well as a biological process and as a culturally informed experience. Developed by social anthropologists such as Margaret Clark (1967), Sharon Kaufman (1986), and Barbara Myerhoff (1992), this conceptualization of aging is evident in an emerging body of scholarship concerned with popular music and aging. As discussed by Cohen (2016) and Jennings (2015), scholars have examined the intersection of music and aging outside of a formal therapeutic context or framework. In doing so, they have challenged the conventional and narrow association of aging with issues concerning health and well-being and offered a counternarrative to age as decline. This is evident in seminal studies of aging youth cultures (Bennett 2013) and of age and aging in US hip-hop culture (Forman 2016). Other examples are studies of the music performances of well-known musicians, whether the "late voice" of well-known singer-songwriters such as Leonard Cohen (Elliott 2015) or the strategies employed by Madonna and other celebrated female musicians to engage with issues and debates concerning public aging (Jennings and Gardner 2012). Particularly relevant for this chapter is the work of ACT scholars who use remembering as a vehicle for investigating age and aging (Grenier and Valois-Nadeau 2020). Moreover, this chapter is closely related to, and seeks to builds on, the seminal work of ACT member and media studies scholar Murray Forman (2012), who conducted ethnographic research on popular music in North American daycare centers.

Part 2. Exploring Music Inheritance with Older Adults in Liverpool

The Inheritance Tracks workshops in Liverpool were envisaged, therefore, as events through which the relationship between musicking, remembering, and aging could be explored. They were also part of a pilot study that successfully led to a new Inheritance Tracks project the three of us subsequently embarked on, which explored transgenerational reminiscence among Liverpool-based Chilean exiles and their families.[4] Yet the hastily improvised workshops at the Liverpool daycare centers were challenging, and we felt that they had gone badly. In retrospect, however, the difficulties we encountered brought to light issues we might not otherwise have noticed, and it is in this spirit that the events from that day are recounted here.

Two Inheritance Tracks Workshops on May 24, 2018

The Liverpool workshops were run as part of regular daycare events organized by a small private company and held in two community centers. One center was attached to a church, and the other to a residential care home. Both were located in neighborhoods that have for many years been ranked among the most deprived areas in England (Liverpool City Council 2019: 7), while Liverpool was the country's local authority with the largest number of the most deprived areas (Ministry of Housing, Communities and Local Government 2019: 13). The older adults who participated in the daycare events did not reside in care homes but were nevertheless in need of care. They traveled to and from the centers in a dedicated minibus that collected them from the areas of the Liverpool City Region in which they lived, so they could participate in the activities staffed by caregivers, all of them women and most of them middle-aged. The participants were predominantly white older adults, the majority of them women, and relatives of these adults sometimes also attended to provide additional support. Lisa and Sara had spent time with some of these adults during previous visits to a daycare center at another community facility but did not know them well, and this time there would be others present whom we had not yet met. We were concerned about the limited time available for planning and preparing the workshops. Ideally, we would have spent time getting to know the group members, developing relationships and rapport, before inviting them to participate. We would also have introduced the idea of Inheritance Tracks to them in advance of the workshop, giving them an opportunity to think about the music or songs they might choose.

Recognizing our apprehension, the daycare organizers tried to reassure us, pointing out that there would be fewer than ten people in each group and the focus on music would go down well. We decided to go ahead and, for a day or two beforehand, tried to rehearse for the workshops by engaging our own parents in conversation about their Inheritance Tracks. Our plan was to begin the workshops by introducing the notion of Inheritance Tracks and encouraging the participants to identify musical choices of their own. Following a refreshment break, we would use Spotify and YouTube to search for and locate the tracks they had identified. Everyone could then listen to the tracks and watch an accompanying video, if available, before the group was invited to discuss the music in question. During the morning drive to the first venue, we checked again that we had brought everything we needed, including tape recorders, speakers, laptops, and a film screen. Each of us also had a set of cards printed with the Playlist for Life "conversation starter" questions, such as "Are there any songs or artists linked to childhood? Can you think of any favorite bands, singers, or shows? Were there any songs sung at family parties or holidays?"

For each workshop we had been expecting a maximum of ten participants, but when we arrived at the first center, we were faced with a group of around twenty-five, three of them caregivers who bustled around, chatting as they went. "How do you want them?" shouted one, with reference to the participants, as we entered the room. She and her colleagues were full of life, with big personalities, and they began moving their charges around with gusto, positioning them along two long rows of narrow Formica tables. The room was bright with fluorescent lighting and vinyl flooring, and the pale walls had a few framed pictures, a couple of noticeboards, and a television screen. The sounds of clattering plates and pans spilled over from the adjacent kitchen, and through the hatch, catering staff could be seen preparing lunch, which, we were informed, would be served at 12:30 p.m. sharp. After spotting the television, we returned the film screen to the car and unpacked the other equipment we had brought. We had checked in advance that the center had in-house Wi-Fi access, but on arrival we discovered that the caregivers did not know how to access the network and had never operated the wall-mounted television. While Jacqueline struggled to get internet access and switch on the TV set, Lisa and Sara attached speakers to a laptop and played excerpts from well-known popular songs of the 1950s and 1960s, in the hope that they would be familiar to the participants and get them in the mood for what we had planned.

As soon as the music started, the caregivers began to sing along and encourage the older adults to join in. Soon, they had managed to get two members of the group to stand up and dance with them. This was a more enthusiastic response than we had envisaged at such an early stage and before the workshop had even started. The volume of the music was turned down once Jacqueline had managed to get the TV and internet working, but it seemed a shame to interrupt the party spirit. In fact, interrupting the proceedings and changing the mood felt like the wrong thing to do. Our hope was that those participating in the workshop would explain, through their Inheritance Tracks, what music meant to them and here, already, was an audible, physical, visceral display of their engagement with music. The energy and devotion of the caregivers were impressive and moving. However, while connections between caregivers and their charges were clearly forged and made visible by the collective listening and singing, we also noticed some older people who were isolated and withdrawn. In addition, many of them were physically unable to stand or move much at all, as evident from the array of walking sticks, frames, walkers, and wheelchairs in the room.

We turned off the music and introduced ourselves and our project to the group. We explained our interest in Inheritance Tracks and how the workshop would run. Lisa then spoke about her own Inheritance Tracks, explaining why she had chosen them before playing them via YouTube. First, there was the song she had inherited from her father ("Green, Green Grass of Home," sung by Tom Jones). Then there was the song she would pass on to others ("I, Yi, Yi, Yi, Yi [I Like You Very Much]," sung by Carmen Miranda). A few participants were talking as she spoke, an early indication that engaging their attention might prove to be a challenge. Given that there were more workshop participants than expected, we encouraged them to break up into smaller groups that each of us could lead. The best way of doing this was to create three groups, two of them seated along one of the two narrow rows of tables but with the group members huddled as close together as possible, and the third group seated at the far end of one of these rows. We each positioned ourselves at the center of one of these three groups, but engaging the group members in discussion was difficult. For starters, there were various distractions, including the noises from the kitchen and the general chatter in the room.

Eventually, participants began to think of songs and request them, and one of the caregivers took over Jacqueline's group so that she could search for and play the tracks. Before long, additional requests were being relayed by Sara, Lisa, the caregivers, and a couple of other participants. Sometimes, these requests were drowned out by the volume of the music being played, which had to be turned up high so the participants could hear it. Also, since the morning had begun with collective singing, there was an expectation that this would continue, and the playing of songs familiar to the participants prompted singing across all three smaller groups. Within these groups, conversation was difficult to generate and maintain in any case. Despite the presence of some daycare center regulars, the participants were generally unfamiliar to one another, and there was little social interaction between them. Some struggled to communicate their thoughts due to cognitive or physical disabilities. Some were hard of hearing, and the wheelchairs and seating arrangements made it impossible for them to move closer together or to lean in to catch a question or comment. Many participants were quiet and soft-spoken, their voices difficult to hear.

Engaging members of the group in conversation, therefore, meant moving close to them while at the same time trying to ensure that the rest of the group did not feel excluded and could follow at least parts of what was being said. Conversation was made more difficult by the need to continually repeat and rephrase questions or comments, to ensure they were heard and understood. Turning to the Playlist for Life questions did not help to move the conversation along. To begin with, identifying songs was inevitably a struggle, given the difficulties people commonly experience when trying to remember particular song titles and lyrics or the names of the artists involved. Some participants were nevertheless able to hum or sing parts of the song, and many of them were able to describe when, where, and with whom a song had been heard. However, there were also the difficulties that some participants experienced with remembering more generally or with talking about their memories of the musical past. For various reasons, therefore, our digital recorders captured very little conversation, and the recordings are broken and muffled.

The workshop had run for a couple of hours, and an hour after it ended, we were at another community center meeting the group assembled for the second workshop. Again, there were about twenty participants, so we divided into three separate groups. Generating group discussion meant grappling with difficulties similar to those encountered during the morning workshop. This time, however, the room was smaller and quieter, and the caregivers, though enthusiastic, were not quite as vocal or lively as those from the morning session. Based on experiences with the morning workshop, we decided that instead of playing a track as soon as it was identified, we would note people's chosen songs and then spend the last part of the session collectively listening to them. We hoped this would facilitate conversation during the first part, but separating the experience of listening to the music from the discussion about it was not ideal. Moreover, as with the morning workshop, the expectation of both participants and caregivers was that we would play songs that could be sung along and danced to. However, a few of the tracks participants chose were not suitable for these purposes, leading some of the participants to lose interest. As with the first workshop, efforts to encourage the participants to talk about music resulted in conversations that were recorded but often stilted. Despite some chatter among a few participants gathered together in pairs or small groups, conversations between participants were anyway limited. More frequent were those that arose between us and the caregivers or among the caregivers.

Inheritance Tracks Troubles and Tales

By the end of the day, we felt that the two workshops had been unsuccessful. This was largely due to the difficulties already described but also due to our focus on the notion of inheritance and Inheritance Tracks. For a start, it was difficult to stick to this focus on music that had been inherited as well as remembered. In the UK, as shown by the POPID research, "inheritance" is not a term that audiences would usually apply to music, whereas references to a music "memory" are more conventional. The questions we posed about Inheritance Tracks called for the participants to not only remember a song but also to trace the lines of connection through which the song had been passed on across past, present, and future. To encourage conversation, we ended up resorting to the Playlist for Life questions sooner than expected, but these were not questions about music inheritance and had instead been designed to prompt a memory of a song and moment from the musical past. Consequently, inheritance kept dropping out of sight during the workshops, and the distinction between music memories and inheritances often became blurred. This is perhaps not surprising; for many people, it might be easier to offer a memory of a song that has personal relevance than to identify a song that has been passed on and lived with over time and pinpoint the contexts in which it has been situated. In addition to this, questions about music inheritance posed particular problems for the participants who had challenges with remembering and with verbal communication. There were those who understood the questions being asked and had memories and ideas to share yet struggled to express them because of physical impairments, such as facial paralysis stemming from a stroke. There were those who understood the questions but were not able to distinguish yesterday from ten years ago. They could not, therefore, conceptualize music from the past or future or travel back and forth in time to a moment when a track was or might have been listened to.

During the first workshop, Sara tried to engage two women who were sitting next to each other in conversation. Mary, articulate and smartly dressed, explained that she was unable to comment on music she had inherited because she could not remember anything. Efforts to encourage her to simply talk about her experiences of music proved unsuccessful. Teresa, in comparison, clearly loved music and was desperate to talk about it. Her smile never waned, her eyes gleamed, her head nodded enthusiastically, and she swayed and sang along to the music. Asked to identify a track she would like to pass on to future generations, she answered immediately, referring to an Elvis song and her nephew. The problem was that she found it difficult to make herself understood. She had memories and experiences she wanted to share, but we struggled to understand what she was saying, forced to grab onto the odd word and rely largely on nonverbal communication. Mary tried to engage Teresa in conversation but had trouble understanding what Teresa was saying. She tried to simplify things by asking Teresa a question requiring a one-word response but then promptly forgot the exchange that had just happened, so she kept asking Teresa the same question again and again (Waldock and Cohen 2020).

Encounters like these heightened our awareness that questions about music inheritance might be frustrating or confusing for some of the workshop participants, and they made problematic any reliance on speech, conversation, and remembering to examine the relationship between music and aging. At the same time, however, such encounters provided a valuable reminder that the musical past can also be remembered, revisited, and conveyed through facial expressions, gestures, or physical movements. Embodied responses of this kind proved important in Lisa's workshops centered on film music in Brazil, where several participants had severe challenges with verbal communication and many were withdrawn and reluctant to participate. When Lisa screened a clip from a 1950s feature film of well-known male singer Orlando Silva performing the hit carnival song "A Jardineira," for example, it prompted smiles and clapping of hands, signaling a pleasure in recognition, among a group of three people in their eighties who were living with dementia and had previously not engaged in the workshop. On another occasion, when someone mentioned another well-known singer from the past, Sílvio Caldas, and began to sing one of his hit songs, a man with severe speech problems and cognitive impairment due to a brain injury joined in with the chorus as best he could, despite having not previously engaged with the workshop at all.

As well as complicating remembering and aging, the Inheritance Tracks theme complicated the workshops' focus on music. For a start, the word "track" is not necessarily familiar to listeners in England, particularly older generations, as a vernacular term for discussing music, and it was also a difficult term to translate into Portuguese and use for the workshops in Brazil. During the Liverpool workshops, therefore, the term was explained through references to inherited "songs" or "pieces of music." Plus, the questions about Inheritance Tracks prompted responses that highlight the difficulty of singling out music in vernacular memory. As illustrated by the POPID research (Cohen 2014, 2016), when invited to share their music memories and inheritances, people respond by remembering not necessarily particular songs but all sorts of other things. Intertwined with music in vernacular memory are the spaces and places in which it was listened to (whether the family car or a live music venue), the technologies that enabled it to be heard (such as a car radio or record player), and the many other factors or "mediations" (Born 2010) through which music exists (people, feelings, emotions, etc.).

Despite these various challenges and complications, the Liverpool Inheritance Tracks workshops were in several respects productive and rewarding. Most importantly, for the purposes of this chapter, the workshops generated song choices (see a list of tracks at the end of this chapter). The chosen songs were generally popular, Anglo-US songs from the 1950s, 1960s, and 1970s. Examples are "A Spaceman Came Travelling" (Chris de Burgh, 1975), "Stand by Your Man" (Tammy Wynette 1969), and "Just Because I'm a Woman" (Dolly Parton 1968). Songs related to other times and music genres include "My Mammy" (Al Jolson 1920), Puccini's aria "O Mio Bambino Caro," and the Irish folk song "(My Own Dear) Galway Bay." Accessing these songs via Spotify and/or YouTube enabled the workshop participants to collectively listen and respond to them and made visible the various ways in which memory is enabled, embodied, and embedded by music (van Dijck 2007).

Most of the Liverpool workshop participants sang along to the music or responded to it by moving their bodies, illustrating the performativity and visceral materiality of music listening. Some also responded by sharing tales of the musical past that illustrated music's embedding in vernacular memory and in the rituals and routines of everyday life. Certainly, the workshops were a powerful reminder that remembering is not simply about constructing the past in the present. It also takes effort and is a selective practice that incorporates forgetting, otherwise referred to as "a means remembering otherwise" (Renan 1990, cited in Raj Isar, Dacia, and Anheier 2011: 6). Through the tales they shared, the participants nevertheless remembered music that used to be played in family homes, in shops, and at weddings and other public events. These tales encompassed different kinds of verbal narratives, from a brief comment or anecdote to more substantial autobiographical stories about the musical past. Sometimes moving and poignant, uplifting and illuminating, they and other aspects of the workshops are discussed in more detail in the remainder of the chapter, along with the ideas about and experiences of aging they prompted us to reflect upon.

Part 3. Aging and Inheritance in Everyday Music Practice

So far, we have explained our interest in exploring music in relation to inheritance, memory, and aging and described two Liverpool-based Inheritance Tracks workshops involving groups of older adults and their caregivers. This final part of the chapter considers what these workshops reveal about the relationship between music and aging. It begins with those who participated in the workshops, their Inheritance Tracks tales, and their construction of an aging self through music. It then moves on to consider the social and institutional contexts that informed the workshops, creating tensions that were evident in how aging was performed, experienced, and understood.

Music Inheritance, Older Adults, and the Aging Self

The study of popular music audiences has traditionally concentrated on youth (Hesmondhalgh 2002; Forman 2012), and although studies of middle-aged audiences have proliferated over the past couple of decades (as illustrated by the work of DeNora 2000 and Bennett 2013), research on older adult audiences is still relatively limited (exceptions include Cohen 1995 and Forman 2012). The work of Susan Crafts, Daniel Cavicchi, and Charles Keil (1993) nicely illustrates the diversity of music and popular music audiences and how music listening is shaped by the intersection of age, ethnicity, class, gender, and location. The focus of our study was groups of older adults in need of care, but there was considerable diversity within these groups. Those participating in the Liverpool workshops, for example, were diverse in terms of their social background and their music tastes and interests and also in terms of their specific care needs and physical or cognitive abilities, including the ability to mentally time travel (chronesthesia). Most of the participants we spoke to were nevertheless able to map their lives through music or relate music to key moments or stages in their lives. In doing so, they showed how music provides a soundtrack to people's lives, enabling tales not only of Inheritance Tracks but also of growing older and aging with music.

Annie told us that she had no music inheritance because until she was in her twenties, she had never even listened to music. Growing up in a convent, she explained, there was no radio, record player, or any other means of music listening. Other participants, however, were able to identify songs that had been passed on from parents to children and from one generation to another, as well as between partners and friends. Sheila, for example, explained that she chose "A Spaceman Came Travelling" by Chris de Burgh as her inheritance track because it was a song favored by her deceased husband. Inevitably, therefore, the questions about music inheritance raised at the workshop prompted further questions about what music had been passed on and by whom, when, and where it had been passed on, and why this music mattered and had value in the present. For Sylvia and Maeve, the songs they chose as their Inheritance Tracks mattered because of their connection to a particular place, community, and way of life. Maeve, quiet and soft-spoken, with a strong Irish accent, chose "(My Own Dear) Galway Bay" as her inheritance track because Galway Bay was where she had grown up. Smiling, she described her life as a child and the cèilidhs she used to go to but how she was forced to leave Ireland in the early 1950s due to a lack of money and opportunity. After arriving in the UK, she suffered a brain hemorrhage that left her paralyzed down one side and wheelchair bound.

In their chapter for the book *Movies, Music and Memory* (Hallam and Shaw 2020), Jacqueline and Sara note that during the Liverpool workshops, "the ability to talk and respond to the music as soon as it was played was important and conversations would often start while the song was playing" (Waldock and Cohen 2020: 105). They refer to Lilly, an older workshop participant who spoke little English; she had immigrated to Liverpool from Hong Kong as an adult. She was nevertheless a passionate fan of Tom Jones and sang along with other workshop participants when the song "Green, Green Grass of Home" was played, illustrating the creation of an impromptu connection between them in the moment through the live listening experience. Sylvia, meanwhile, sat apart from everyone else for much of the workshop. Although a regular at the daycare center, she was reluctant to join in the singing and stayed at the back of the room. Eventually, toward the end of the workshops, she identified "O Mio Bambino Caro" as her inheritance track. As the song was played, she suddenly joined in, eyes closed and head thrown back, singing with passion in her native Italian. When Sara told her how much she admired her singing, she explained that when she lived in Italy, they all used to sing outdoors together, "the older and the younger" (Waldock and Cohen 2020: 105). They no longer do this, she added, explaining that she lives in Liverpool now, but when her son comes to visit, he encourages her to sing.

Based on autobiographical remembering, Inheritance Tracks tales like these were inevitably tales of self, showing how people narrate and produce themselves through acts of remembering (Murray and Järviluoma 2020) and storytelling (Surr 2006). A sense of self was clearly evident in the reliance on first-person pronouns ("I," "me," "my," and "mine") to locate the source of music experiences. As pointed out by Steven Sabat and Michelle Collins (1999), this use of first-person pronouns is a common feature of narratives of selfhood. Also common are narratives concerning an individual's attributes and beliefs and their social persona as a friend, parent, spouse, and so on (Sabat and Collins 1999, cited in Surr 2006: 1722).[5]

What the Inheritance Tracks methodology also enabled was observation of an "embodied selfhood," described by Kontos (2005: 559) as involving "a complex interrelationship between primordial and sociocultural characteristics of the body, all of which reside below the threshold of cognition, grounded in the pre-reflective level of experience, existing in primarily corporeal ways." Drawing on her ethnographic research with an Orthodox Jewish long-term care facility in Ontario, Kontos argues that this selfhood emanates "from the body's power of natural expression, manifesting in the actual movements of the body" (561). One of the examples she offers is of a resident who clapped his hands and tapped his feet in excitement when music was played. At the Liverpool workshops, the use of Spotify and YouTube to play excerpts from songs, many of them well-known, provided both an aural and a visual stimulus, allowing participants to interact with music and moving images through their bodies, whether swaying to the music, singing along, or smiling and laughing.

The four workshops Lisa conducted at the residential care home in Petrópolis, Brazil, suggest that an older adult's sense of personhood is drawn out most effectively by musical stimuli in a group context, where they are prompted by musical cues and memories to perform their sense of self to others (Shaw and Giebel 2020: 112–13). These workshops were run weekly, allowing time for the participants to become more comfortable and relaxed in each other's presence and more willing to share with each other tales of their autobiographical past. What struck Lisa after conducting the workshops was how clips from musical films had elicited animated verbal responses and interjections from older adult audiences, including people with dementia, which tended to begin with an assertive "I" (129). While those participating in the Liverpool workshops did not necessarily have a dementia diagnosis, there was a marked similarity in how their music-related memories were framed ("I Am a Buddy Holly Fan," "I Am a Mother," etc.). By bringing the recollection directly back to the self, the participants evidenced how music-centered group reminiscence, generating interaction and connection, encourages a sense of personhood.

Our interpretation of these "I statements" supports the conclusions of other scholars such as the psychologist Claire Alice Surr, who shows how people with dementia understand and contextualize themselves as people or "selves" through storytelling and/or self-narration, what Surr terms as "the storied reconstruction of elected biographical life events and experience" (Surr 2006: 1721–2). In the Brazil workshops, it became clear to Lisa that songs were a medium to connect people living with dementia with their own life stories and allowed them to form meaningful connections with each other. These connections with lived experiences in the past and with other people, we would argue, strengthened the participants' sense of selfhood or identity. They also provided a positive boost to well-being "in-the-moment," as evidenced by embodied responses to the songs, such as moving to the music, singing along, smiling, and laughing.

Similarly, at the workshops in both Liverpool and Petrópolis, the collective music listening encouraged embodied and verbal interactions, both serving to ignite or reignite a sense of self and of being connected to others. In addition, this listening enabled the construction, through memory, of an aging self. Based on her ethnographic research with older adults in the northern English village of Dodworth, the social anthropologist Catherine Degnen (2012) shows how this aging self is constructed not only through narrative and social interaction with others "but also cumulatively through past experiences" (3) in the present day. Her research participants commonly spoke, for example, of "what used to be where, who used to inhabit those spaces, and how those people and places are connected to the current day" (142). Citing Hekkinen's work with adults from age eighty-five to ninety years, Degnen describes how memories of childhood and youth begin to filter through into narratives of self, so that the past, present, and future do not unfold in a linear fashion but instead become nested together (Hekkinen cited in Degnen 2012: 20). Consequently, as observed during the Liverpool workshops, "both narrativity and temporality are elements of selfhood that are at times differently weighted for older people than younger people" (7), with past, present, and future sitting together in different ways. The selection of songs from the 1950s as Inheritance Tracks by participants at the Liverpool workshops helps to illustrate this by illustrating the so-called reminiscence bump (Rathbone, Moulin, and Conway 2008), whereby music from an older person's youth and adolescence (when they were between ten and thirty years of age) evokes stronger autobiographical memories and emotions than music from later in life.

Music Inheritance and the Tensions of Aging

Acts of music listening and remembering among the older adults who participated in our workshops have been described, along with their Inheritance Tracks choices and tales. The workshops offered glimpses into the richness and diversity of the participants' music tastes and experiences and the construction of the aging self through music. Yet they also highlighted the regulated use of popular music and entertainment for older adults with care needs and the various ways in which the participants' engagement with music was constrained and restricted. In this sense, the workshops illustrate the "dual purpose" of popular music and music events (such as concerts and sing-alongs) in the care settings observed by Forman (2012: 248), acting "as factors of self-definition or subjective identity construction and as an outlet for the pursuit of elder-oriented entertainment and leisure in the shared company of peers." The workshops also illustrate certain tensions that have characterized ideas and experiences of aging, and are discussed in the remainder of this chapter. The discussion focuses in particular on tensions between narratives of aging as decline and of successful, "healthy aging"[6] and between the losses and gains of aging and its freedoms and constraints.

While only some of those participating in the Liverpool workshops chose Inheritance Tracks that could be shared with other participants, given more time, we would undoubtedly have had the opportunity to engage other members of the group directly and learn about their Inheritance Tracks. As discussed earlier, the tales of these tracks offered perspectives on *aging with* music, but the participants were at the same time *aged by* music and by the social and ideological contexts in which they listened to it. To mark the start of the Liverpool workshops, for example, we played a medley of songs that had been popular in the UK during the 1950s, when the workshop participants would generally have been teenagers or young adults. Our choice of songs was based on the so-called reminiscence bump referred to earlier but might also have encouraged a few participants to choose popular songs from the 1950s as their Inheritance Tracks (see track list at the end of the chapter). It cannot wholly account for these choices, however, and other Inheritance Tracks chosen during the workshop hint at the diversity of the participants' music tastes. At the same time, our chosen medley aged the participants while also reinforcing conventional assumptions about the music tastes of older adults. These assumptions were evident at the daycare events Forman participated in where he observed the "casual yet damaging attributions of nostalgic yearning" evident in the repertoire chosen for music concerts, sing-alongs, and social dances, arguing that such choices "delegitimise the musical interests or tastes of older citizens" (2012: 245). It is as if older adults, he writes, "are deemed incapable of locating music from their past within the present or of making sense of it in relation to time, culture and change" (247).

Forman associates such assumptions about the music tastes of older adults with the work of the aging studies scholar Margaret Gullette, who argues that in contemporary society, "ageing equals decline" (Gullette 2004: 7, cited in Forman 2012: 247). While this ageist "decline narrative" constrains older adults, putting pressure on them to conform by "acting their age" (247), it is nevertheless a narrative that older adults often promote themselves. At one of the Liverpool workshops, Betty chose "My Mammy" sung by Al Jolson as her inheritance track because "It was just in the house" when she was a child. After further prompting, she explained that she had grown up on Liverpool's Scotland Road, a road known at the time for its large number of Irish-Catholic residents and sectarian divisions, poor housing, and cultural vibrancy. For Betty, the road was associated with family and community and a tradition of collective and pub sing-alongs. Conveying a sense of dismay through her tone of voice and facial expression, she added, "It's not like that today. And the younger generation just like the modern stuff." Much like Betty's Inheritance Tracks tale, the tales of other workshop participants also illustrated the construction of an aging self through comparisons between then and now and between younger and older selves. These comparisons were not necessarily driven by a sense of nostalgia. As noted by Forman, citing Kimberly Smith's work on nostalgia (2000): "[R]emembering positive aspects of the past does not necessarily indicate a desire to return there. Remembering the past should instead be seen as a way to express valid desires and concerns about the present—in particular, about its relationship (or lack of relationship) to the past" (2012: 256).

At the same time, however, the construction of an aging self by participants at the Liverpool workshops often conveyed a sense of loss, as illustrated by Betty's reference to a community and way of life that no longer exist. This was particularly evident when workshop participants remembered musical sounds and performances, or music spaces and technologies, to which they no longer had access. These participants had health conditions that were complex and diverse but meant that their access to music could be restricted, and they depended on intermediaries to help them to gain access, whether a volunteer caregiver or relative. Rob, for example, was passionate about music, and whenever a song was mentioned, he could not stop himself from singing it out loud. While this made it difficult to hear other people speaking, Rob's love for singing was infectious and often led to a short impromptu "sing-along." Despite being able to sing along to almost every track that was played, he did not choose his own inheritance track and struggled to remember song titles or the names of the artists involved. When talking about his favorite song, however, he referred to a singer he loved, describing her as having "a beautiful voice" and mentioning that she could "sing anything." When asked who this singer was, he replied, "She sings on a Wednesday, down on the Dock Road, the second pub on the left." When asked if he stills goes down to the Dock Road, he told us that he can't get there anymore: "[I]t's too difficult."

Tales like these highlight experiences of change, from the active pursuit of music and a sense of agency and control concerning access to it to engagements with music that were more restricted. Similarly, John told us, "I used to listen to music in the car with the kids. Always my music, my car, my rules," adding, "I can't drive now, not since the stroke." His comments reflect the significance of this listening space in vernacular memory, something that other scholars have also commented on (see, e.g., Cohen 2016). The cultural studies scholar Michael Bull states, "For many drivers the time spent in the car may well be the only regular opportunity for reflection, voluntary solitude, and concentrated listening to the radio or to record music, the only chance to do nothing without having to appear to be doing something else" (2003: 364). Consequently, Bull refers to the "automobile sanctuary," although for John's children, obliged to listen to their father's music on car journeys, their memories of this experience might be quite different. Similar restrictions on and difficulties with music listening were evident in Inheritance Tracks tales that referred to music technologies. For example, a few workshop participants mentioned their collection of LPs and the fact that they no longer had the technology to play them, while one or two participants referred to music stored in digital format but said they did not feel confident about accessing it without support from someone else.

In his article on music in care settings, Forman refers to such difficulties with music listening technologies, explaining, "I witnessed on many occasions at various residences during the research phase, failing dexterity complicates the most basic physical processes such as handling vinyl albums, cassette tapes or CDs or operating a stereo component. The desire to listen to music may, therefore, be thwarted by physical limitations" (2012: 250). One of the tracks played at the Liverpool workshops was Elvis Presley's "Suspicious Minds," which prompted Maria to explain, "I never liked him. Me, I was a Buddy Holly fan. Me and my husband, we used to listen to Buddy Holly every night in the kitchen doing the washing up." When Jacqueline asked whether she still listened to Buddy Holly, Maria replied, "No. I used to have all the songs, suppose they might be in the loft. The record player stopped working, [and] I didn't know how to fix it after Charlie [her husband] passed." Rosie happily tapped her foot and sang along to the songs that her fellow group members chose, chipping in with little comments about them ("That's a good one, I like that one."). This indicated a wide engagement with music in the past, but when it came to the track she chose herself, Andrea Bocelli's "Time to Say Goodnight," Rosie explained that she chose it because it was the only CD she could listen to. Having lost her sight some years ago, she struggled to change the CD in the CD player, with no one around to change it for her. The Bocelli recording just happened to be the one CD that had been left in the player, and it had subsequently become a significant song, a song that now accompanied her quotidian life.

Tales like these suggest a loss of agency, and as illustrated earlier, some workshop participants explained that they could not identify an inheritance track due to their loss of memory. In the introduction to their edited book on cultural mediations of memory and aging, Line Grenier and Fanny Valois-Nadeau critique common associations made between memory and aging, such as the conventional association of aging with memory loss. They point out that "memory would appear as a variable dependent on the aging process: either lost or in the process of being lost or becoming more or less faulty due to the physiological aging of the body that carries it, or on the contrary thickened and enriched thanks to accumulated lived experiences and the care taken to prolong its proper functioning" (2020: 10). Other scholars specializing in the study of cultural aging have likewise critiqued and countered the narrative of aging as loss and decline, and the ageism that informs it, as illustrated by the work of Forman (2012) and Gullette (2011). Yet for Degnen, "Denying the experience of loss is to silence and erase portions of the wide range of important experiences that inform one's sense of self in older age" (2012: 145). During her research in Dodworth, Degnen's research participants spoke openly about their experiences of loss, whether connected to changes in their social and physical environment or in what the body could do. Referring to anthropological work aimed at countering negative stereotypes of old age as decline, loss, and disease, Degnen argues that conceptualizing old age in such terms is not something that only younger people do but "something that older people themselves engage in at times" (145).

These characterizations of aging as loss can be related to a tension between narratives of aging as decline and of successful aging. Over recent years, policy-makers in the UK and in other countries with an aging population have increasingly promoted the notion of "healthy aging." In doing so, they have encouraged and supported the commodification and marketization of products designed to improve the health and well-being of older adults and reinforced the common association of aging with health and well-being. This association provides a dominant framework for scholarship on age and aging (much of it based in the sciences), one that ACT has sought to challenge (see introduction to this book). It has led to the medicalization of aging, as evident in the increasing emphasis on the "prescribing" of arts and cultural activities to promote wellness among older adults and provide low-cost forms of prevention or treatment. Examples include the Museums on Prescription project of the Arts and Humanities Research Council in the UK,[7] part of a more general move toward "social prescribing" in the UK (Hallam, Shaw, and Waldock 2020: 5). Research by popular music scholars shows how this "healthy aging" agenda has become integrated into the recreation activities of older adults in institutionalized care settings (Forman

2012; Forman and Fairley 2012; Grenier, Sawchuk, and Valois-Nadeau 2020). In care homes and adult daycare centers, live music performances and other musical activities have provided entertainment for "ostensibly idle and potentially bored residents" while also serving as a "desirable facet of marketing and promotion for the facilities" they offer (Forman and Fairley 2012: 196).

At the Liverpool Inheritance Tracks workshops, the daycare center staff clearly regarded music as a mood booster, while the older adults assumed it was something they should sing along to. The workshop participants could refuse to join in or choose to ignore what was going on, but there was nevertheless a collective expectation and understanding, facilitated by the staff, of how music should be experienced by the group. In this respect, the role, responsibility, and knowledge of the daycare center staff were important factors. One example is how the caregivers engaged with the idea of music and listening, where their role and preferences became quite prominent. They would call out for songs that they liked to sing to encourage others to sing and dance with them. On one occasion, a caregiver encouraged us to turn off Sheila's chosen inheritance track, "A Spaceman Came Travelling," a song loved by her husband, because it did not fit the sing-along genre. There was an unspoken expectation that music's purpose in this setting was for singing, dancing, and having a good time. This resonates with the notion of "busy bodies" discussed by the aging studies scholar Stephen Katz (2000), in relation to the ideal of activity in the wider political context of a neoliberal "active society." As noted earlier, the emphasis on group singing sometimes challenged our efforts to encourage the sharing of personal experiences based on autobiographical remembering.

The "healthy aging" agenda and funding scheme of the UK government can be connected to this neoliberal "active society," and it supported and informed our pilot study. Consequently, the scheme provided a context that shaped the study's core aims and its concern with multimedia, digital tools for promoting reminiscing and well-being. The workshops with older adults that we ran in Liverpool and Petrópolis were part of this pilot study, which explored reminiscence tools cocreated with older adults and their caregivers and families, particularly adults living with dementia, and the well-being effects of group reminiscence based on music and musical film. As a powerful focus for group reminiscence, music listening has been shown to improve the well-being and mental health of institutionalized older adults (Shaw and Giebel 2020: 113). Sharing inherited music and attendant memories with others can help foster an emotional connection between group members, including those living with dementia, as well as reduce anxiety by providing focus and distraction (ibid.). Connecting with others and with their own earlier lives can clearly trigger a positive response, a sense of well-being "in the moment." Whether the memory of this connection or recognition lasts or not is immaterial; what is key is an emotional element. As Habib Chaudhury

(1999) argues, for those living with a dementia diagnosis, who can access memories associated with emotions more than other kinds of memories, feelings are potentially the pivotal points of their sense of self. For Lisa and Clarissa Giebel (Shaw and Giebel 2020), fostering and preserving a sense of self (often referred to as "personhood") are essential for increasing the well-being of those living with dementia. It reassures them "that they are individuals with a past and a continued identity who have stories that we are interested in and thus have 'something to offer'" (110–11).

Unlike the Liverpool workshops, Lisa's weekly musical film club workshops at the care home in Petrópolis did not focus on music inheritance. Yet both sets of workshops illustrated the power of song to stimulate personal memories and a sense of personhood as well as group interaction and visible, embodied well-being benefits. During one workshop session in Petrópolis, Lisa screened the performance of the carnival song "Madureira Chorou" ("Madureira Cried") by the male singer Joel de Almeida in the film *É de chuá* (*It's Fab*, 1958). Instantly many participants began to smile, move to the music, and start singing along to the chorus. Although they struggled to remember many of the lyrics, they hummed to the music to fill the gaps, some of them moving to the rhythm as they sat in their chairs, and most joined in again whenever the memorable refrain was repeated. When the clip ended, they began to chat animatedly with their neighbors, and the chatter did not die down for several minutes. No one could identify the singer on-screen or recall who had written or previously recorded the song, but one woman with dementia began talking about Madureira, the neighborhood of Rio de Janeiro that is the subject of the lyrics, and the place where she had spent her childhood.[8] On hearing the same song, a male participant in his late seventies, who had taken part in an earlier intervention using musical films that Lisa had run for a medical doctor's practice in Brazil, and who had lost his sight a year or so earlier, began to beat a rhythmic accompaniment on his knee in time with the music and joined in the chorus. He was visibly moved by his unexpected encounter with a song that clearly meant a great deal to him and his life story, and his tears initially caused Lisa concern. However, he soon reassured her that it had been a very positive experience for him. "I travelled through time," he said. "It took me back to the carnival of my youth in Rio," he confessed, now smiling affectionately, and to the year when he met his future wife.

The social contexts of musicking that we have mapped out, such as the policy agenda concerning "healthy aging," play an important part in shaping practices, experiences, and understandings of aging. Yet the specificities and complexities of these contexts matter, including the intersection of age with class, location, gender, and ethnicity. At the Liverpool workshops, we were struck by the social and digital inequalities that shape music listening and aging. The workshop methodology called for the use of music streaming services such as Spotify and YouTube, but access to digital technologies was problematic. The daycare users and staff were unfamiliar with these technologies, and although one of the community centers did have an internet connection, the staff did not know the Wi-Fi access code. The center also had a television, but it was never used for the daycare events. Both centers nevertheless had a portable CD player that was used for the daycare events, and we were eventually able to overcome the lack of internet connection and access YouTube and Spotify by using mobile data. Such difficulties highlight issues concerning digital access within care settings, which became more urgent and apparent with the arrival of the Covid-19 pandemic in 2020. Access to and adoption of digital technologies are not simply age-related issues, and digital inclusion is not simply a case of affordability and provision of digital technologies. As noted by Elinor Carmi and Simeon Yates (2020), social and cultural issues must also be taken into account, since digital inequalities are as much about the provision of social support and digital skills as about technological provision (Carmi and Yates 2020).

The so-called digital divide is influenced by a range of socioeconomic factors (Lloyd, Given, and Hellwig 2000). As noted by Robinson et al. (2015: 569), "the significance of digital inequalities is clear across a broad range of individual-level and macro-level domains, including life course, gender, race, and class, as well as health care, politics, economic activity, and social capital." Inequalities between developed and developing nations are also marked, with 20 million households in Brazil having no internet access—a problem that predominantly affects the poorest sectors of society and Afro-Brazilians in particular—and 58 percent of the population having internet access only through a smartphone (BBC World Service 2020). In spite of the central government's efforts to foster digital inclusion in Brazil, chiefly via the creation of telecenters, the older population is not included in this process, and most of the country's aging adults have never accessed the internet (Ferreira, Sayago, and Blat 2016). Lisa was surprised to discover that there was no internet access, for example, in the residential care home where she carried out her musical film club activities despite it being a well-funded center of excellence for dementia care. For the daycare staff participating in the Inheritance Tracks workshops in Liverpool, their lack of internet access was related to not only an absence of the necessary technical apparatus but also a lack of the skills and technical literacy required to operate that apparatus and navigate the digital world. Our use of YouTube and Spotify for the purposes of the workshops prompted the staff to ask us for written instructions on how to access the technology in the future. They were subsequently provided with a step-by-step guide that will be useless at this center until internet access has been enabled.

The 2020–1 "stay home" campaign by the UK government was accompanied by a series of national "lockdowns" designed to tackle the Covid-19 pandemic. Residents with existing health conditions and a large swath of older adults were instructed to shield, which involved minimizing all social contact. These "stay home" restrictions led to the closure of community support groups, including the daycare centers we visited in Liverpool, and to restricted visiting in care homes. The digital realm became the predominant medium for education, social interaction, work, and socializing. In their paper "COVID-19 and Digital Inequalities: Reciprocal Impacts and Mitigation Strategies," Elisabeth Beaunoyer, Sophie Dupéré, and Matthieu Guitton (2020) discuss how the pandemic has intensified digital inequalities. They draw attention, for example, to how access to the internet has been restricted for many due to the closure of public spaces and how technological support has decreased due to social distancing or social isolation requirements. Clearly, these circumstances made the difficulties with digital access that we encountered during the Liverpool workshops even more pronounced.

Conclusion

Throughout this chapter, two Inheritance Tracks workshops in Liverpool have provided a basis for investigating musicking, remembering, and aging. In explaining how these workshops were approached and came about, and what happened at them, we have highlighted the limitations of this investigation. As a one-off event (or "music intervention"), the workshops bore little resemblance to the kind of detailed, in-depth ethnographic research we are planning to conduct with older adults, to investigate their everyday experiences of music and how they remember the musical past. Both workshops nevertheless generated productive insights that helped us to develop a follow-on project exploring music reminiscence among older adults. They also enable three concluding points about Inheritance Tracks, music reminiscence, and aging.

The first point is that understanding how aging is performed, experienced, and understood through music means examining the tensions that characterize this process. The chapter has focused in particular on tensions between the notion of aging as decline and that of "healthy aging." Along with the pilot study they were part of, the workshops illustrate aspects of musicking in UK care settings that are comparable with Forman's (2012) observations on popular music and eldercare in Canada. In such settings, care providers and institutions typically offer limited and highly regulated engagements with music and homogenized forms of music entertainment. The choice of repertoire for these events, for example, often illustrates an association of older adults with nostalgic leanings and with music tastes that are stuck in the past. Moreover, the care providers organizing such events do not always consult the participants in advance, to check whether or not they want to participate. In this sense, music plays a part in the process of "identity stripping" discussed by the aging studies scholar Margaret Gullette as so often befalling those aging in a "hostile environment" (2018: 265; see also 2004), and it reinforces the association of aging with decline. Older adults participating in these events can resist or confound this association but might also promote it, as suggested by the Inheritance Tracks tales associating aging with loss. Simultaneously, the aging population represents an expanding market for tailored products and services, including those focused on music. In the UK, music performances and sing-alongs are increasingly used to advertise care services, while commercial music products and events designed for older adults are becoming more diverse, catering to niche markets. The "healthy aging" agenda, promoted through a partnership between the UK government and the industry, is part of this process, and advocates for the arts have been making a strong case for inclusion of the arts in this agenda. Increasingly, a wealth of evidence has been supplied for the health and well-being benefits of music and for its advantages as a low-cost means of addressing aging-as-decline.

While music has become increasingly popular as a tool for improving well-being and enabling remembering, the emphasis has overwhelmingly been on live music. In contrast, the workshops in Liverpool focused on recorded music and Inheritance Tracks, and the second point is that despite their difficulties and limitations, these workshops supported findings from those in Brazil regarding the benefits of collective music listening and reminiscence for older adults in need of care. Based on workshops in both the UK and Brazil, Lisa, Jacqueline, and Julia Hallam argue that for people living with a dementia diagnosis, reminiscence "allows them to make use of a skill they still have, rather than dwelling on what they have lost, fostering a sense of confidence, self-esteem and competence. The fact that they can actively share something with others, instead of depending on them passively, and actually inform and interest others, gives them a sense of dignity and purpose" (Hallam, Shaw, and Waldock 2020: 31). As an activity for older adults, collective music listening and reminiscence provide connections, via a song, with their lived experiences in the past, and with other people, that can strengthen older adults' sense of identity framed in their lived musical experiences. In this way, music and music reminiscence can enable a positive construction of a sense of self or "personhood." Whether stemming from a recognition of the loss of a past self or an opportunity to share fandom with another, this building of identity and personhood in the present challenges the association of music and older citizens with a homogenized nostalgia. The workshops also show that "[l]istening is not necessarily a passive experience but an activity that everyone can engage with and participate in. It can therefore bring people together and enable a shared experience. Through this listening, individuals can connect with others in the present, while also connecting with a self that existed in the past" (Waldock and Cohen 2020: 106). Moreover, the embodied responses to music at the workshops, such as moving to the music, singing along, smiling, and laughing, suggest a positive boost to well-being "in the moment."

Moving beyond arguments for the well-being effects of music reminiscence, the final point is that Inheritance Tracks is a productive methodology for investigating the relationship between music and aging. First, the emphasis on collective listening at the workshops in Liverpool and Petrópolis prompted remembering while also encouraging a sharing of music memories. Second, the association in the UK of "inheritance" with value, and with gains as well as losses, meant that the workshops provided insights into memories that the workshop participants considered to be particularly meaningful. Third, because "inheritance" is also associated with the process of passing on, and with connections between past, present, and future, the notion of "Inheritance Tracks" enabled insights, through remembering, into the construction of an aging self. Examining this process, and reflecting on the difficulties and challenges encountered while running the workshops in Liverpool, this chapter highlighted tensions that have been fundamental to aging and the specific situations and contexts that inform them.

Notes

1 Running from 2010 to 2013, POPID was supported by the Humanities in the European Research Area Joint Research Programme run by a network of twenty-six national funding agencies. In England, the research was conducted by Sara Cohen, Les Roberts, and Gurdeep Khabra, and this chapter draws on the second phase of this research, which was conducted with audiences. In particular, it draws on data from face-to-face, audio-recorded interviews. Quotes taken from these interviews are provided, and pseudonyms are used to refer to the interviewees.
2 https://www.liverpoolmuseums.org.uk/house-of-memories. Accessed May 2021.
3 The UK is one of only a few countries that abstained in the vote on the 2003 UNESCO convention (see Kurin 2004: 66) and did not sign the UNESCO intangible heritage agreement (namely, the Convention for the Safeguarding of the Intangible Cultural Heritage), signaling a reticence to fully embrace the idea of intangible heritage.
4 This project, led by Shaw since 2019, has been supported by the Northern Network for Medical Humanities Research. It has explored music-based transgenerational reminiscence as a route to well-being, with people who arrived in Liverpool as exiles from the Pinochet regime in Chile in the late 1970s and the 1980s and their descendants. One of the project participants, a musician and poet, introduced his daughter to the project team. He and his daughter then met with the researchers to discuss their Inheritance Tracks and how their musical memories both connected and diverged. Additional Inheritance Tracks workshops were planned but had to be put on hold due to the Covid-19 pandemic.

5 Notions of self and social identity connected with music have also been explored by Bennett (2013), Frith (1996), and McDonald, Miell, and Wilson (2005).
6 This tension can be related to what Marshall, drawing on McHugh's (2003) work on ageism, refers to as the "bipolar" media images of aging (Marshall 2015: 210) that have emerged along with the aging of the population in Western countries. For example, media images of those who have successfully fought against the ravages of time, such as marathon runners over eighty years of age, contrast starkly with those of the frail or sick elderly in need of care.
7 https://www.ucl.ac.uk/culture/projects/museums-on-prescription. Accessed May 2021.
8 This song was one of the biggest hits of the 1958 carnival in Rio, and its catchy refrain and melody had clearly cemented the song in the participants' memories. As what is known as a *marcha carnavalesca* (carnival march), it would have subsequently been performed in street carnivals in the city and beyond on an annual basis, ensuring that like other carnival classics, it still features in the repertoire of even the youngest revelers. The ages of the participants in this session ranged from sixty-five to ninety-three years; in other words, in 1958, they would have been between five and thirty-three years of age. Some of them would have taken part in the street carnival and listened to the radio (details of their personal histories that they discussed in other sessions), and thus been repeatedly exposed to "Madureira Chorou," which won the official prize for best carnival song that year. The song evidently also won the popular vote, as various newspaper articles from the time printed its lyrics and featured items relating to its lyrics.

Track List

"A Spaceman Came Travelling"—Chris de Burgh, 1975
"Buttons and Bows"—Bob Hope, 1948
"Don't Fence Me In"—Bing Crosby, 1944
"Funny Girl"—Barbra Streisand, 1968
"(My Own Dear) Galway Bay"—John Gary, 1965
"I've Got You under My Skin"—Frank Sinatra, 1966
"Just Because I'm a Woman"—Dolly Parton, 1968
"My Mammy"—Al Jolson, 1920
"O Mio Bambino Caro"—Maria Callas, aria by Giacomo Puccini and Giovacchino Forzano (libretto) from the opera *Gianni Schicchi*, 1918
"Only the Lonely"—Roy Orbison, 1960
"Rave On"—Buddy Holly, 1958
"Stand by Your Man"—Tammy Wynette, 1969
"Summer Holiday"—Cliff Richard, 1963
"Suspicious Minds"—Elvis Presley, 1969
"The Black Hills of Dakota"—Doris Day, 1954
"Time to Say Goodnight"—Andrea Bocelli, 1996
"West Side Story: Act 1: America"—Leonard Bernstein, 1957

References

Antze, Paul, and Michael Lambek (eds.). 1996. *Tense Past: Cultural Essays in Trauma and Memory*. London: Routledge.

BBC World Service. 2020. "Digital Exclusion in Brazil." *Digital Planet*. June 2. https://www.bbc.co.uk/programmes/w3csz97z.

Beaunoyer, Elisabeth, Sophie Dupéré, and Matthieu J. Guitton. 2020. "COVID-19 and Digital Inequalities: Reciprocal Impacts and Mitigation Strategies." *Computers in Human Behaviour*, 111(October). https://doi.org/10.1016/j.chb.2020.106424.

Bennett, Andy. 2013. *Music, Style, and Aging: Growing Old Disgracefully?* Philadelphia: Temple University Press.

Born, Georgina. 2010. "Listening, Mediation, Event: Anthropological and Sociological Perspectives." *Journal of the Royal Musical Association*, 135(1): 79–89.

Bull, Michael. 2003. "Soundscapes of the Car: A Critical Study of Automobile Habitation." In Michael Bull and Les Back (eds.), *The Auditory Culture Reader*, 357–74. Oxford: Berg.

Carmi, Elinor, and Simeon J. Yates. 2020. "What Do Digital Inclusion and Data Literacy Mean Today?" *Internet Policy Review*, 9(2). https://doi.org/10.14763/2020.2.1474.

Chaudhury, Habib. 1999. "Self and Reminiscence of Place: A Conceptual Study." *Journal of Aging and Identity*, 4: 231–53.

Clark, Margaret. 1967. "The Anthropology of Aging: A New Era for Studies of Culture and Personality." *The Gerontologist*, 7: 55–64.

Cohen, Sara. 1995. "Sounding Out the City: Music and the Sensuous Production of Place." *Transactions of the Institute of British Geographers*, 20(4): 434–46.

Cohen, Sara. 2014. "'Going to a Gig': Remembering and Mapping the Places and Journeys of Live Rock Music in England." In Karen Burland and Stephanie Pitts (eds.), *Coughing and Clapping: Investigating Audience Experience*, 131–47. Farnham: Ashgate.

Cohen, Sara. 2016. "Music as Cartography: English Audiences and Their Autobiographical Memories of the Musical Past." In Johannes Brusila, Bruce Johnson, and John Richardson (eds.), *Memory, Space, Sound*, 107–23. Bristol: Intellect Books.

Cohen, Sara. 2020. "Music, Memory and Ageing: Stories from the Archives." In Line Grenier and Fannie Valois-Nadeau (eds.), *A Senior Moment: Cultural Mediations of Memory and Ageing*, 33–76. Bielefeld, Germany: Transcript Verlag.

Crafts, Susan D., Daniel Cavicchi, and Charles Keil. 1993. *My Music: Explorations of Music in Daily Life*. Middletown, CT: Wesleyan University Press.

Degnen, Catherine. 2012. *Ageing Selves and Everyday Life in the North of England: Years in the Making*. Manchester: Manchester University Press.

Dennison, Stephanie and Lisa Shaw. 2004. *Popular Cinema in Brazil*. Manchester: Manchester University Press.

DeNora, Tia. 2000. *Music in Everyday Life*. Cambridge: Cambridge University Press.

Elliott, Richard. 2015. *The Late Voice: Age and Experience in Popular Music.* London: Bloomsbury.
Ferreira, Susan M., Sergio Sayago, and Josep Blat. 2016. "Going beyond Telecenters to Foster the Digital Inclusion of Older People in Brazil: Lessons Learned from a Rapid Ethnographical Study." *Information Technology for Development,* 22(suppl. 1). https://doi.org/10.1080/02681102.2015.1091974.
Forman, Murray. 2012. "'How We Feel the Music': Popular Music by Elders and for Elders." *Popular Music,* 31(2): 245–60.
Forman, Murray. (2016, May 11–13). "Every Day a Pioneer: Aging Artists and Hip-Hop Legacies." Paper presented at the Music, Ageing, Technology Symposium, University of Eastern Finland.
Forman, Murray, and Jan Fairley (eds.). 2012. "'Introduction' to Special Issue on Ageing." *Popular Music,* 2: 193–7.
Frith, Simon. 1996. "Music and Identity." In Stuart Hall and Paul du Gay (eds.), *Questions of Cultural Identity,* Chap. 7, 108–27. London: Sage.
Grenier, Line, and Fanny Valois-Nadeau (eds.). 2020. *A Senior Moment: Cultural Mediations of Memory and Ageing.* Bielefeld, Germany: Transcript Verlag.
Grenier, Line, Kim Sawchuk, and Fanny Valois-Nadeau. 2020. "Resoundingly Entangled: Ageing and Memory in Étoile des aînés in Quebec." In Line Grenier and Fannie Valois-Nadeau (eds.), *A Senior Moment: Cultural Mediations of Memory and Ageing,* 195–220. Bielefeld, Germany: Transcript Verlag.
Gullette, Margaret M. 2004. *Aged by Culture.* Chicago: University of Chicago Press.
Gullette, Margaret M. 2011. *Agewise: Fighting the New Ageism in America.* Chicago: University of Chicago Press.
Gullette, Margaret M. 2018. "Against 'Ageing'—How to Talk about Growing Older." *Theory, Culture and Society,* 35(7–8): 251–70.
Gusman-Castillo, Maria, Sara Ahmadi-Abhari, Piotr Badnsoz, Simon Capewell, Andrew Steptoe, Archana Singh-Manoux, Mika Kivimaki, Martin J. Shipley, Eric J. Brunner, and Martin O'Flaherty. 2017. "Forecasted Trends in Disability and Life Expectancy in England and Wales up to 2025: A Modelling Study." *Lancet Public Health,* 2(7): 307–13.
Hallam, Julia, and Lisa Shaw (eds.). 2020. *Movies, Music and Memory: Tools for Wellbeing in Later Life.* Bingley: Emerald.
Hallam, Julia, Lisa Shaw, and Jacqueline Waldock. 2020. "Introduction: Mapping the Terrain—Film and Music in Third-Age Care." In *Movies, Music and Memory: Tools for Wellbeing in Later Life,* 1–35. Bingley: Emerald.
Hesmondhalgh, David. 2002. "Popular Music Audiences and Everyday Life." In David Hesmondhalgh and Keith Negus (eds.), *Popular Music Studies,* 117–30. London: Arnold.
Jennings, Ros. 2015. "Popular Music and Ageing." In Julia Twigg and Wendy Martin (eds.), *Routledge Handbook of Cultural Gerontology,* 77–84. Abingdon: Routledge.
Jennings, Ros, and Abigail Gardner (eds.). 2012. *"Rock On": Women, Ageing and Popular Music.* Farnham: Ashgate.
Katz, Stephen. 2000. "Busy Bodies: Activity, Aging, and the Management of Everyday Life." *Journal of Aging Studies,* 14(2): 135–52.

Kaufman, Sharon R. 1986. *The Ageless Self: Sources of Meaning in Late Life*. Madison: University of Wisconsin Press.

Kontos, Pia. 2005. "Embodied Selfhood in Alzheimer's Disease: Rethinking Person-Centred Care." *Dementia*, 4(4): 553–70.

Kurin, Richard. 2004. "Safeguarding Intangible Cultural Heritage in the 2003 UNESCO Convention: A Critical Appraisal." *Museum International*, 56(1–2): 66–77.

Liverpool City Council. 2019. "Executive Summary." *The Index of Multiple Deprivation 2019: A Liverpool Analysis*. Liverpool.

Lloyd, Rachel, Jock Given, and Otto Hellwig. 2000. "The Digital Divide: Some Explanations." *Agenda: A Journal of Policy Analysis and Reform*, 7(4): 345–58.

Marshall, Barbara A. 2015. "Anti-Ageing and Identities." In Julia Twigg and Wendy Martin (eds.), *Routledge Handbook of Cultural Gerontology*, 210–17. Abingdon: Routledge.

McDonald, Raymond, Dorothy Miell, and Graeme Wilson. 2005. "Talking about Music: A Vehicle for Identity Development." In Dorothy Miell, Raymond MacDonald, and David J. Hargreaves (eds.), *Musical Communication*, 321–38. Oxford: Oxford University Press.

McHugh, Kevin E. 2003. "Three Faces of Ageism: Society, Image and Place." *Ageing and Society*, 23(2): 165–85.

Ministry of Housing, Communities and Local Government. 2019. *Indices of Deprivation 2019*. London: UK Government. https://www.gov.uk/government/statistics/english-indices-of-deprivation-2019.

Murray, Lesley, and Helmi Järviluoma. 2020. "Walking as Transgenerational Methodology." *Qualitative Research*, 20 (2020): 229–38.

Myerhoff, Barbara. 1992. *Remembered Lives: The Work of Ritual, Storytelling, and Growing Older*. Ann Arbor: University of Michigan.

Playlist for Life. 2019. "About Us." https://www.playlistforlife.org.uk/about-us.

Raj Isar, Yudhishthir, Viejo-Rose Dacia, and Helmut K. Anheier. 2011. "Introduction." In Yudhishthir Raj Isar and Helmut K. Anheier (eds.), *Heritage, Memory and Identity*, 1–20. London: Sage.

Rathbone, Clare J., Chris J. A. Moulin, and Martin A. Conway. 2008. "Self-Centered Memories: The Reminiscence Bump and the Self." *Memory & Cognition*, 36(8): 1403–14.

Renan, Ernest. 1990. "What Is a Nation?" In Homi Bhabha (ed.), *Nation and Narration*, 8–22. New York: Routledge. English translation of lecture delivered in 1882.

Roberts, Les. 2018. *Spatial Anthropology: Excursions in Liminal Space*. London: Rowman & Littlefield.

Roberts, Les, and Sara Cohen. 2014. "Unauthorizing Popular Music Heritage: Outline of a Critical Framework." *International Journal of Heritage Studies*, 20(3): 1–21.

Robinson, Laura, Shelia R. Cotten, Hiroshi Ono, Anabel Quan-Haase, Gustavo Mesch, Wenhong Chen, Jeremy Schulz, Timothy M. Hale, and Michael J. Stern. 2015. "Digital Inequalities and Why They Matter." *Information, Communication & Society*, 18(5): 569–82.

Sabat, Steven R., and Michelle Collins. 1999. "Intact Social, Cognitive Ability and Selfhood: A Case Study of Alzheimer's Disease." *American Journal of Alzheimer's Disease and Other Dementias*. https://doi.org/10.1177/153331759901400108.

Shaw, Lisa. 1999. *The Social History of the Brazilian Samba*. Aldershot: Ashgate.

Shaw, Lisa. 2013. *Carmen Miranda*. London: BFI/Palgrave Macmillan.

Shaw, Lisa, and Clarissa Giebel. 2020. "Music and Film in Dementia Care in Brazil and on Merseyside." In Julia Hallam and Lisa Shaw (eds.), *Movies, Music and Memory: Tools for Wellbeing in Later Life*, 109–42. Bingley: Emerald.

Shaw, Lisa, and Julia Hallam. 2020. "Cinema, Memory and Wellbeing: Pilot Projects in Liverpool and Brazil." In Julia Hallam and Lisa Shaw (eds.), *Movies, Music and Memory: Tools for Wellbeing in Later Life*, 37–72. Bingley: Emerald.

Small, Christopher. 1998. *Musicking: The Meanings of Performing and Listening*. Middletown, CT: Wesleyan University Press.

Smith, Kimberly K. 2000. "Mere Nostalgia: Notes on a Progressive Paratheory." *Rhetoric & Public Affairs*, 3/4: 505–27.

Surr, Claire A. 2006. "Preservation of Self in People with Dementia Living in Residential Care: A Socio-Biographical Approach." *Social Science & Medicine*, 62(7): 1720–30.

van Dijck, José. 2007. *Mediated Memories in the Digital Age*. Stanford, CA: Stanford University Press.

Waldock, Jacqueline, and Sara Cohen. 2020. "Music, Memory and Wellbeing: A Pilot Project in Liverpool." In Julia Hallam and Lisa Shaw (eds.), *Movies, Music and Memory: Tools for Wellbeing in Later Life*, 73–107. Bingley: Emerald.

7

Journeys of Attachments, Trajectories of (Mis)fitting: Musicking in Deaf Communities in Montreal

Line Grenier and Véro Leduc

In our audist societies, where superiority is ascribed to those who hear or behave like those who do (Humphries 1977), music is deemed an auditory art form, one that Deaf people cannot fully perform as artists, have access to, or appreciate (Maler 2016). The effectivity of the hearing-centric episteme extends to Deaf cultures in which music, although experienced by many and through different media (Cripps, Rosenblum, and Small 2015a; Maler 2016), is nonetheless often conceptualized as a cultural expression of hearing people (Holmes 2017). As our research suggests, while this limited approach is increasingly contested, it mediates the present and past musical practices of those who grew up in Deaf communities, where saying that you like music was neither a banal nor an inconsequential statement.

This chapter offers a critical analysis of an Inheritance Tracks workshop held in February 2018, in the wake of *La musique au bout des doigts* (Music at the Fingertips), a research project located at the intersection of music, aging, and Deaf studies.[1] In this pilot project, we had explored the experiences and understandings of music by Deaf adults through interviews with members of the Quebec sign language (LSQ) and American Sign Language (ASL) communities in Montreal. The interviews we had conducted, especially those with older adults (sixty to ninety years old), highlighted the complex and at times challenging nature of the participants' relation to music across their life course. They had also brought forth the affective, cultural, and political significance ascribed by some individuals, especially younger adults (thirty- and forty-year-olds), to music over time, and the workshop gave us an opportunity to look into this further.

We brought together a group of Deaf adults willing to share meaningful musical "tracks" and exchange ideas and experiences about something deemed a sensitive, contentious matter if not a taboo within the Deaf communities to which they belong. For indeed, music tends to represent the epitome of hearing culture and symbolizes its hegemonic dominance over Deaf people (Holmes 2017). The gathering prompted testimonies and discussions that raised broad questions concerning the changing intersections of music and Deafhood[2] and, more specifically, the different ways in which these individuals got to incorporate music into Deaf identification, albeit to varying extent.[3] The event provided a window into how, as Deaf people, these individuals are aging with music in ways that would have been improbable, if not altogether unfathomable a few decades ago, an argument we elaborate in our conclusion. From our perspective, aging is a "trajectory whose forms vary according to individual and collective pathways" (Grenier and Valois-Nadeau 2020: 16). It is a plural process shaped notably by social class, sexuality, language, gender, physical capability, ethnicity, and geographical location, which involves a constant negotiation of sociohistorical expectations and norms. We are "aged by culture," as Margaret Morganroth Gullette (2004) claims. This means, in the case at hand, to be aged by Deaf culture as well as by the ambient audist—not to mention ageist (Gullette 2011)—hegemonic culture. It also means acknowledging the media, technologies, cultural objects, and practices that, as they render our changing relationships to the world and to others possible, mediate how we age and are aged. The workshop highlighted the performative role that music can play in Deaf aging.

What the participants ended up sharing during the workshop was not so much their recollections of particular songs—though some favorites were commented on—as their different ways of "doing music," what Christopher Small (1998) calls "musicking." In the process they uncovered some common experiences that marked their respective history with music. These common experiences, we suggest, are best construed as significant moments in their journeys of attachment. Working as mnemonic practices (Olick and Robbins 1998), the anecdotes they recounted and the stories they told wove together, in the present, the lines of the open-ended, unpredictable becoming that characterizes journeys as ambivalent back-and-forth and up-and-down movements (Bissonnette 2020). A three-hour-long animated discussion unfolding in an atmosphere of camaraderie rekindled the "wow" moments, the confrontations and misunderstandings, as well as the surprises and mind-boggling realizations that punctuated the journeys through which their multifarious attachments to music had been forged. Materialized, mediated, and embodied through recollections, attachments have to be "continuously done and re-done," experienced as both "a constraint and a resource," as conceptualized by Antoine Hennion (2017: 118).[4] Drawing on feminist work in critical disability studies and cultural studies, we will problematize these journeys of attachment as changing trajectories of (mis)fitting (Garland-Thomson 2011) and orientations (Ahmed 2006a) to music that may be more integral to what Deaf adults have inherited and pass on than songs, repertoires, or favorite artists. In this respect, the workshop lent full credence to Jacques Derrida's aphorism that "[i]nheritance is never a given, it is always a task" (1994: 54), which, as we will discuss, is rife with power dynamics.

At the beginning of the workshop, participants took turn introducing themselves by sharing recollections of their earliest experiences with music. It has inspired us to present them to the readers by focusing on the different musicking they consider integral to their present-pasts (Allor 1997). Drawing from some of the most interactive segments of the evening, we move on to moments of common identification, mutual recognition, or shared concern around some of the participants' recollections that strongly resonated with other members of the group. We wrap up the chapter by highlighting how individual trajectories of attachments to or with music intersect with the sedimented histories of the Deaf communities as well as the broader milieu that mediate Deaf musicking as embodied, lived, situated experiences. But before we go any further, let us first recall how this memorable and thought-provoking workshop unfolded.

Retracing Steps, Setting the Scene

It is a cold mid-February weeknight in 2018, in downtown Montreal. As the Atwater Library and Computer Centre is about to close for the day, we are getting ready for our Inheritance Tracks workshop. We have privileged "after-hours" access to the heritage building where the library is housed, thanks to our host and co-organizer, Eric Craven, coordinator of its Digital Literacy Program. For nearly four years, Line and Eric—Eric is also a professional musician—have been collaborating on different participatory research-creation projects dealing with music and aging. Together they have facilitated two Inheritance Tracks workshops, one with seniors involved in the Downsizing and Honouring Memories: Seniors Helping Seniors project and another with older Black members of the Anglican Church congregation of Westmount, the borough where the library is located, marking Canada's Black History Month. Tonight's event fits into one of Eric's most recent projects, the Living History Collection designed to link Montrealers to their past, present, and future.[5]

It is almost 6:00 p.m., and final preparations for our workshop are almost completed. The front section of the large auditorium on the second floor of the heritage building has been equipped with all the gear Eric thought we could need: cassette deck, turntable, DVD player, computer with Wi-Fi connection, amplifier, mixer, large speakers, and big screen. At the opposite end, near the entrance to the room, a table with refreshments and snacks awaits our guests—something included regularly in the extensive outreach activities hosted by the library's Digital Literacy Program, which are often attended by people with limited financial means.[6] Although most participants have yet to arrive, the place is already buzzing as the support teams are already at work. Eric has enlisted Wendy, a senior volunteer, and Kira, a student trainee, to record the discussion. While they are making last-minute adjustments to their video cameras, we remind them not to start shooting before ethics are discussed with the participants and consent forms are signed.[7] The team of interpreters composed of Geneviève Bujold, Véro's designated interpreter, and five of her colleagues—Sara Houle, Jordan Goodman, Liz Scully, Suzanna Oppedisano, and Julie Laroche—is finalizing the reconfiguration of the area where participants will be sitting. Pushing aside the long benches that formed a square, they set individual chairs distanced enough from one another to form a large circle, thereby allowing unhindered movement by the person who is signing and an unobstructed view of this person and, where appropriate, the interpreter. They are discussing where each team member would be best positioned given their specific role this evening: Geneviève and Sara, and Jordan and Liz will alternate "doing voice," interpreting French and English in LSQ and ASL, respectively, and vice versa, and will sign when Line speaks, while Suzanna and Julie will take turns "doing signs," interpreting LSQ in ASL and vice versa. They are also finalizing their preparation by sharing LSQ and ASL signs for "Deaf music," "signed music," "signed-song," and other specialized vocabulary that may be used during the workshop.

A little after 6:00 p.m., seven of the eight confirmed participants (who will be introduced in the next section) have arrived. We decide not to wait for the latecomer, who joined us subsequently. As a whole, the group is equally divided between LSQ and ASL signers, able-bodied Deaf adults in their late thirties to early forties, otherwise differently positioned in terms of gender, familial background, education, national origin, occupation, and race.[8] They are all friends or acquaintances of the Deaf members of our research team, but they do not all know each other. Those who do know one another congregate as they move toward the seating area, chatting. They have answered the invitation we circulated through email and Glide, a video application, which provided a detailed presentation of the workshop, including information on how its format is inspired by the segment of a BBC radio show and how its objectives relate to our research projects. It specified that each participant was to use audio or video equipment available on-site to introduce their chosen "inherited" song or tune or track to others, who would be invited to comment and discuss this music and the accompanying stories shared by the participant. The invitation also specified that if time permitted, there would be another round of sharing, focused this time on music that participants would like to pass on.

Everyone is choosing their place in the discussion area. Véro and the participants take seats that allow them to best see the LSQ or ASL interpreters. The LSQ-ASL interpreters as well the video recorders are also part of the circle. Together with the LSQ-French and ASL-English interpreters, Line is standing outside the circle, while Eric has settled near the sound console, a few steps back. There is excitement and some nervousness in the air: no one knows exactly what to expect. We welcome everyone—Véro in LSQ, Line in French—reminding everyone of the objectives and format of the workshop as well as the importance of informed consent and inviting questions on ethical issues or the consent forms. There are none; every participant has signed a form allowing us to record them and use their name in forthcoming research dissemination activities. After Véro has made sure that everyone understands who is doing what, who is interpreting what for whom, Line asks for a volunteer to share their inherited music of choice.

Following these introductory remarks, we become engaged observers. We limit our interventions to greeting the latecomer participant, announcing a short pause to give interpreters a well-deserved break and, once we realize we were running out of space on the memory cards of our recording equipment almost three hours into the discussion, wrapping up the workshop and thanking everyone for participating. The workshop unfolds organically, so to speak. No enticement or encouragement is needed for people to offer testimonies and interact. It is clear from the very first story shared, however, that the participants are more or less ignoring the proposed script, taking matters into their own hands. They are giving the event a different orientation, a new "starting point" (Ahmed 2010), upon which the following analysis aims to shed some light.[9]

Recollecting "Doing Music": Diversified Acts of Musicking

Daz Saunders leads us off. Thinking about the theme of the evening's workshop, he explains, brings him back to his childhood years in the UK.

> I grew up in a Deaf family. I had two Deaf parents. There was music in my milieu—it was a hearing milieu. At home, there were poetry books for

kids, in English. When I went to bed, my mother would tell me stories. We did not call it music, it was signs. Short, two- to three-minutes-long stories. A story with a horse; it is galloping, there's wind, its head is moving. These were very short stories. Later it was a boat, the movement of the sails. ... A time for the two of us. For me it was music, my first experience of music. (Daz)

The particular movement and rhythm of the signed bedtime stories, as well as the particular connection they created between him and his mother, sketch the contours of how Daz approaches music as an embodied performance. It might well be that Daz has had other memories of these intimate moments with his mother, given that remembering is a "do-over" process (Aden et al. 2009), an emplaced "processual action by which people constantly transform the recollections they produce" (Zelizer 1995: 218). On this particular occasion though, his recollection can be said to configure bedtime storytelling not as a literary genre but as an act of musicking.[10]

The de-nominalization popularized by music educator Christopher Small is shorthand for music considered not as a reified thing but as "something that people do" (Small 1998: 2). The notion of musicking highlights the collective character of musical participation: acts of musicking are "socially inter-connected doing(s)" (Churchill 2015: 21). It also acknowledges its heterogeneity: "[t]o music is to take part, in any capacity, in a musical performance," not only as composers, instrumentalists, or spectators but also, as Small specifies, as roadies, janitors, and ticket counter clerks, who "are all contributing to the nature of the event that is a musical performance" (Small 1998: 9). From this perspective, extending the meaning of musicking to people who tell or respond to stories makes sense, provided, however, that the performance to which they contribute is deemed musical even if it does not comprise audible sound, as appears to be the case of Daz's "first experience of music."

To experience music as a form of storytelling is integral to many genres and traditions, notably rap (Marsh 2012).[11] To experience storytelling as "doing music" is more unusual, outside of Deaf cultures, that is. It defies the dominant view of music as an essentially auditory art form, a challenge that many Deaf people consider necessary to "understand[ing] what music is in all its performative diversity" (Cripps, Rosenblum, and Small 2015b: 3). Within Deaf communities, however, closely connecting music and storytelling is coherent with a long history of music-making based solely on signs. Described initially as "art-sign" (Klima and Bellugi 1976),[12] entirely visual acts of musicking are performed by Deaf individuals who make aesthetic use of sign language,[13] incorporating sequences of words that function as lyrics or performing more abstract, nonreferential hand and facial movements (see, e.g., Cripps 2016).

While Daz is not the only participant to evoke sign-based musicking, a few recall acts of musicking where auditory-based music is present. Although the idea does not sit well with some Deaf music scholars and members of the Deaf community, for whom the notion refers exclusively to the performance art form "fundamentally based on visual-gestural performances that emerge from the Deaf community" (Cripps, Rosenblum, and Small 2015a: 703), "signed music" is commonly used to refer to a range of practices. Creations initially developed in the sign modality by Deaf signers, accompanied or not by audible text or sounds, and translations in sign language of songs originating from an aural language, performed either by hearing interpreters or Deaf signers, also referred to as *chantsigne* (Despeyroux 2017), are the most common forms of signed music or signed-song (Bahan 2006).

Matthew Kuntz's practice falls into the latter category. Inspired perhaps by Daz, Matthew recalls his experiences as a child, more precisely, memories of his schoolboy years in the province of Alberta. He attended a Deaf school where he and his classmates were encouraged to sign pop songs to be later performed live during school pageants. He continued to do song signing through high school. Matthew recounts how Céline Dion ("I don't know if you know Céline Dion, a famous French singer, she's from Quebec," he adds, not assuming that other participants are familiar with mainstream pop music) was sent a video recording of his ASL rendition of one of her hit songs: "We wanted her to come to school, [but] she was not able to make it." He appears quite proud to share that he and his schoolmates were more successful with Canadian country singer Jann Arden, who accepted their invitation. Matthew performed a song with Arden in front of what he describes as a "large audience." This experience, he adds, gave him a taste of public performance. Whether he is putting on shows for kids in school contexts or performing as a drag queen at fundraising events, his relationship to music is the same: "Figure out what to do with the lyrics, … how to really get the idea of the lyrics across, remove that [language] barrier, so that as audience, [people] can experience the song" (Matthew).

Suzanne Laforest's early experiences of music also predominantly involve Anglo-American pop. "I grew up liking music a lot," she explains, "but it was very much linked to the hearing world" until she turned twenty-one and decided that "so what, I'm through with the hearing world." She grew up in Quebec City, in an all-Deaf family, with parents who were not aware of what was going on in the world of music. Members of her extended family introduced her and her sister to music by way of a toy instrument and an audio output device.

> There were hearing people among uncles and aunts, who played music, guitar. They gave my sister one of those small pianos, you know the ones that made sounds. You touched the keys and it made sounds. How I loved the keys and listening to the sounds that piano made. Later, she received a

> radio, so we listened to music. We are both profoundly deaf, so even with our hearing aids we did not understand the words. But we nevertheless enjoyed listening to music. (Suzanne)

The enjoyable listening that she recalls experiencing with her sister challenges the widely held audist assumption that Deaf people are trapped in total silence (Best 2023). As Suzanne points out though, as Deaf individuals, she and her sister formed their own appreciation of the "hearing people's music" they listened to: "It was another perspective on music," one which frames the pop songs broadcast on the radio less as meaningful texts to decode ("understanding lyrics and all that, it is not necessary"), more as bundles of sounds that make you dance ("It made us dance. We had fun with this").[14] During their teenage years, the sisters' musicking gravitated toward fandom. Becoming pop music fans meant adopting practices typical of the mainstream bedroom culture (McRobbie 1991) through which many middle- and upper-class young girls in the most economically developed countries have been socialized.

> We bought records, cassettes, we played the music over and over, even to try to understand the lyrics. … And then there was New Kids on the Block. We were crazy about the New Kids. We had their posters everywhere in our bedroom. We were obsessed with them. (Suzanne)

In the 1980s and early 1990s, experiencing music as a young person in places like Montreal often still meant consuming commodities produced mostly by transnational recording companies, whose dominant position within the music industries had not yet been significantly challenged. The record as popular music's "form of communication" (Frith 1988) was also central to the musical participation of Pierre-Olivier Beaulac-Bouchard as he grew up in a hearing family in Lac Saint-Jean, Quebec. But as he remarks, his connection to recorded music differed from that of his friends.

> In elementary school, there were hearing kids, I was the only Deaf. My friends were buying CDs, cassettes and all of that, and I would buy the same ones. I did not know any better. I had no other knowledge of music. One day, my brother asked me: "Why do you buy these CDs? You never listen to music." I said that my friends shared their music with me. So … But I had no identity in relation to that. (Pierre-Olivier)

Other objects mediate the acts of musicking through which many participants relate to the sound of aural-based music as an intersensorial experience (Best 2023), irreducible to hearing alone. While for Suzanne a toy piano and a radio transistor played an important role in the first explorations of music, for Sera Kassab, a self-identified Lebanese Canadian who was raised among hearing siblings, it was a violin. Sera shares an anecdote involving her eight-year-old sister (she was seven), who took violin lessons:

> She would practice, I remember her standing ... I remember staring at her and saying to myself: "What is this all about?" She took a break, put the violin down, and left the room, and I stared at it. I played with the strings, felt the vibration of my arm. I had put in on my shoulder, and put the bow to it, and was striking it back and forth .... My sister came back, and she was like "What are you doing? Awful sound!" But I had such a good time! [disappointed expression] When she picked up the violin, one of the strings snapped. Bashfully I ran, completely scared. (Sera)

Sera recollects a similar moment that occurred a year later, when her sister, who had abandoned the violin, had started taking piano lessons. She remembers how, one day, she took advantage of her sister leaving the room during practice and experimented with the piano keys:

> I just sat there, looking at this instrument, and I could not help the curiosity ... inside me. I approached the bench, pressed a key, and went over and over again. ... I was like, "Ah, this looks like fun." Who cares about the violin? I took both fingers and I went to another key and another key, another key, and all ten fingers, and again, my sister comes into the room: "What are you doing? Horrible, horrible sound." But when she left again, I continued playing, enjoying myself. (Sera)

Dancing is another way of "doing music" through which experiencing sound "involv[es] a wider spectrum of senses" (Loeffler 2014: 451). Hodan Youssouf tells the group that she has vivid memories of her childhood in Somalia, where she lived until she was eight, the only Deaf person of the household. In her reminiscence, village get-togethers and festivals function as sensory encounters.[15]

> In Somalia, in our culture, we danced a lot. Me, I would feel the vibration. I sat, and watched people dancing. I remember this so well. I was invited to participate in these events. The pleasure of music was already in me, probably because of my culture which I had interiorized. Women danced in a circle, like this [gesture], and then moved to the center. I watched. It was highly visual for me, the movement, the vibration, dancing and all of that. (Hodan)

Dancing is also Jack Volpe's passion. Born and raised in Montreal by Italian parents, the only Deaf member of a hearing family, Jack is especially attached to Latin dances. "Cha-cha, salsa, rumba, merengue. ... This is what

I really enjoy." For him, this musical activity is first and foremost a visual experience.

> I love dance because it is so visual. ... Music does not drive my dance. I have the dance, the steps, and then I follow. Can we make it a little louder? Sometimes I am a step behind. ... My memory is pretty good, it is just a matter of steps and, you know, my partner is there with me. (Jack)

Jack's testimony reminds Matthew of a singular occasion when lyrics, which are usually his point of reference, did not matter. "It was not dancing," he explains, but doing gymnastics. "A group of us was doing a gymnastic routine to the soundtrack of the Teenage Mutant Ninja Turtles theme song. It was a visceral experience" (Matthew).

When his turn arrives, Jordy St-Jacques introduces himself as a 3-D animator who does not have much experience with music. There are two experiences he remembers well, he explains: learning the recorder in school and discovering bass. Both turned out to be among the acts of musicking to which many other participants relate, as discussed in the next section.

Recognizing Commonalities and Affinities: Significant Moments of Musicking

As the evening progresses, participants' testimonies prompt more and more reactions in the group, and dynamic discussions get intertwined with additional individual recollections. The workshop unfolds in ways that resemble what Sverker Hyltén-Cavallius observed during meetings of a (hearing) pensioners' study circle in music-listening in Sweden: a sort of "joint storytelling" (Young 1987, quoted in Hyltén-Cavallius 2012) through which a memoryscape is assembled out of the different recollections shared by participants. Although some artists and songs are mentioned in the process, this particular memoryscaping pivots mostly around moments of musicking that appear to have particularly affected the participants' journeys of attachments to music albeit to varying degrees. Whether they contribute their own remembering, offer their perspective on its meaning or importance, or simply manifest their understanding and sympathy toward the experiences that are communicated, participants recognize, and often identify with, these particularly significant, impactful moments. The group's memory-making not only reconstructs particular acts of musicking. It also hints at the broader context embedding the people, media, technologies, discourses, and institutions involved. The "storyworld" collectively established by participants, to borrow loosely from narrative theorist David

Herman, "transports" participants into particular space-times within which they can "imaginatively (emotionally, viscerally) inhabit a world in which things matter, agitate, exalt, repulse, provide grounds for laughter and grief, and so on" (Herman 2010: 570). In the process, as individual life courses intersect with collective trajectories, the complexity of their shared inheritance as Deaf adults and how they negotiate what has often not been passed on through filiation but through community belonging becomes apparent.

Taking Recorder Lessons in School

During his early school years at the Montreal Oral School for the Deaf (MOSD), Jordy remembers taking recorder lessons.[16]

> I do remember taking recorder lessons, using a recorder. I have no idea why I took that, to be honest. I think it was something I was told to do by instructors, because it would practice, it would work out my vocal cords, in order to produce speech. (Jordy)

His recollection appears familiar to many participants, including Jack, who nods in agreement. He had a similar experience, which he recalls in a humorous and mocking way that has Daz and Suzanne laughing, Sera and Pierre-Olivier smiling ("Yeah, that's it," they sign):

> I, too, was at MOSD, the same school, and learned the recorder. I hated it. The teacher, well, she forced us. We had to practice with a recorder. You know [mimicking placing the record to his lower lip], and practice, even with your tongue [exaggerating tongue movements], where you are placing it ... before we open our mouth, we had to do this exercise [moving his lips to mimic blowing in the recorder] ... And at the same time, all the students, prepare the recorder on our lips, 1, 2, 3, go. (Jack)

On a more serious note, he expresses the discomfort he remembers experiencing:

> They [teachers] just said it will be a good experience for you, and I did it. ... I wasn't comfortable playing it. I certainly couldn't hear it, you know. ... Keep going, keep practicing, so of course, I flowed with it, I played with it, but I ... [a]s a Deaf person, I never really felt comfortable. But I played as a Deaf person playing music. (Jack)

Jack's recollection suggests that the discomfort he experienced during recorder lessons is not related to the school's intention of having students learn music. There is a good chance that the memories he recalls would have been different had he been studying drums or other percussion instruments or had he been allowed to play recorder the way he wanted to. It is likely that his discomfort has to do with the underlying oralist agenda of the recorder classes: to teach Deaf individuals the codes and mores of the hearing population. Indeed, over the past fifty years or so, many Québécois children have learned to play the recorder in schools. Deemed especially affordable, easy to carry, sturdy, and quite accessible even to younger students, the recorder has become a vehicle for the democratization of music education, and culture and arts education more generally—a national priority established in the wake of the Commission d'enquête sur l'enseignement des arts of 1968. The curricula of many schools continue to include recorder lessons, which are said to contribute to the overall development of children and, more specifically, help them strengthen their lungs and respiratory system, as well as develop their auditory and hearing skills.[17] For Jordy and Jack, culturally Deaf signing adults looking back on their childhood music-related memories, the prospective benefits of the recorder lessons that marked their musical awakening classes may appear questionable. But in the context of the school they attended, they were the very objectives of the whole curriculum.

MOSD is among the specialized schools for the Deaf with an auditory-verbal approach that include music in a program designed to teach students with "a hearing loss" to listen and to speak.[18] While music education programs for Deaf children are no longer all focused on auditory perception (at least not exclusively), most were from the nineteenth century onward (Schmitt 2012). These programs were inspired by research such as that of French otologist Jean-Marc Gaspard Itard, who, in 1802, studied the impact of musical instruments on the development of auditory discrimination skills of deaf and hard of hearing students (Solomon 1980). In the United States, an influential tradition sprung from William Wolcott Turner and David Ely Bartlett's 1848 article advocating music instruction for the same children on the basis of its benefits for auditory skills development as well as articulation, speech, and language improvement (Darrow and Heller 1985). However, by the end of the 1800s, in the wake of the Milan Congress and the institution of oralism that ensued, teaching deaf kids how to speak through various speech therapies had become not only the objective pursued in music classes but also the very definition of what education for the Deaf has to be.

While Jack and Jordy neither make explicit reference to this history nor criticize the pedagogical and ideological foundations of the school their parents chose for them, their recollections are specifically about how Deaf individuals had to learn the recorder as part of an oralist program developed by hearing educators. The present-past of these lessons, we argue, articulates this musicking to particular educational programs and embodied civilizing practices situated in specific collective histories. Audism (Humphries 1977), "the normative system that subordinates Deaf and hard of hearing persons to a range of practices, actions, beliefs and attitudes that valorizes hearing people and their way of life" (our translation, Leduc 2016: 1), runs through these histories. It is largely responsible for the systemic oppression experienced by Deaf people, "not because a tyrannical power coerces them, but because of the everyday practices of a well-intentioned liberal society," as Iris Marion Young argues (Young 2015: 41). How much of the recalled discomfort of the participants has to do with this particular musicking acting as a normalizing device and being experienced as "ordinary" oppression?[19]

As Jordy explicitly questions the underlying intentions of these teaching practices, he frames musical instruments as belonging ipso facto to the hearing world, hence as something from which Deaf people would be estranged by definition.

> I remember when they used to test our hearing based on music, and how … we were taught music in order to practice our hearing muscles, whether it was through a wind instrument or otherwise. … It is so interesting to me, like, is the expectation that we would love, pick up an instrument and keep with it for the rest of our lives? This hearing artifact, put on to me, as a Deaf person, I am supposed to keep up with it? What's the idea behind this? (Jordy)

His interrogations contribute to assemble a memoryscape that moves beyond the recorder lessons forced upon some Deaf students in school to include, more broadly, other musical instruments that participants remember being encouraged to learn and take on as a hobby or leisure activity. Guitar is briefly evoked by Daz, a (nonspecified) wind instrument by Jack, and the organ by Suzanne. Their experiences with these instruments were short-lived, and so was Pierre-Olivier's flirtation with the violin, which, as he recalls, was imposed on him by his mother when he was a teenager.[20]

> I have been implanted when I was sixteen years old. It was basically my mother who decided: "You will take lessons!" She took me to a class: it was a violin lesson. *Certainly not!* [I thought]. The teacher said OK, and my mom left. In fact, the violin was sort of my mom's dream. Sol, re, and all of this. Time went by, I had no confidence. I did not understand how it worked, and the Christmas show was fast approaching. I was not alone; I think there was also four hearing individuals. … The teacher would look at us, directing us. I was lipreading, trying to follow. After the show, the teacher came to see me and told me that it was excellent. It was very difficult for me to believe this. My mom asked: "Do you want to continue?" I said no. She understood that it would not work. (Pierre-Olivier)

Teaching Deaf students to play the recorder (or another instrument) "the right way" through programs and initiatives developed by well-intentioned hearing educators illustrates how schools designed as democratic instruments of social mobility also function as mechanisms of social reproduction (Bourdieu and Passeron 1970). In this case, maintaining the status quo meant encouraging Deaf students to speak as hearing people do and, by the same token, to music just like the hearing majority does. Although it is part of their inheritance, this dual injunction did not sit well with the participants who lived their teenage years and reached adulthood in the aftermath of social and rights movements that, from the 1970s onward, challenged the legacy of oralism and paved the way to a generation of individuals who take pride in their Deaf belonging, languages, and cultures.

Discovering Bass

It is through Jordy's initial comments that another field of affinities and commonalities is brought to the table. Having explained how no real appreciation of music emerged from recorder lessons, he adds, "It did not go far until I discovered bass instruments and the vibration they made." Some participants have had similar "turning point" experiences: how they look back at how their life with music has changed over time follows a before-bass and after-bass periodization. Sera, for example, learned about pitch and, more specifically, about bass sounds in the dance classes she took when she was six to seven years old. She recounts how she was initiated to music through ballet lessons in a class where she was the only Deaf kid:

> So, what does that look like? you might ask yourself. Really, I just spent the time looking at everyone's feet, including my own. I tried desperately to copy exactly what the instructor was doing.... But then I wouldn't be able to follow. ... It made it really difficult to look graceful. ... It wasn't successful, it wasn't a great integration for me. (Sera)

She quit ballet, she explains, and joined a Lebanese folk dancing class through which she began appreciating music very differently.

> [There was] much more bass, there were drums used, and when I was close to the drums in class, I felt the music so much stronger than I ever did in ballet, where the music feels like miles and miles away, it is like a flute, and it is so distant ... you are like dancing on clouds, it is not a comfortable feeling. When you are dancing to drums, to bass, it is so ... it is just a different experience entirely. And so, I feel like it was magic to me, a great deal more. (Sera)

Jack also recalls the moment when, at twenty-one, he discovered bass. Becoming fully aware of the power of bass, he explains, made him realize that the louder bass is, the stronger vibrations are and the better "you can really feel" music.

> I didn't really know about bass. My best friend had me try bass [guitar]. He himself is hard of hearing, and his brother is a guitarist in a band. ... And so, through that, I was able to learn about bass. Even on speaker, you can turn up the bass. There is treble, bass, and something else, I don't know all these different aspects. ... But turn up the bass! That's the one you want. Bass is going to give you the feel of the music. (Jack)

Judging from another anecdote shared by Jack, bass could be said to impart musicality even to a newscast. He did make the group laugh when he told us about the time when he had been dancing on his seat to the beat of the loud sound that was coming from his car radio only to have his (hearing) partner indicate that he was "grooving" to the newscast!

Given how much nodding is going on, many participants appear to concur that bass sounds are key to experiencing music, an opinion also expressed by the older Deaf adults we had interviewed. While Deaf people in general tend to hear bass more easily than higher pitched sounds, almost all Deaf can feel the vibrational sensations of music. The popularity of this form of musicking among Deaf people (Schmitt 2012; Loeffler 2014) is such that it inspires artists as well as researchers to experiment with various vibrotactile technologies (such as vibrating floors, electrodynamic shakers) and conductors (balloons, pillows) to further develop the sensory experiences that they afford.[21] Challenging the widely held view that Deaf people go through life in silence, some Deaf musicians discuss vibrations as a listening medium. For example, renowned Deaf professional percussionist Dame Evelyn Glennie calls "touching sound" the vibrational listening she advocates, one which "engages the whole body as a 'resonating chamber' by which to sense, distribute, and digest the sounds while simultaneously integrating visual cues, movement, and imagination" (Glennie 2003, quoted in Holmes 2017: 171). Often misconceived as Deaf people's only access to music, the enjoyment of vibration as a mode of "sensing sound" (Eidsheim 2015) is, needless to say, no more "natural" for Deaf musickers than the dominant notion of listening as a strictly auditory act (Holmes 2017) that it challenges is "natural" to the hearing majority. All forms of listening occur in particular sociohistorical environments within which particular sensory attunements are "based on culturally situated sensory priorities" (Sirvage 2016: 294, quoted in Best 2023: 3).

During the workshop, discussions about discovering bass sounds and feeling music as vibration brought to the fore one particular sociohistorical environment that mediates and shapes the participants' aging with music: automotive culture and, more precisely, car culture. Allow us to quote at some length parts of a reconstructed exchange that begins with Jack elaborating on how he "cranks up the bass."

> JACK: I do that [crank up the bass] in my car, for example, or in my office.
> JORDY: I've done that before, where I've totally left it on, and then [a hearing person] would get in the car and say: "What the hell!"
> JACK: Yeah, [his hearing partner] knows … I had my favorite cassette, I'd say, "Can you record this song, that song …" Really, any music is good. I don't care who the musician is, or whether it is spoken word or not. … What I want is bass, any music with bass. And you know, like in the club, like club dancing, there is a lot of base there involved. … So I ask [his hearing partner] to put that on, then I'll put that in my car, and drive along, crank it up, and then I can feel it through me … through the car. Until someone comes in, you know, who can hear. And then I forget. [laughter]
> DAZ: This is so pleasant, so enjoyable! It makes me want to put some in my car, tonight. Crank up the volume as much as possible. That's it … On the weekend … As if you are in your own bubble, in your car.
> JORDY: I remember one time. … I was getting closer to the car, and you started the car. I wasn't even in it yet, and I could feel the vibrations, like what's that?
> JACK: Yeah … I have a Bose sound system in my car.
> DAZ: Wow, a Bose system! Fancy, very fancy.

Through their exchange, the participants configure the car as a significant musicking space and context, thereby foregrounding a connection that has a long history. In North America, the articulation of car and music dates back to the 1950s, when automobility came to symbolize "the good life" and a pivotal focus for citizenship and mobility in what was then a booming consumer society (Urry 2004). As Mark Duffett argues, "[A]s parallel commodities, car and popular music became instrumental in *catalysing America's shift into an era of high modernity*" (Duffett 2020: 3; emphasis in original). Twenty years after the introduction of the first commercially successful car radio in a luxury vehicle produced in the United States, automobiles were deeply intertwined with music (especially pop music). AM/FM in-car transistor radios that had evolved into a standard feature of increasingly affordable cars and allowed popular music to be the driver's soundtrack of choice were instrumental in the process. In the context of rapidly changing urban and suburban landscapes, musicians and car manufacturers were inspired by commuting, cruising, and escaping as the driving force of the emerging cultural imaginaries. With the flourishing of consumption and its linkage of identity to consumption, cars and music "in tandem" came to function as "markers of personal style" (Duffett 2020: 8).

The exchange about the car as a space of musicking raises issues of control, technological mediation, and branding as well as gender and social class that allude to significant dimensions of car stereo culture. It brings attention to the agency of the driver, who gets to decide what music is played in the car and how loud it will be played—in the case at hand, how much louder than what would be "acceptable" for hearing people. As Jonathan Bell explains, "Car stereo culture offers not only another means of self-expression, but also allows the driver to control their surroundings, producing sounds so intense that the bystander is literally physically moved" (Bell 2001: 115, quoted in Duffett 2020: 8). The participants' interactions also hint at the in-car playback technology as a condition of possibility of turning the driver's car into an efficient boom box through which control over one's sonic surroundings can be exercised.[22] More precisely, they point to the branding that occurs across the automobile, music, and technology sectors. It is not any "good," "powerful" sound system that produces the intense sounds that will be sensed as vibrations. It is Bose, the brand name associated with the first designer sound system introduced in 1982, that for many represents quality, distinction, performance, and refinement. Finally, we might see in who took part in this exchange and who did not traces of the ingrained and long-lasting gendering of car culture (Walsh 2008; Lumsden 2010; Balkmar 2012; Lezotte 2013). The participants' allusion to the pleasure of going for a drive "just for fun," to enjoy loud beat-driven music, is coherent with the automotive culture's view of car travel as sensory experience, one that can generate "automotive emotions" (Sheller 2004). But as Katie Milestone (2020) reminds us, this "just for fun" type of travel has always been far more accessible to men than to women, exemplifying what she describes as the "patriarchal modus operandi" of a cultural formation within which a car tends to represent "freedom, escape, and status for men, compared with service, care, and chores for women" (74).

The strong albeit different connections between cars, masculinity, and music performed in Anglo-American rock, heavy metal, and especially hip-hop and rap cultures have been documented—musical genres that may or may not be what the participants listen to in their car. Murray Forman has explored how these relations in hip-hop involve the fetishization of bass and volume and how this process has in fact transformed the soundings of contemporary urban cities in the United States, thanks in part to "the rolling bass beats of hip hop music booming from convertibles, Jeeps, customized low riders and tall SUVs, luxury cars and sedate family sedans" (Forman 2002: xvii). Needless to say, we are not suggesting that Jack's, Jordy's, and Daz's cars are "'pimped' to judder in time to the beat" (Milestone 2020: 75). What they are discussing is not a form of musicking designed first and above all to attract attention (although their "cranking up the bass" may), at least not necessarily as it may be of some hip-hop, rock, or heavy metal fan drivers. However, in our view, the exchange in which they took part suggests that through their entanglements with the mainstream automotive culture they have inherited, the musicking trajectories of Deaf men is also gendered.[23]

Watching Music (Videos)

If some of the participants' musicking takes place in cars and in public places (e.g., in schools and recital halls), they also often occur in the home, in front of a small or a big screen turned music media. By contrast with the older Deaf adults we interviewed, who, for example, tuned into popular American television shows featuring their favorite big band orchestras, the adults who took part in the workshops not so much watch television programs with music content as they experience music as something to be watched, a visual medium.

As was already mentioned, pop music occupied an important part of Suzanne's teenage years. The New Kids on the Block became the object of her and her sister's infatuation, thanks to the attention their songs were getting not only from local radio stations they listened to but also from the highly popular music television specialty network they watched. When she mentions the other boy bands she became a fan of after watching their music videos, other participants are quick to add their own recollections of favorite artists and clips.

> SUZANNE: My sister and I, we watched Musique Plus. ... It is there that we discovered the Backstreet Boys, by accident.[24]
> DAZ: The Backstreet Boys! You say this and I had forgotten them. ... There was also Janet Jackson, she was expressive, her choreographies were interesting.
> HODAN [after recalling her childhood years in Somalia]: When I arrive in Canada ... you mentioned Janet Jackson. I really liked her.
> I liked Black handicapped artists, rappers. [And] MC Hammer! You remember? He danced like this [she makes circular movements with her hips; many people laugh]. You can still see it on YouTube. It would be a good idea to show this material.
> MATTHEW: You want to watch it?
> DAZ: Let's watch it. The song "U Can't Touch This."

Eric finds the video on YouTube, and we all watch it on the big screen as many participants laugh, smile, and comment to one another.

In their early years, music videos were used by labels as marketing tools designed to promote the latest LP record of already known artists or as a part of more long-term strategy to introduce new talents to the public and establish their public image (Banks 1997). They indeed appear to have worked as a form of advertisement for the workshop participants, whose musical trajectory is marked, from the 1980s on, by their avid viewing of Musique Plus, MuchMusic, and the like: they all remember "discovering" their favorite bands and singers through their consumption of music videos on television. However, as promotional products, the videos might have played a limited role considering that, in their recollections, these individuals pay little attention, if any at all, to the LPs whose sales the videos they appreciated helped to promote.[25] In fact, as Suzanne hints during the discussion, Deaf individuals developed their own Deaf experiences of music, which may rely on a particular approach to videos considered a full-fledged musical creation in its own right, rather than a secondary product, strictly subordinate to the record—which, at the time, was not only the key commodity produced by the music industries but also the very "form of communication which determines what songs, singers and performances are and can be" (Frith 1988: 12).

In a way, this particular Deaf musicking might have anticipated the future of music videos, which progressively turned into a pivotal feature of music production, circulation, and consumption practices. Economic, technological, and cultural changes since the 1980s have indeed made it possible for music videos to be omnipresent on a range of public and private screens and widely accessible through various digital platforms and social networks. Moreover, having become the musical media par excellence for many enthusiasts, videos have made it more difficult to maintain any clear-cut distinction between music as a primarily aural work and music as an (audio)visual creation. These developments around music videos had (hearing) rapper-producer Didai observe that "today [early 2000s], music is watched more than it is listened to. We only listen to clips" (Mehdi 2011, quoted in Kaiser and Spanu 2018: 8). Reframing the observation with Deaf musicking in mind, we could rather suggest that, perhaps more intensely in a video-centered era, music is watched to be listened to: watching means engaging in a multisensorial mode of listening that is visually—rather than aurally—driven.

The other music video played at the workshop is requested by Pierre-Olivier, who expresses his appreciation of Australian singer-songwriter Sia: "I really like her. She is very good. 'Soon We'll Be Found' ... The colored hands! It's so beautiful. Can we put it on and watch it?" As he joins Eric to help him find his favorite version of the 2008 pop song on YouTube, a couple of participants mention knowing and liking the video. We watch the critically acclaimed video, which features (hearing) Sia, signing while singing (some segments) in ASL, her hands and those of the six actors who sign, dance, and do shadow puppets with her covered in as many colors of fluorescent paint. What appears to have attracted Pierre-Olivier's attention—as it attracts ours—is not so much the semantic content of the signed segments as the largely prosodic movements of the colored hands (and bodies) in action and the rhythm they visually embody, hence render discernible, enjoyable, recognizable.

Enjoying music visually is not, of course, limited to watching videos. References to visuality abound in the participants' testimonies concerning their musicking practices more broadly. It is integral to Jack's love of dancing to Latin music, Hodan's appreciation of Somalian women folk dances, Matthew's understanding of choreographed gymnastics routines, and Daz's fondness for bedtime childhood rituals with his mother, for example. In each case, the emphasis is on how delightful music can be for the eyes, if neither necessarily nor primarily for the ears. Jack associates this approach to music with that of Deaf artist Christine Sun Kim, who is known for creations and performances through which, refusing to consider sound and music as the sole purview of hearing people, she reclaims the ownership of sound: "In Deaf culture, movement is equivalent to sound. ... I know sound, I know it so well. It does not have to be something just experienced through the ears. It could be felt tactually, or experienced as a visual or even as an idea. So I decided to reclaim the ownership of sound" (Kim 2015). This is an excerpt from Kim's 2015 TED talk, which, on Jack's suggestion, the group watches the first few minutes of. "I've seen this many times, and we actually studied her in one of my classes at university," explains Jack. Other participants are also familiar with the artist's talk, her work more generally, and her argument that for Deaf people, "[m]usic can be an exclusively visual-spatial experience" (Holmes 2017: 195).

In fact, this penchant for watching music is coherent with the importance of sight and seeing in Deaf cultures. Deaf people are referred to as a "people of the eye,"[26] not to signal some natural heightened visual sense they share but rather to bring attention to their practices of "seeing," which, as Carol Padden and Tom Humphries (2005: 2) argue, "follow a long history of interacting with the world in certain ways—in cultural ways." Sign languages, as spatial and visual modes of expression, are central to these "cultural ways."

Having Mixed Feelings toward Signed Music

Given that for decades Deaf people have claimed broader recognition for signed languages, including as official languages, it is tempting to assume that musics signed in a variety of sign languages occupy a prominent place in their musical repertoire of choice. The situation is, however, more complex.

The participants who expressed their opinions on the topic appeared to welcome the existence of music with sign languages, of which they became increasingly aware with the advance of the internet, and YouTube more specifically. By contrast, unless they attended Gallaudet University, were deeply involved in Deaf community organizations, or lived in the broader urban centers where a vast majority of the latter were located, older generations of Deaf people did not have that kind of access to signed music. For some participants, discovering music in signed language was a memorable experience. In Sera's case, it was a life-changing moment:

> I saw "O Canada" signed, it was … it was also signed language as I never had seen it before. And I saw how music could influence sign language, and how sign language could make music accessible, and that was kind of the starting point of me wanting to be an artist, and choosing the type that I am on now, why art is sacred to me, why color and imagination, to me, is music visualized. (Sera)

But for the most part, signed music sparked less enthusiasm than questions and critical reflections.

Participants expressed their reluctance to songs in signed language (*chantsignes*) created by hearing people. There is indeed an unprecedented rise in translated English-to-ASL songs circulating on the web and a similar albeit not as extensive hype surrounding French-to-LSF (*langue des signes française*) songs. In the United States, where most of the former are produced, the hearing signers and translators who are responsible for these songs tend to "believe that they are helping deaf people listen to music performances" (Cripps and Lyonblum 2017: 81). Moreover, an increasing number of hearing students taking lessons in sign language create signed songs as an exercise. Although fueled by good intentions, these compassion and pedagogy-driven songs do not necessarily appeal to Deaf people, many of whom "express apprehension over the proliferation of unskilled hearing song signers on YouTube, who, they feel, are appropriating tokens of Deaf culture in order to harness its novel appeal" (Holmes 2017: 199).

Not all signed songs or musics using sign language are created equal, so to speak, and participants find problematic that differences between translations and original creations are not acknowledged or taken seriously into consideration. The following segment of the discussion, which follows Hodan's mention of the influence of hearing people on Deaf people through music, illustrates this line of reasoning.

> HODAN: I notice that what often happens with songs in ASL is that they are too close to the hearing text, on the song's lyrics. … There are musics that are more ASL, not so tied to French or English. And there are many videos on the internet that follow English or French lyrics too closely. They should be separated.
>
> DAZ: Do I applaud [that there are more signed songs]? Yes. However, I am sometimes under the impression that people steal our culture, our language, all of it. It's OK, but when you look at the videos that are produced … they are stealing from us.

SUZANNE: At the same time, consider the TV singing contest *La Voix* [*The Voice*], lots of contestants are Francophones but they sing in English. They understand the English songs. They could sing in French, but they don't. It is the same thing with LSQ, we take songs created in other languages. ... However, Deaf people don't express themselves. When music stars are appropriating our language rather than encouraging Deaf people to create themselves, it is not all bad, but I am tired of seeing this from lots of hearing individuals.

The discussion draws interesting parallels between the situation of hearing and Deaf linguistic minorities and their relation to hegemonic languages. It also echoes the tensions and confusions observed by Pierre Schmitt (2016) in his study of artistic approaches in the media and on stage in France, between sign languages considered an accessibility device and a medium of expression and creation. While the former is designed to allow Deaf people to experience audible music through signed songs produced *for* Deaf by hearing people, the latter is about signed music-making *by* Deaf people in modalities that are in keeping with Deaf experiences of the world. "When signed language, visual-gestural performance and multisensorial input are used to express artistic performances within the Deaf community, the result is called Signed Music" (Cripps, Rosenblum, and Small 2015a: 702).

The creation of a specific ASL sign for music signed by Deaf individuals is testament to the growing appeal of this musicking. This appeal is particularly in the United States, where, although ASL lacked official recognition until the 1970s and the 1980s (Cripps and Lyonblum 2017), it has a relatively long history—which intersects, at least in part, with that of Gallaudet University, where music, signed and audible, has been part of the artistic components of curricular and extracurricular activities for a long time.[27] By contrast, in Quebec, and within the LSQ community especially, signed music remains an emergent practice that appeared to raise some interest among some workshop participants. References were made to only one specific musician, Pamela Witcher, a renowned Deaf artist and performer, a Montrealer of many years, and whose 2008 clip "Experimental Music" makes her a precursor to contemporary signed music.[28]

Judging from the workshop as a whole, most of the participants' musickings so far have involved making do in various ways with audible or hearing musics, which have provided the soundtracks of their lives as Deaf signers. Signed music might well be too recent and marginal a practice to figure in their inheritance or musical attachments. But who knows, as a Deaf way of experiencing music in the making, does it not have the potential to become a practice worth passing on?

Musical Attachments as Breeding Ground for Harmonious and Disjunctive Encounters

Although the Inheritance Tracks workshop lasted only three hours, it brought to the fore an array of questions and issues of an impressive scope. How can we come to grips with the rich cartography of musical attachments, still in the process of being made (Hennion 2017), that the experiences, rememberings, and reflections shared by the participants contour? How can we best appreciate the different acts of musicking through which these contingent attachments to audible and signed music have developed and changed over time? How can we make sense of the affects, tensions, and power relations that, as they link individual and collective trajectories, further problematize the articulation of aging, memory, and inheritance through music? We turn to the concepts of fitting and misfitting theorized by Rosemarie Garland-Thomson (2011) to explore these issues, given that, in our view, they offer relevant guidelines to understand the contingent and complex effectivity of the practices and experiences at hand.[29]

The feminist scholar developed these notions in the context of her materialist understanding of disability as a lived, a situated, and an embodied experience shaped by the spatial and temporal aspects of one's environment.[30] She wrote:

> Fitting and misfitting denote an encounter in which two things come together in either harmony or disjunction. When the shape and substance of these two things correspond in their union, they fit. A misfit, conversely, describes an incongruent relationship between two things: a square peg in a round hole. The problem with a misfit, then, inheres not in either of the two things but rather in their juxtaposition, the awkward attempt to fit them together. When the spatial and temporal context shifts, so does the fit, and with it meanings and consequences. (Garland-Thomson 2019: 225)

The interrelated dynamics of fitting and misfitting, she argues, take into account the "particularity of varying lived embodiments and avoid a theoretical generic disabled body" while "confer[ring] agency and value" on disabled subjects (Garland-Thomson 2011: 592).

Garland-Thomson's concepts guide our critical analysis of Deaf people's relations to music as multiple, situated, and unstable and of their musicking practices as carved in particular material, social, cultural, and sonic environments where the "discrepancy between ... that which is expected and that which is" matters (593). Rid of the cliché that music is inaccessible to Deaf people because it is auditory, and free of the misleading assumption that original signed music is surely the favorite of Deaf signers, our approach to Deaf people's musicking can embrace the historicity of the simultaneously oppressive and agentifying forces of sound and music today. For a long time, music was strictly a matter of concern for hearing people living in a world largely conceived, built, and organized for them or for those who could behave like them. Even though sound and music have been the objects of reappropriation by Deaf people for some time—but particularly in the past decade or so (Kim 2015)—they still constitute a field fraught with wounds, microaggressions, and unutterable affects. Let us briefly explore how, in different situations, they can become the breeding ground for Deaf people's more or less incongruent relationships to their environment.

Some of the acts of musicking that participants have recalled developed out of more or less deliberate efforts to fit in. Pierre-Olivier mimicking his friends and buying CDs he never listened to and Suzanne becoming a pop fan and tuning in to mainstream radio programs she understood only partially exemplify a fit emerging from practices that can be construed as "passing." As Véro Leduc (2016) explains, "Woven with complexities, passing generally involves the attempt to hide an identity or certain elements of an oppressed identity in order to be perceived as a member of the dominant group, to access social privileges, to mitigate the effects of oppression or to be seen as a full human person" (our translation, 52). Not all passing is successful or achieved once and for all, dependent as it is on contexts, situations, and others' reactions. When the relevance of Pierre-Olivier's consumption of CDs is questioned by his brother, his passing is challenged. Sometimes, passing loses its relevance or importance, such as when Suzanne, at twenty-one years old, decided she had had enough of the hearing world and distanced herself from her mainstream pop-driven musicking.

But as many other shared recollections suggest, fitting is neither always connected to passing nor deliberately sought. Rather, harmonious encounters may derive from the multiple belongings that individuals experience. Hodan and Daz, among others, discovering boy bands by watching MuchMusic might have experienced a fit that could be said to emerge from their belonging to, at one and the same time, Deaf and Québécois cultures. As Québécois young adults who liked music, they partook to varying degrees in the hegemonic Anglo-American pop to which they were willy-nilly exposed. It may be the case, as Schmitt (2012) observed in France, that Deaf youths in Montreal, including those who may not have liked music, have acquired basic knowledge of the most popular musical styles and renowned musicians of their times and, in some cases at least, of their parents' musical culture. But given the ambivalent relation that Deaf people have had with music, this familiarity cannot be taken for granted, as in Matthew wondering whether participants knew about Céline Dion illustrates.

During the workshop, many acts of musicking were introduced through memoryscaping, which highlighted the strangeness and awkwardness of the recalled experiences. The recorder lessons are best understood in terms of misfit, in at least two different ways. On the one hand, as Jack rendered explicit, the Deaf kids were not producing the right sounds, the ones that were expected to come out from the instrument in the context of a music class. On the other hand, as Jordy's intervention also made clear, the class heightened a clash of identities: as a disciplinary technology, the recorder materialized and intensified the differences between a Deaf person's and a hearing person's experiences of the instrument: the sound it produces and the music it is meant to create.

Misfitting inheres in juxtapositions that, in particular contexts, may be experienced by the two entities involved albeit differently. Just as fitting can be experienced as oppressive (especially when it is linked to passing) and/or affirmative (when it yields a feeling of belonging), misfitting does not only characterize the experience of Deaf people when they do not meet hearing standards or expectations. Given that the misfit emerges from or in an encounter, it can evoke the moment of clash when two ways of musicking collapse. When Jack's partner gets into the car and realizes Jack is dancing to the beat of the newscast, misfit could have been experienced, if only fleetingly, by Jack, who is "caught" doing something "wrong" from a hearing perspective. But some sense of misfit could also have been experienced by his partner, who may not be able to imagine dancing to the evening news.

The experience of misfitting is often destabilizing, at least at first. However, the participants gave many examples of a misfitting encounter being short-lived as it is reclaimed through reappropriation, a performative act that challenges ostracism through creative and affirmative practice (Leduc 2016). Consider, for example, Sera's recollection of the time when, after her sister had caught her playing "awful sounds" on the piano, she resumed musicking in her own way.

This possibility of reclaiming music is not only a matter of taking back power in the face of hearing people. It is also an issue of self-affirmation for Deaf people within their own community. The social movement promoting Deaf pride, which was in full swing in the 1970s and 1980s—a historic moment described as Deaf Awakening (Ladd 2003)—did help to valorize how Deaf people perceive and experience the world differently from hearing people (Jankowski 1997; Padden and Humphries 2005). In the wake of this movement, music became associated strictly with the hearing world. One could not like music and be Deaf—the capital letter being recently used to distinguish the spelling of the words "deaf" (according to the medical paradigm) and "Deaf" (as a cultural affiliation). The following remarks made about ASL signers in the United States could apply to other Deaf communities: "[D]eaf individuals who are fluent in ASL and part of deaf culture have frequently accepted the notion that music belongs to hearing people. Society's perceptions that deaf people are associated with silence, and that music is reserved to the audible form, clearly has created an impact on the deaf community's consciousness about music in general" (Cripps and Lyonblum 2017: 82).

The relationship between the Deaf and music has, since, remained quite tense. For many Deaf people, music is not only controversial but also taboo: "It almost seems dangerous to say that I love music, because not everyone will understand and I will be judged. While the majority of the Deaf Community will say they don't enjoy music at all, there are plenty of us that do love music. Even when we cannot hear it. ... In the Deaf Community, we usually don't talk about it" (Deaf blogger J. Parrish Lewis quoted in Holmes 2017: 200).

New Orientation and Renewed Inheritance in the Making?

This workshop turned out to be a fruitful memory-making *dispositif* that enabled participants to rekindle their respective journeys of attachment to or with music. Through often funny anecdotes and many moving testimonies, they recollected some of the meaningful, albeit not always strictly harmoniously experienced, acts of musicking in which they have engaged as Deaf individuals since their childhood. Moments of mutual recognition fueled particular dynamic segments of the discussion, which brought out affinities and commonalities that the participants' different biographical trajectories might have overshadowed.

The musical present-pasts of the participants are not only intertwined with the cultural histories of, among others, mainstream Anglo-American pop, music celebrity, playback technologies, automobile culture, and girl fandom. They are also inflected by the collective trajectories of Deaf communities and the charged historicity of Deafhood. Bits of conversations, knowing smiles, and exchanged glances hint at their malaise or discomfort as Deaf individuals who have been oppressed or at least marked to varying degrees by their common experience of oralism, in its many guises—an ideology that remained otherwise tacit throughout the workshop. Their uneasiness permeates the participants' musicking as well as their recollection of the ways in which music has contributed to "orient" Deaf people mostly toward a hearing way of being in the world.

We draw here on feminist critical phenomenologist Sara Ahmed, for whom orientation is "not only about how we 'find our way' but how we come to 'feel at home'" (2006b: 6) and disorientation is "the feelings that build up when we lose our sense of who we are" (20). The embodied iterative practices that constitute acts of musicking can be said to have affected how, as Deaf people, participants "found their way" at times and got lost at others. For as Ahmed argues, "Bodies ... acquire orientation through the repetitions of some actions over others, as actions have certain 'objects' in view, whether they are physical objects required to do the work ... or the ideal objects that one identifies with" (2010: 247). Workshop participants remembered moments of pleasure, joy, and fun brought about by their own Deaf engagements with music on the radio, on TV, on the stage, and in their cars: far from feeling "out of place," the return of different beautiful dance moves, inspiring hand movements, invigorating sound vibrations, and nice-looking rhythms brought them "home." But they also recalled and discussed various moments when their experience of music had been unsettling, if not painful: disorientation speaks to the effectivity of repeatedly being told you are playing the "wrong" piano notes, not following the "right" dance rhythm, not managing to produce a "pleasing" sound with the recorder—in short, not doing music the way it is expected to be done, according, of course, to hearing mores, traditions, and values.

Very few songs, genres, or repertoires were mentioned during the workshop, which, in our view, indicates that they are not the most significant attractive objects in view, hence not pivotal to what participants recognize as their inheritance. In the words of Ahmed (2010: 248): "We inherit the proximity of certain objects. ... The objects are not only material: they may be values, aspirations, projects, and styles. We inherit proximities." We suggest that what these Deaf individuals have been handed down is an orientation defined by the proximity of the wide range of objects that are deemed meaningful according to a strictly aural notion of music. However, given the shared stories and the discussions that took place during the workshop, we feel there are ample reasons to believe that this orientation is increasingly called into question and may not be what these people will pass on.

Through their life course, participants have developed heterogeneous musical attachments that appear to articulate a twofold refusal: to submit to a strictly aural notion of music and to recognize only signed music as "their own." They are negotiating differently the tension between a conception of Deaf signed music as having to be based solely on visual-gestural performance and an approach that recognizes and even valorizes various modes of reappropriation of audible sound-based music by Deaf people.

In contrast to older Deaf signers we interviewed and for whom music was either a taboo, hence kept at a distance, or had no particular bearing on their aging, these individuals have aged with music, have aged liking music. For them, aging with music has meant claiming their particular experiences of music, an undertaking that, as expressed by Schmitt (2012), "poses the double challenge of extricating oneself from the explicit and implicit prohibitions of which the previous generations of the [D]eaf were victims, and of reconfiguring individually and collectively, for oneself and in front of others, the limits of [D]eaf identity" (224–5). We are inclined to deem the workshop participants' practices, attitudes, and values the germs of a novel orientation, one that may well be instrumental in how a new generation of Deaf people, increasingly aware of its own history and culture as well as its "ability to act upon the social understanding they have developed," is "contribut[ing] to its historically conditioned social situation" (Burnett 2010: 41) through music.

A myriad of contingent transformations have occurred over the past thirty years or so, in the wake of the Deaf pride movement and the deinstitutionalization that ensued, in Quebec as elsewhere. The workshop taught us that, as the legacies of oralism and audism continue to be contested and problematized, relationships to music and acts of musicking are indeed redefined, charting the way to the new proximities of which tomorrow's inheritance will be made.

Notes

1 We are grateful for the financial support that this research has received from the Ageing + Communication +Technologies (ACT) partnership funded by the Social Sciences and Humanities Research Council (SSHRC) of Canada, the Fondation des Sourds du Québec, as well as the Université de Montréal.
2 In 1990, Paddy Ladd coined this term to refute "deafness" and the medical model it encapsulates. Integral to the cultural-linguistic model proposed, the term refers to the "existential state of Deaf 'being-in-the-world,' " deemed not "as a finite state but a process by which individuals come to actualize their Dead identity, positing that those individuals construct that identity around several differently ordered sets of priorities and principles, which are affected by various factors such as nation, era and class" (Ladd 2003: xviii).
3 Echoing Ladd's insistence on process, Stuart Hall (1996: 2–3) privileges the concept of identification, which, in contrast to the notion of identity, refers to "a process never completed—always 'in process.' It is not determined in the sense that it can always be 'won' or 'lost,' sustained or abandoned. Though not without its determinate conditions of existence, including the material and symbolic resources required to sustain it, identification is in the end conditional, lodged in contingency."
4 Hennion (2017: 119) falls back on "to experience" for lack of a better translation of *éprouver*, which "in French means both to try and to feel, like 'to experience' in English, but even more strongly: to put to the test and to be afflicted."
5 For a short description of the Downsizing project, go to https://www.atwater library.ca/computer-services/digital-literacy-project/digital-literacy-projectdow nsizing-and-honouring-memories-seniors-helping-seniors. The Living History Collection is a permanent collection accessible at http://livinghistory.atwaterlibr ary.ca.

6 Community outreach is a key part of the mission of the Atwater Library and Computer Centre since its establishment in the 1920s. See https://www.atwaterlibrary.ca/about-us.
7 LSQ and ASL versions of the consent form were made available to participants and interpreters a week before the workshop. French or English printed copies of the document were signed that evening.
8 These were the axes of identity and positionality mentioned by the participants. Participants did not rely on them systematically to introduce themselves, and we did not ask them to do so. We will take them into account only insofar as they are explicitly included in the participants' stories.
9 Eric and his team have produced a montage of excerpts from the workshop. Each video shows the participants who are expressing themselves in LSQ or ASL, with the LSQ-ASL interpreter side by side; it also includes the voice of interpretation in French for LSQ participants and in English for ASL participants. These videos form part of the Living History Collection (see URL in note 5). We are especially thankful for these videos, given that they make at least parts of the workshop accessible not only to the Francophones and Anglophones but also to members of the LSQ and ALS signing Deaf communities. They allow us to give back to these Deaf communities from whose knowledge and experiences we are learning. Moreover, while we do quote participants (quotations that consist of either transcriptions of interpretations of ASL in English or English translations of interpretations of LSQ in French, done by a Deaf person), we are well aware of the issues raised by this practice, as discussed in Leduc (2016) and Schmitt (2016), among others. Video remains the most appropriate medium given the multimodal attributes of sign languages.
10 Signed language storytelling is a popular literature genre, "distinct and evolved from both ASL poetry and from translated signed songs which initiated from spoken language. It may incorporate ASL literary poetic features such as lines, meter, rhythm and rhyme while also incorporating basic elements of music like harmony, rhythm, melody, timbre, and texture, which are expressed as a visual-gestural artistic form" (Cripps et al. 2017: 1).
11 According to Ben Bahan (2006), what he calls "signed song" (which is discussed further in the chapter) is one of many face-to-face storytelling traditions in Deaf culture.
12 As we discuss later, contrary to what the title of Killman and Bellugi's article suggests, sound remains an integral part of the life of many Deaf people who, however, do not necessarily experience it aurally.
13 The presence of signing distinguishes these practices from those associated with both silent versions of visual music or color music, an art form that combines musical structures and visual imageries (Garro 2012), and avant-garde performances such as the *Theater of Music Optics* composed by John Zorn (https://jfgraves.tripod.com/General/theatre.html).
14 In our interviews with older Deaf adults, Julie-Élaine, an LSQ signer who considers music (by which she meant aural-based music) one of her lifelong passions, expressed a drastically different view. Siding with the

singer-songwriter tradition of *chanson*, which remains culturally more valued than others in Quebec (Grenier 1993, 1997), she defined music as meaningful, poetry-inspired lyrics with accompaniment.

15 This phrasing is inspired by Gavin Andrews and Viv Wilson (2020), who, after interviewing seniors who experienced the Second World War coastal action firsthand, wrote about how "respondents recollect event as sensory encounters" (23).

16 The three most common modes of schooling available for Deaf children are integration into a regular (i.e., hearing) school, with interpreters in class and/or various assistive hearing technologies; enrollment in a school for Deaf children, where teaching is done in one sign language or another; and registration in an oralist school, whose pedagogical mission is centered on speaking and lipreading. The latter type of institution developed in the wake of the oralist movement, which dates back to the nineteenth century. "Oralism is the idea that deaf individuals should be educated through the means of lipreading, mimicking mouth shapes, and practicing certain breathing patterns as well as vocal exercises that were meant to help deaf individuals produce oral language. This concept was also referred to as the oral method. Supporters of oralism believed that it was important for the deaf community to assimilate into the 'hearing world' " (Oralism and the Deaf Community n.d.). At the second international conference of deaf educators held in Milan, Italy, in 1880, oral education was declared superior to manual education, and a resolution was passed that banned the use of sign language in school. These deemed attempts to eradicate sign languages and deaf cultures are considered major events of historical and cultural violence (Ladd 2003), key points of reference for deaf historicity (Gaucher 2009: 130, quoted in Leduc 2016: 32) and becoming (Leduc 2016).

17 These are the specific benefits of learning the recorder, according to a music teacher who responded in a post (co-signed by 250 of her colleagues) to the Facebook post of a concerned mother who was questioning why the recorder is still taught in school. The response was reproduced in the popular magazine *Urbania* (Paquette 2019).

18 "You can teach a child with hearing loss to listen and speak. At the Montreal Oral School for the Deaf, we've been teaching children with hearing loss to listen and speak since we were founded in 1950" (MOSD 2015: para. 1).

19 Experiences of "ordinary" oppression, often not perceived as oppressive by hearing people, include being regularly told by passers-by who see a group of Deaf individuals signing together in a public place, what a "nice" language it is—referring to sign language in French as *langage* (the ability to communicate) rather than *langue* (a form of expression shared by members of a linguistic community), having to explain why all Deaf people do not use the same sign language, being questioned about why Deaf signers do not have a cochlear implant, and being asked if LSQ or ASL allows people to say everything (implying that it is not a full-fledged language but a limited collection of gestures).

20 He refers to cochlear implants, which are surgically implanted neuroprosthetic devices that replace the acoustic hearing process with electric signals conceived to stimulate the auditory nerve. Objects of intense debates around corporal and cultural normalization, implants remain highly controversial and are considered by some culturally Deaf people as "a treason to deafhood in favor of privileges of the hearing world" (Leduc 2016: 53n42). While implants enhance speech understanding, they do little for music perception, which is difficult, if not unpleasant, for many users (Au et al. 2012). Given that "'there is no easy way to encode pitch as an electrical stimulation patterns,' current cochlear implant models are poorly equipped to process music" (Holmes 2017: 203).

21 See the University of Liverpool project Musical Vibrations in the United Kingdom (https://www.liverpool.ac.uk/arts/sota-research/research-impact/musical-vibrations) and VibraFusionLab in Toronto, Canada (https://vflvibrations.com).

22 Agency and technological mediation are mentioned also by Sera though not in connection to car, beat, or vibration. She confided that her enjoyment grew significantly when, thanks to a particular playback technology, she started listening to the music of her choice: "I got my first earphones that I could use with my hearing aids, and I could finally use them to listen to music. ... From that day on, ... I've been able to take music into my own personal space, because before that, music was something that I had to experience outside of the home, as I came across it, so often because I happened to be there." Notice that she does not provide the brand name of the earphones.

23 Although no women took part in the exchange around bass during the workshop, one Deaf older woman we interviewed in 2019, Thérèse, told us how much she enjoyed going for car rides with music played very loudly and the bass of her sound system cranked up.

24 Created in 1986, Musique Plus was a French-language cable TV network station whose early programming focused on music videos. It was the Montreal (Quebec) antenna of MuchMusic, a Canadian English-language specialty TV channel located in Toronto (Ontario).

25 This does not mean that audio recordings were altogether absent from the spectrum of the participants' musicking practices. For example, Pierre-Olivier bought records during his teenage years, and Daz played with records in his deejaying.

26 The expression was coined in 1910 by the president of the US National Association of the Deaf, George Veditz, for whom Deaf people were "first, foremost and for all time, people of the eye" (quoted in Straus 2011: 168). *Le people de l'oeil* (*The People of the Eye*) is also the title of an exhibition about "160 years in the history of the Deaf community" that was presented first in Montreal, in 2015, and then in different cities across Canada (see https://ecomusee.qc.ca/evenement/peuple-de-loeil).

27 Created in 1864, Gallaudet is the only higher education institution in the world to cater to Deaf and hard of hearing individuals and where the language of instruction is ASL. In the interviews we conducted in the context of *La*

musique au bout des doigts (Music at the Fingertips) project, some of the Deaf signers who expressed the strongest attachment to music, in its various modalities, had attended Gallaudet, where they were introduced to music with signed language.

28 Witcher's early work is analyzed in Cripps (2016) and Cripps et al. (2017). Although it was not mentioned during the workshop, Véro, Daz, and Hodan have been creating signed music. Together with Pamela Witcher, they conducted a research-creation, including workshops, to explore signed music. Their creations were initially presented in 2018 at the symposium Vibe: Confronting Audism and Ableism through the Arts. They share their thoughts on the process and on Deaf music more generally in Leduc et al. (2021).

29 We follow cultural studies scholar Lawrence Grossberg's (1992) concept of effectivity, which "describes an event's place in a complex network of effects—its effects elsewhere on other events, as well as their effects on it; it describes the possibilities of the practice for effectuating changes or differences in the world" (50).

30 Socially regarded as disabled people, Deaf people usually define themselves as a cultural and linguistic minority.

References

Aden, Roger C., Min Wha Han, Stephanie Norander, Michael E. Pfahl, Timothy P. Pollock Jr., and Stephanie L. Young. 2009. "Re-Collection: A Proposal for Refining the Study of Collective Memory and Its Places." *Communication Theory,* 19(3): 311–36.

Ahmed, Sara. 2006a. "Orientations: Toward a Queer Phenomenology." *GLQ: A Journal of Lesbian and Gay Studies,* 12(4): 543–74.

Ahmed, Sara. 2006b. *Queer Phenomenology: Orientations, Objects, Others.* Durham, NC: Duke University Press.

Ahmed, Sara. 2010. "Orientations Matter." In Diana H. Coole and Samantha Frost (eds.), *New Materialisms: Ontology, Agency, and Politics,* 234–57. Durham, NC: Duke University Press.

Allor, Michael. 1997. "Locating Cultural Activity: The 'Main' as Chronotope and Heterotopia." *TOPIA: Canadian Journal of Cultural Studies,* 1(1): 42–54.

Andrews, Gavin J., and Viv Wilson. 2020. "Sensing Health and Wellbeing through Oral Histories: The 'Tip and Run' Air Attacks on a British Coastal Town, 1939–1944." In Sarah Atkinson and Rachel Hunt (eds.), *GeoHumanities and Health,* 23–38. Cham, Switzerland: Springer.

Au, Agnes, Jeremy Marozeau, Hamish Innes-Brown, Emery Schubert, and Catherine J. Stevens. 2012. "Music for the Cochlear Implant: Audience Response to Six Commissioned Compositions." Abstract. *Seminars in Hearing,* 33(4): 335–45.

Bahan, Ben. 2006. "Face-to-Face Tradition in the American Deaf Community: Dynamics of the Teller, the Tale, and the Audience." In

H.-Dirksen L. Bauman, Jennifer L. Nelson, and Heidi M. Rose (eds.), *Signing the Body Poetic: Essays on American Sign Language Literature*, 21–50. Oakland: University of California Press.

Balkmar, Dag. 2012. *On Men and Cars: An Ethnographic Study of Gendered, Risky and Dangerous Relations*. Linköping, Sweden: Linköping University.

Banks, Jack. 1997. "Video in the Machine: The Incorporation of Music Video into the Recording Industry." *Popular Music,* 16(3): 293–309.

Bell, Jonathan. 2001. *Carchitecture: When the Car and the City Collide*. London: August.

Best, Katelyn E. 2023. "Ethnocentrism 2.0: The Impact of Hearing-Centrism on Musical Expression in Deaf Culture." In Brenda Romero, Susan Asai, David McDonald, Andrew Snyder, and Katelyn E. Best (eds.), *At the Crossroads of Music and Social Justice*. Bloomington: Indiana University Press.

Bissonnette, Joëlle. 2020. "Devenir entrepreneur culturel en contextes sociaux marginaux: tensions et pratiques d'agencement chez les entrepreneurs musicaux en situation linguistique minoritaire." PhD diss., HEC Montréal, Université de Montréal.

Bourdieu, Pierre, and Claude Passeron. 1970. *La reproduction*. Paris: Minuit.

Burnett, Judith. 2010. *Generations: The Time Machine in Theory and Practice*. Surrey: Ashgate.

Churchill, Warren N. 2015. "Deaf and Hard-of-Hearing Musicians: Crafting a Narrative Strategy." *Research Studies in Music Education,* 37(1): 21–36.

Cripps, Jody H. 2016. *Signed Music: A Symphonious Odyssey* [Documentary]. Towson, MD: A Cripps Production. https://www.youtube.com/watch?v=2JjFCM8UZHM.

Cripps, Jody H., and Ely Lyonblum. 2017. "Understanding Signed Music." *Society for American Sign Language Journal (SASLJ),* 1(1): 78–96.

Cripps, Jody H., Ely Rosenblum, and Anita Small. 2015a. "Music, Signed." In Genie Gertz and Patrick Boudreault (eds.), *The Sage Deaf Studies Encyclopedia*, 702–5. Thousand Oaks, CA: Sage.

Cripps, Jody H., Ely Rosenblum, and Anita Small. 2015b. "Signed Music: An Emerging Inter-Performative Art." *MIT's Performance Art*. https://www.academia.edu/33721421/Signed_Music_An_Emerging_Inter-performative_Art.

Cripps, Jody H., Ely Rosenblum, Anita Small, and Samuel J. Supalla. 2017. "A Case Study on Signed Music: The Emergence of an Inter-performance Art." *Liminalities: A Journal of Performance Studies,* 13(2): 1–25.

Darrow, Alice-Ann, and George N. Heller. 1985. "Early Advocates of Music Education for the Hearing Impaired: William Wolcott Turner and David Ely Bartlett." *Journal of Research in Music Education,* 33(4): 269–79.

Derrida, Jacques. 1994. *Specters of Marx: The State of the Debt, the Work of Mourning, and the New International*. Translated by Peggy Kamuf. New York: Routledge.

Despeyroux, Charly. 2017. "Les pratiques artistiques dans le théâtre musical bilingue français/langue des Signes: enjeux et techniques." Master en arts de la scène et du spectacle vivant, Université Toulouse Jean Jaurès.

Duffett, Mark. 2020. "Introduction." In Mark Duffett and Beate Peter (eds.), *Popular Music and Automobiles*, 1–14. London: Bloomsbury Academic.

Eidsheim, Nina S. 2015. *Sensing Sound: Singing and Listening as Vibrational Practice*. Durham, NC: Duke University Press.

Forman, Murray. 2002. *The 'Hood Comes First: Race, Space, and Place in Rap and Hip-Hop*. Middletown, CT: Wesleyan University Press.

Frith, Simon. 1988. *Music for Pleasure: Essays in the Sociology of Pop*. New York: Routledge.

Garland-Thomson, Rosemarie. 2011. "Misfits: A Feminist Materialist Disability Concept." *Hypatia*, 26(3): 591–609.

Garland-Thomson, Rosemarie. 2019. "Misfitting." In Gail Weiss, Ann V. Murphy, and Gayle Salamon (eds.), *50 Concepts for a Critical Phenomenology*, 225–30. Evanston, IL: Northwestern University Press.

Garro, Diego. 2012. "From Sonic Art to Visual Music: Divergences, Convergences, Intersections." *Organised Sound*, 17(2): 103–13.

Gaucher, Charles. 2009. *Ma culture, c'est les mains. La quête identitaire des sourds au Québec*. Québec: Presses de l'Université Laval.

Glennie. Evelyn. 2003. "How to Truly Listen." TED2003. https://www.ted.com/talks/evelyn_glennie_how_to_truly_listen#t-453457.

Grenier, Line. 1993. "The Aftermath of a Crisis: Quebec Music Industries in the 1980s." *Popular Music*, 12(3): 209–27.

Grenier, Line. 1997. "'Je me souviens' … en chansons: articulations de la citoyenneté culturelle et de l'identitaire dans le champ musical au Québec." *Sociologie et sociétés*, 29(2): 31–47.

Grenier, Line, and Fannie Valois-Nadeau. 2020. "Introduction: Thinking Memory *with* Ageing, and Ageing *with* Memory." In Line Grenier and Fannie Valois-Nadeau (eds.), *A Senior Moment: Cultural Mediations of Memory and Ageing*, 7–32. Bielefeld, Germany: Transcript Verlag.

Grossberg, Lawrence. 1992. *We Gotta Get Out of This Place: Popular Conservatism and Postmodern Culture*. New York: Routledge.

Gullette, Margaret M. 2004. *Aged by Culture*. Chicago: University of Chicago Press.

Gullette, Margaret M. 2011. *Agewise: Fighting the New Ageism in America*. Chicago: University of Chicago Press.

Hall, Stuart. 1996. "Introduction: Who Needs 'Identity'?" In Stuart Hall and Paul du Gay (eds.), *Questions of Cultural Identity*, 1–17. London: Sage.

Hennion, Antoine. 2017. "Attachments, You Say? … How a Concept Collectively Emerges in One Research Group." *Journal of Cultural Economy*, 10(1): 112–21.

Herman, David. 2010. "Storyworld." In David Herman, Manfred Jahn, and Marie-Laure Ryan (eds.), *Routledge Encyclopedia of Narrative Theory*, 569–70. New York: Routledge.

Holmes, Jessica A. 2017. "Expert Listening beyond the Limits of Hearing: Music and Deafness." *Journal of the American Musicological Society*, 70(1): 171–81.

Humphries, Tom. 1977. "Communicating across Cultures (Deaf/Hearing) and Language Learning." PhD diss., Union Institute & University, Cincinnati, OH.

Hyltén-Cavallius, Sverker. 2012. "Memoryscapes and Mediascapes: Musical Formations of 'Pensioners' in Late 20th-Century Sweden." *Popular Music*, 31(Special Issue 2): 279–95.

Jankowski, Katherine. 1997. *Deaf Empowerment: Emergence, Struggle and Rhetoric*. Washington, DC: Gallaudet University Press.

Kaiser, Marc, and Michael Spanu. 2018. "'On n'écoute que des clips!' Penser la mise en tension médiatique de la musique à l'image." *Volume! La revue des musiques populaires,* 14(2): 7–20.

Kim, Christine S. 2015. *The Enchanting Music of Sign Language* [TED talk]. https://www.youtube.com/watch?v=2Euof4PnjDk.

Klima, Edward S., and Ursula Bellugi. 1976. "Poetry and Song in a Language without Sound." *Cognition,* 4(1): 45–97.

Ladd, Paddy. 2003. *Understanding Deaf Culture: In Search of Deafhood*. Bristol: Multilingual Matters.

Leduc, Véro. 2016. *C'est tombé dans l'oreille d'une Sourde. La sourditude par la bande dessignée*. Thèse de doctorat inédite, Université de Montréal.

Leduc, Véro, Daz Saunders, Hodan Youssouf, and Pamela Witcher. 2021a. "Nos mains qui vibrent. Un texte à huit mains sur une recherche-création en musiques sourdes." *Canadian Journal of Disability Studies* https://cjds.uwaterloo.ca/index.php/cjds/article/view/792/1019.

Lezotte, Chris. 2013. "Born to Take the Highway: Women, the Automobile, and Rock 'n' Roll." *Journal of American Culture,* 36(3): 161–76.

Loeffler, Summer. 2014. "Deaf Music: Embodying Language and Rhythm." In H.-Dirksen L. Bauman and Joseph J. Murray (eds.), *Deaf Gain: Raising the Stakes in Human Diversity,* 436–56. Minneapolis: University of Minnesota Press.

Lumsden, Karen. 2010. "Gendered Performances in a Male-Dominated Subculture: 'Girl Racers,' Car Modification and the Quest for Masculinity." *Sociological Research Online,* 15(3): 75–85.

Maler, Annabel. 2016. "Musical Expression among Deaf and Hearing Song Signers." In Blake Howe, Stephanie Jensen-Moulton, Neil W. Lerner, and Joseph N. Straus (eds.), *The Oxford Handbook of Music and Disability Studies,* 73–91. Oxford: Oxford University Press.

Marsh, Charity. 2012. "Bits and Pieces of Truth: Storytelling, Identity, and Hip Hop in Saskatchewan." In Anna Hoefnagels and Beverley Diamond (eds.), *Aboriginal Music in Contemporary Canada: Echoes and Exchanges,* 346–71. Montreal: McGill-Queen's University Press.

McRobbie, Angela. 1991. *Feminism and Youth Culture: From* Jackie *to* Just Seventeen. London: Macmillan Education UK.

Mehdi. 2011. "Interview Rimcash et Didai." Abcdrduson. July 15.

Milestone, Katie. 2020. "The Passenger? Gender, Cars, Mobility and Dance Music." In Mark Duffett and Beate Peter (eds.), *Popular Music and Automobiles,* 71–82. London: Bloomsbury Academic.

Montreal Oral School for the Deaf (MOSD). 2015. "History." https://montrealoralschool.com/about/history/.

Olick, Jeffrey K., and Joyce Robbins. 1998. "Social Memory Studies: From 'Collective Memory' to the Historical Sociology of Mnemonic Practices." *Annual Review of Sociology,* 24: 105–40.

Oralism and the Deaf Community. n.d. "What Is Oralism?" https://oralismandthedeafcommunity.weebly.com/what-is-oralism.html.

Padden, Carol, and Tom Humphries. 2005. *Inside Deaf Culture*. Cambridge, MA: Harvard University Press.

Paquette, Lorie. 2019. "Pourquoi apprend-on encore la flûte à bec? Lettre ouverte d'une enseignante de musique au primaire." *Urbania*. February 25. https://urbania.ca/article/pourquoi-apprend-encore-la-flute-bec.

Schmitt, Pierre. 2012. "De la musique et des sourds. Approche ethnographique du rapport à la musique de jeunes sourds européens." In Talia Bachir-Loopuyt, Sara Iglesias, Anna Langenbruch, and Gesa zur Nieden (eds.), *Musik, Kontext, Wissenschaft: Interdisziplinäre Forschung zu Musik / Musiques—contextes—savoirs: perspectives interdisciplinaires sur la musique*, 221–34. Frankfurt am Main, Germany: Peter Lang.

Schmitt, Pierre. 2016. "Sourds et interprètes dans les arts et médias: mises en scène contemporaines de la langue des signes." *Glottopol: Revue de sociolinguistique en ligne*, 27: 13.

Sheller, Mimi. 2004. "Automotive Emotions: Feeling the Car." *Theory, Culture & Society*, 21(4–5): 221–42.

Sirvage, Robert T. 2016. "Deaf_Space." In *The SAGE Deaf Studies Encyclopedia*, edited by Genie Gertz and Patrick Boudreault, 292–5. London: Sage Publications

Small, Christopher. 1998. *Musicking: The Meanings of Performing and Listening*. Middletown, CT: Wesleyan University Press.

Solomon, Alan L. 1980. "Music in Special Education before 1930: Hearing and Speech Development." *Journal of Research in Music Education*, 28: 45–47.

Straus, Joseph N. 2011. *Extraordinary Measures: Disability in Music*. Oxford: Oxford University Press.

Turner, William W., and David E. Bartlett. 1848. "Music among the Deaf and Dumb." *American Annals of the Deaf and Dumb*, 2(1).

Urry, John. 2004. "The 'System' of Automobility." *Theory, Culture & Society*, 21(4–5): 25–39.

Walsh, Margaret. 2008. "Gendering Mobility: Women, Work and Automobility in the United States." *History*, 93(3): 376–95.

Young, Iris M. 2015. "Five Faces of Oppression." In S. N. Asumah and M. Nagel (eds.), *Diversity, Social Justice, and Inclusive Excellence: Transdiciplinary and Global Perspectives*, 3–35. New York: State University of New York Press.

Young, Katharine G. 1987. *Taleworlds and Storyrealms: The Phenomenology of Narratives*. Dordrecht: University of Martinus Nijhoff.

Zelizer, Barbie. 1995. "Reading the Past against the Grain: The Shape of Memory Studies." *Critical Studies in Mass Communication*, 12(2): 214–39.

8

Sharing and Reflecting on Inheritance Tracks: Some Afterthoughts

Murray Forman

Music shapes us and fundamentally changes us. Once we have listened we do not stop. We do not ever recover from music.
(Rickie Lee Jones 2021: xii)

Sharing

This is a book about sharing. Its conceptualization was born from an awareness that music carries across time and between people in varied and unique ways and that individual and collective meanings, values, legacies, and identities can be nurtured and conveyed through processes of musical exchange. It is also a book about memory and the resonant character of music as a mnemonic apparatus that facilitates the conjuring of the self that are, in turn, introduced and offered up to others.[1]

These themes, among others that permeate the narratives and analyses throughout the book, extend the study of age and aging and the dynamics between music and memory that has accelerated in the past decade. Indeed, there is a familiar resonance in several instances with earlier findings from my own research forays (Forman 2012) among older men and women living in "seniors residences" and "nursing homes" (complicated terminology to be sure but also common in North America). In my previous ethnographic study, I witnessed institutional forces at work that both facilitated and inhibited social interaction and the casual exchange of music such as that which is recounted in these chapters. Then, as now, it was amply clear that people love to talk about the music they love, and the tunes they hold closest are often formative and foundational components of their individual identities. Since then, the theoretical sophistication in the study of age and aging has evolved considerably, and with a broad array of research methods at hand, scholarship in this field exhibits intensified rigor and, as a result, throws new light onto the processes of everyday musical reception and its attendant meanings.

The underlying concepts of the book—inheritance and bequeathal—are certainly examples of sharing (handing down, passing on, and similar terms of exchange), yet in social and legal contexts, they are also easily associated with life and death, which do permeate many of the chapters herein. The discourse of "inheritance" evokes the issue of late life and generational conferral in a manner that different terms may not, and, thus, there is an inherent potential for sadness and lament associated with loss and departure of loved ones. Despite this, however, the acts of memory, song selection, and narrative testimonial on display here combine as pronounced articulations of vitality, expressions of sustained resonance across time and throughout the life course.

Troubling Inheritances was, from the beginning, imagined as a collaborative project focused on sharing songs and stories about their relevance in peoples' lives. Throughout its nascent phase, the project was oriented toward notions of "multi-modal connectivities ... across multiple differences,"[2] with the authors physically convening (in the pre-pandemic era) to discuss objectives, exchange research strategies, and explore various means of motivating musical memories that, in turn, bubbled in rich and illuminating dialogue. In those early conversations, the Inheritance Tracks model[3] was explicitly addressed as a research methodology, a mechanism through which to engage individuals from a range of international and social backgrounds and to get them listening, remembering, and talking about their lived experiences with music. It was immediately clear to all involved that *people age with music* just as they *age with memory* (Grenier and Valois-Nadeau 2020); the global cohort of project authors and participants reinforced this over and over, indicating that the phenomenon of musical remembering occurs throughout the world in ways that are impressively similar. As the project took shape, the initial conversations were themselves steeped in considered reflection as the authors shared their own memories about the music that was—and remains—most significant to them. The sharing, it would seem, began immediately.

Among the central themes of *Troubling Inheritances* is the issue of "ageing with music" and the interrelated aspects of age, memory, and identity. Delineating the contours of critical age studies, Stephen Katz, a pioneer in the field, explains:

> Research requires careful observation and participation, discourse analysis, qualitative interviews, deconstruction of images and texts, and close attention to the ordinary. Narrative is particularly important because it anchors the inside of aging, bringing together self and society and animating our biographies as we borrow, adapt, interpret, and reinvent the languages, symbols, and meanings around us to customize our personal stories (2014: 20)

As this suggests, people are storytellers; this is a key facet in the construction of human relations, and it is also how we make sense of ourselves in the social realm, talking our identities into the world and articulating the tones and timbres of existence.

Music comprises a powerful ingredient in the shaping of the self, providing reference points that others can identify and serving as information that others can, in turn, identify with. As Katz indicates, it is essential to pay particular attention to the terms and references and the operative discourses that are narratively generated, in this case by the workshop participants, for it is through their narrative expression that musical experience and recollection are rendered comprehensible and made socially meaningful. Lawrence Grossberg, however, adds an additional aspect to the expression of selfhood and experience, noting how songs deemed somehow important or meaningful to oneself can also function in an assistive role in the articulation of identity: "By making certain things or practices matter, the fan 'authorizes' them to speak for him or her, not only as a spokesperson but also as surrogate voices (as when we sing along to popular songs)" (Grossberg 1992: 59).

There are, as one might expect, musical absences here, which is also an indication of certain priorities that can exceed the musical discussions themselves. While rock and pop music (encompassing such genres as disco, which was also discussed by participants) are very well represented, along with classical music, folk tunes, calypso, and soca, several other prominent musical genres go entirely unmentioned; rap music is not present in the narratives here, nor are funk and soul music; R&B and reggae were mentioned indirectly. Less surprising is the absence of jazz and its various subgenres (hard bop/post-bop, fusion, smooth jazz, free jazz, etc.) or more abstract forms of experimental composition. The discussions herein are not always or even necessarily about music per se, even as they coincide with aspects of music, age, memory, and identity. The privileging of certain discourses over others reveals much about the ideological values that inform the subjective self, including social dynamics and familial relations, and that correspondingly inflect one's status within larger frames of cultural experience.

Embodiment and Location

As the chapters in this book make abundantly clear, there is no single modality or determining factor guiding the apprehension of music in everyday life. Music, in its plural forms and genres, enters one's sensibilities within multiple social contexts, merging with mundane routines and patterns and interweaving with quotidian social rhythms. Several chapters here discuss this in relation to Tia DeNora's analysis of "music in everyday life" (2000) or Christopher Small's (1998) concept of "musicking," which, in its active verb construction, encompasses a range of practices that simultaneously refute the authority of the music as a composed "piece" or a "work" while emphasizing the varied ways in which people interact with the music they encounter. The participants explain their thoughtful reflections about the music they love, describing their lifelong musical experiences in the situational contexts of work and leisure, days and nights, and solo and social musical engagement. Importantly, their vibrant testimonies are frequently communicated while *grooving* to the music they selected: humming, singing, toe-tapping, and dancing. "Groove" is itself a multifaceted term, and the embodied response to musical feeling can be merged with the emplacement of the affective self whereby one is situated "in the groove," immersed in and encompassed by the music in all its emotional swirl.

This physical, embodied mode of experiencing music is of crucial importance, revealing how deeply entwined music is with the corporeal expression of existence, whether in elaborate gestural flourishes and robust laughter among the group or more minutely pitched responses, registered in a subtle nod of the head and a gentle smile that may indicate recall and familiarity, individual pleasures, or some unprofessed intimacy. The participants are described sitting (in most cases) and experiencing the tracks, but they displayed other physical dispositions too ("eyes closed," "swaying," "dancing," "singing along," "tearing up," etc.), highlighting the embeddedness of being in the moment even as the tracks from their past are recalled and reintroduced in the company of others. In some cases, participants explicitly stated that their musical selections had been resounding for a lifetime, with the accompanying suggestion that while the music may be emotionally moving, they were also quite literally *moved* at the level of synapse, sinew, and muscle for much of their lives. And while age may affect the physical comportment of the human subject, the enduring capacity to adjust and maintain an embodied relationship to the music cannot be ignored.

There are, in the accumulated reminiscences among the workshop participants, other kinds of physicality that emerge quite profoundly. This can be discerned, for instance, within the situated design of the workshops whereby participants were positioned adjacent to one another in close physical proximity, easily allowing for shared glances and gestures and the expression of mirth or melancholy as they discussed their selected tracks. In these circumstances, music's undeniable communality is on full display, and the circle of shared experience is wound tighter.

The chapters also describe locations of bodies in relation to technological components—the mediating audio speakers and computer screens of the listening sessions, each with their own inherent histories (van Dijck 2009)—and in a narrative mode, the thresholds, borders, landscapes, and territories that inform the evolution of the social subject. If, in a temporal sense, we might identify music in relation to rites of passage—a dimension in the processes of individual *becoming*—in a spatial sense the music can facilitate one's mobile passages, providing a sense of stability as they navigate through the physical world, relocating in unfamiliar realms.

Tracks associated with radio broadcasts heard in a car or songs experienced live at the local pub, club, or concert space arise frequently, with each musical context positioning the social subject some*place* that constitutes a sonic environment. The book's impressive scope encompasses the experiences of music of Deaf subjects, which include engaging sensually through "vibrations" (summoning notions of what, in 1966, the Beach Boys famously called "good vibrations" or what Bob Marley referred to a decade later as "positive vibrations") emanating from a nearby speaker or sound system. With their specific orientation toward music as concatenation of sound or vibration and as a social connector, however, the inheritance workshops do not seem to accommodate the possibility of inheriting or bequeathing silence and quietude. While John Cage's 4'33" might be a viable—if unlikely—inclusion in this regard, the fact remains that subsonic, inaudible tones or simple silence was not a consideration among participants as an adjunct or remedy for the cacophony and hurly-burly of the social environment.

The matter of physical positioning also crucially involves the "home," whether articulated in reference to an actually existing domicile (at times evoked with a whiff of wistful nostalgia) or symbolically as an ideological construct. Participant reflections abound of songs heard as a child, sung softly in the home by a nurturing parent, or heard in the comfort of a kitchen or salon with the family arrayed around a radio's "ethereal hearth" (Czitrom 1982) or a small phonograph. The technological circumstances of musical apprehension emerge as they introduce factors such as volume or sound quality that influenced the musical experience and memory, acknowledging in some passages that the musical technologies that are most fondly remembered are either no longer extant or grievously outdated. In these instances, it is often not an individual song rendition or track that spurs memory, initiating reminiscence and perhaps nostalgia, but recall of the contextual conditions of the track's acquisition and reception as well as other sensory cues that correspond with the sonic event. This realization invites us to rethink the primacy of the music itself and, rather, to more closely interrogate the ways in which music is interwoven with myriad experiential factors that buffet or caress the subjective soul.

The discussion of borders that frequently arises in the narratives adds a further geo-cultural element to the analysis. This is especially noteworthy in view of how some music is inexorably aligned with the narrowed contours of cultural formations or national identities (e.g., folk music or highly idiosyncratic national music genres, such as Trinidadian calypso and soca, which might be conceived as the music from "home" in the contexts of diaspora and displacement), whereas some musical tracks (pop music in its various generic forms) resonate more widely across cultural "scapes" (Appadurai 1990), unanchored and widely circulating through global systems of technological diffusion, corporate industrial networks, and physical transport via tourism and international travel. In a world seemingly pushing toward ever more remote and virtual experiences, inclined to incessant mobility and characterized by an apparent diminishment of spatial significance, the participants' emphasis on locations and sited musical engagement is a notable rejoinder, articulating the perspective that, in fact, place (still) matters.

Affect and Aging with Music

The facets of musical reception and "aging with music" correspond with the issue of affect, a concept that is traced across the participants' reminiscences, emerging palpably in the workshop discussions while also being explicitly embraced in the authors' analyses. Within a broader theoretical frame, affect is conceived "as an intensity that variously energizes, contradicts, deconstructs, and overwhelms the narratives through which we live," not as a thing and not simply as emotion but "as momentum and force" (White 2017; 178) that is measured in "intensity" (Massumi 1995; Zournazi and Massumi 2015). As the participants gathered together to share their musical selections, inherited and bequeathed, it might be regarded as a harnessing of energies that occurred within a collectivity of individual subjects. The accumulated affective intensity within the context of the workshops was given free rein to roam, ooze, or erupt according to the impetus of the group dynamic.

As one of the first scholars to focus on popular music's affective capacities, Lawrence Grossberg writes, "Affect is closely tied to what we often describe as the feeling of life. ... Affect is what gives 'color,' 'tone' or 'texture' to our experiences" (1992: 56–7). He argues that affective intensities are structured within differences that are registered across a panoply of lived practices, distilling the dynamic to the relatively simple equation, "some things feel different from others, some matter more, or in different ways, than others" (Grossberg 1992: 56).

The song tracks described here serve as mnemonic catalysts among the participants. They spur reactions, fomenting an outpouring of affect and discourse that merges remembered pasts with present dialogue, bridging temporal distances and social differences.

Individuals harbor their own inner feelings toward music, processing what it might mean to them, sometimes over decades. What seems less certain in these chapters is a prior certainty about how bringing the affective sensibilities into language and discourse might resonate, both in terms of how others might react to the tracks they have identified and how they themselves might respond in a particular moment or context. There is no guarantee that how one once reacted and interacted with any given song in the past will occur again with any predictability. In the accounts captured here, there are numerous instances where the telling of the tale—explaining the rationale for playing this track or that, in public and among a group of strangers—is a tentative act. This involves an emotional translation, a framing of affect that exceeds easy expression. This process might be explained as being prone to a kind of latency, an affect-in-waiting, whereby the force of affective intensity is simultaneously untethered by the sonic encounter with the musical tracks within the group listening context and remobilized by the subsequent narrative articulation.

There are in these pages numerous examples of musical "tracks" having entered peoples' lives with transformative impact, comprising what might be defined as "wow!" moments wherein the soundtrack converges with some monumental life event in a manner that fuses the music to the event in memory *forever*. The events' significance is deeply engrained: where one was, who they were with, what they were doing, and what music played. The seeming banality of music in everyday life can be deceptive, and we may not fully realize the deeper implications of a song in the moment, but over time and upon further reflection, as we age with the music, we might gain a new appreciation for its relevance to our sense of self and others.

The participants cited in these pages remind us that music constitutes a crucial but often imperceptible force that binds and connects people within families, across social networks, and, more broadly, to the more ambiguous and arguably more fraught strands of nation and culture. For all the commonalities that can be perceived among participants from varied backgrounds, however, the language and expressive terms about musical reminiscence also offer important insights about reverberating differences, revealing nuanced distinctions within the broader ideological forms of knowledge and the construction of meaning and value. We know from experience that, while music can create a binding force, it is also often provocative and can be a source of pointed conflict about, for example, genre and taste preferences, perceived aesthetic quality, and tone and volume, among other things (Washburne and Derno 2004; Trotta 2020). Music harbors the potential for affective eruption and disruption, something that also occasionally seeps through the memories and narratives here. Participants and the authors-cum-session facilitators frequently address the ways in which particular songs had, in the past, presented disruptive influences in their lives, upending their sensibilities, altering attitudes and emotions, and providing grounds for new ways of apprehending the world in full, for better and perhaps for worse.

The listening circles adhered to a prevailing sense of civility and politesse, with the participants' remarks reflecting a rather consistent social propriety of acceptance—or, at least, tolerance—of the selections of others. Yet as history has shown, music can be grounds for heated dispute. While in these inheritance sessions, there were apparently no outright quarrels about the songs' meanings or values, about the aesthetics and perceived social relevance of a given track or artist, we know that differences in musical taste and related cultural inflections can be the source of marked *dis*unity. This is commonly cited in cases where, for example, intergenerational music preferences collide and generational dissonance ensues (something addressed by Andy Bennett [2013] in his study among aging hippies, punks, and dance music aficionados and that I have witnessed as well in my own research among intergenerational hip-hop fans). It is also true that music can catalyze memories that are measured in extremes (relating, e.g., to corrosive pain, inordinate fear, or deeply damaging shame, among many other possible dispositions). Music can, thus, be aligned with unspeakable horrors that, in turn, portend unforeseen emotional responses in individuals; some things can barely be imagined, let alone uttered or narrativized. That such narratives do not appear here does not necessarily mean that these extremes are absent among the participants.

Ultimately, *Troubling Inheritances* illustrates the numerous ways that music is retained in our lives through memory, carried with us and in us (in this sense, everyone can "carry a tune") over the years even as it carries us over undulating and sometimes difficult social terrain. And while the scholarly, analytical rigor in these pages is apparent throughout, it is important not to lose track of the pure fun in the inheritance model, acknowledging the many insights and pleasures that accrue when individuals gather to share the music they care about and to tell the stories of why.

Notes

1 As Tia DeNora writes, "[M]usic comes to the fore, as part of the retinue of devices for memory retrieval (which is, simultaneously, memory construction). Music can be used as a device for the reflexive processes of remembering/

constructing who one is, a technology for spinning the apparently continuous tale of who one is" (2006: 141).

2 The term "multi-modal connectivities" was introduced by Ros Jennings at the ACT Music Working Group's "Symposium on Popular Music and Ageing," Brunel University, October 30, 2018.

3 It would be remiss to underplay the catalytic impetus of BBC Radio's Inheritance Tracks segments aired on BBC Radio 4. Most of the authors featured here live in countries where publicly funded national radio networks (under political, economic, and technological duress) serve a crucial role in informing the population about news and events while, in the language of the Canadian Broadcasting Corporation/Radio Canada mandate, "actively contribut[ing] to the flow and exchange of cultural expression" (https://cbc.radio-canada.ca/en/vision/mandate). The BBC's stated mission is "to act in the public interest, serving all audiences through the provision of impartial, high-quality and distinctive output and services which inform, educate and entertain" (https://www.bbc.com/aboutthebbc/governance/mission).

References

Appadurai, Arjun. 1990. "Disjuncture and Difference in the Global Cultural Economy." *Theory, Culture & Society*, 7: 295–310.
Bennett, Andy. 2013. *Music, Style and Aging: Growing Old Disgracefully?* Philadelphia: Temple University Press.
Czitrom, Daniel J. 1982. *Media and the American Mind: From Morse to McLuhan.* Chapel Hill: University of North Carolina Press.
DeNora, Tia. 2000. *Music in Everyday Life*. Cambridge: Cambridge University Press.
DeNora, Tia. 2006. "Music and Self-Identity." In Andy Bennett, Barry Shank, and Jason Toynbee (eds.), *The Popular Music Studies Reader*, 141–7. New York: Routledge.
Forman, Murray. 2012. "How We Feel the Music: Popular Music by Elders and for Elders." *Popular Music*, 31(2): 245–60.
Grenier, Line and Fannie F. Valois-Nadeau (eds.). 2020. "Introduction: Thinking Memory *with* Ageing, and Ageing *with* Memory." In Line Grenier and Fannie Valois-Nadeau (eds.), *A Senior Moment: Cultural Mediations of Memory and Ageing*, 7–32. Bielefeld, Germany: Transcript Verlag.
Grossberg, Lawrence. 1992. "Is There a Fan in the House? The Affective Sensibility of Fandom." In Lisa A. Lewis (ed.), *The Adoring Audience: Fan Culture and Popular Media*, 50–67. New York: Routledge.
Jones, Rickie L. 2021. *Last Chance Texaco: Chronicles of an American Troubadour*. New York: Grove Press.
Katz, Stephen. 2014. "What Is Age Studies?" *Age, Culture, Humanities* (1): 17–23.
Massumi, Brian. 1995. "The Autonomy of Affect." *Cultural Critique*, 31 (Autumn): 83–109.

Small, Christopher. 1998. *Musicking: The Meanings of Performing and Listening.* Middletown, CT: Wesleyan University Press.

Trotta, Felipe. 2020. *Annoying Music in Everyday Life.* New York: Bloomsbury.

Van Dijck, José. 2009. "Remembering Songs through Telling Stories: Pop Music as a Resource for Memory." In Karen Bijsterveld and José van Dijck (eds.), *Sound Souvenirs: Audio Technologies, Memory and Cultural Practices,* 107–19. Amsterdam: Amsterdam University Press.

Washburne, Christopher, and Maiken Derno (eds.). 2004. *Bad Music: The Music We Love to Hate.* New York: Routledge.

White, Daniel. 2017. "Affect: An Introduction." *Cultural Anthropology,* 32(2): 175–80.

Zournazi, Mary, and Brian Massumi. 2015. "Navigating Movements." In Brian Massumi (ed.), *Politics of Affect,* 1–46. Malden, MA: Polity.

AUTHOR AND CONTRIBUTOR INFORMATION

Andy Bennett is Professor of Cultural Sociology in the School of Humanities, Languages and Social Science at Griffith University, Australia. He has written and edited numerous books including *Popular Music and Youth Culture* (2000), *Music, Style and Aging* (2013), *British Progressive Pop 1970–1980* (2020), and *Music Scenes* (2004, co-edited with Richard A. Peterson). He is a Faculty Fellow of the Yale Center for Cultural Sociology, an International Research Fellow of the Finnish Youth Research Network, a founding member of the Consortium for Youth, Generations and Culture, and a founding member of the Regional Music Research Group.

Sara Cohen is Professor at the University of Liverpool, UK, where she holds the James and Constance Alsop Chair in Music and is Director of the Institute of Popular Music. She has a DPhil in Social Anthropology from Oxford University and is author of *Rock Culture in Liverpool* (1991), *Decline, Renewal and the City in Popular Music Culture* (2007), *Harmonious Relations* (coauthored with Kevin McManus, 1994), and *Liverpool's Musical Landscapes* (coauthored with Robert Kronenburg, 2018) and coeditor of *Sites of Popular Music Heritage* (2014). She specializes in interdisciplinary research on popular music, with a particular interest in ethnographic approaches and research on place, heritage, memory, and aging.

Murray Forman is Professor of Media and Screen Studies at Northeastern University. He is the author of *The 'Hood Comes First: Race, Space and Place in Rap and Hip-Hop* (2002) and *One Night on TV Is Worth Weeks at the Paramount: Popular Music on Early Television* (2012). He is also co-editor (with Mark Anthony Neal) of *That's the Joint! The Hip-Hop Studies Reader* (1st ed., 2004; 2nd ed., 2011). In 2003–4, he was awarded a U.S. National Endowment for the Humanities Fellowship, and he was an inaugural recipient of the Nasir Jones Hip-Hop Fellowship at the Hutchins Center for African and African American Research, Harvard University (2014–15).

Abigail Gardner is Reader in Music and Media at the University of Gloucestershire, UK. She writes on music, gender, and aging and produces community film and media. Key publications include *Ageing and Contemporary Female Musicians* (2020), *Aging and Popular Music in Europe* (2020), *PJ Harvey and Music Video Performance* (2015), and *Rock On: Women, Ageing and Popular Music* (2012). She has led Erasmus+ projects on digital storytelling, media literacy, and music and migration, as well as running digital storytelling projects with Age UK and public sector organizations.

Line Grenier is Professor at the Département de communication at Université de Montréal in Montréal, Québec (Canada), where she teaches predominantly in the areas of media theory, memory and media, and popular culture. Her work on the history and politics of local music and music industries, the Céline Dion phenomenon and the figures of fame it embodies, and the business and politics of live music, has been published in several journals, including *Popular Music, Cultural Studies, Recherches féministes, Ethnomusicology, Recherches sociographiques,* and *Musicultures*. More recently, in the context of the research partnership Ageing + Communication + Technology (ACT) funded by the Social Sciences and Humanities Research Council of Canada, and of which she is one of the cofounders, her research focuses on intersections of aging and music. Her current project focuses on Deaf cultures of aging and deaf musics.

Jocelyne Guilbault is Professor of Ethnomusicology at the University of California, Berkeley, United States. Her work is concerned with power relations, global industrialization, labor practices, politics of aesthetics, and work ethics in Caribbean popular musics. Stressing a multidisciplinary approach, she addresses these issues in the scholarly intersections of music, anthropology, cultural studies, and history. Her research in Saint Lucia, Martinique, Guadeloupe, Dominica, and Trinidad is reported in articles and in *Zouk: World Music in the West Indies* (1993), *Governing Sound: The Cultural Politics of Trinidad's Carnival Musics* (2007), and *Roy Cape: A Life on the Calypso and Soca Bandstand* (2014, coauthored with Roy Cape). Her latest project, co-edited with Timothy Rommen, is titled *Sounds of Vacation: Political Economies of Caribbean Tourism* (2019).

Elina Hytönen-Ng is an ethnomusicologist and cultural researcher. She holds a docent title in ethnomusicology at the University of Turku, Finland. She has not only specialized in research on performance venues in the contemporary British jazz scene but also studied musical experiences related to contemporary shamanism. She has been an academic visitor at the Faculty of Music, University of Oxford, and a visiting research fellow at King's College London. She was awarded a PhD in 2010 at the University of Eastern Finland (UEF) with Professor Steven Feld (University of New Mexico, United States) being the external examiner while professor Helmi Järviluoma-Mäkelä (UEF) was the supervisor. She is currently the primary investigator on a three-year project funded by Kone Foundation, focusing on lamenting rituals in contemporary Finnish society.

Helmi Järviluoma is Professor of Cultural Studies at the University of Eastern Finland and the Principal Investigator of ERC AdG "Sensory Transformations" (SENSOTRA). Her research spans the fields of sensory remembering, qualitative methodology (especially regarding gender), environmental cultural studies, music, sound and radio art, and fiction writing. Järviluoma is probably best known for her work in the field of soundscape studies. Decades of research on this topic culminated in the publication of *Acoustic Environments in Change* (2009). Currently, her research focuses on sensobiographies, as well as the themes of mobilities, aging, remembering, technologies, and displacement. Among her 180 publications, *Gender and Qualitative Methods* (2003/2010) continues to draw attention.

Ros Jennings is Professor in Cultural Studies, Director of the Centre for Women Ageing and Media (WAM), and Head of Postgraduate Research at the University of Gloucestershire, UK. She is a founder member of the European Network in Ageing Studies (ENAS), author of the *WAM Manifesto* (2012), and contributor to the UK Charter against Ageism and Sexism in the Media (launched October 3, 2013). She is coeditor with Abigail Gardner (2012) of *Rock On: Women, Ageing and Popular Music* and leader of the annual WAM International Summer School. Her research interests are older women and popular culture (in particular, popular music, television, and film).

Véro Leduc is an artist and engaged scholar as well as a professor in the Département de communication sociale et publique at Université du Québec à Montréal, Canada. She is the first Deaf university professor in Quebec and holds a PhD in Communication and an MA in Social Work. Associate researcher at (ACT), Testimonial Cultures, Groupe de recherche sur la médiation culturelle, Community and Differential Mobilities Cluster and Critical Disability Studies Working Group, her projects and practices are anchored in research creation as well as critical, feminist, queer, intersectional, crip, and Deaf perspectives. As a researcher at ACT, she is working on intersections of Deafhood and aging, especially regarding technologies and music.

Sonja Pöllänen is a PhD student of cultural anthropology in the "social and cultural encounters" doctoral program at the University of Eastern Finland. Simultaneously, she is working as a project researcher (2017–21) in an ERC adv. grant (GA 694893) project SENSOTRA. The project aims at producing new understandings of the changes in people's sensory environmental relationships in three European cities during a particular period in history, 1950–2020. Sonja's research interests are in anthropology of the senses and affect theory. Sonja is also a member and an affiliated student of ACT at the Concordia University.

Lisa Shaw is Professor of Brazilian Studies at the University of Liverpool, UK. She is author of the books *Carmen Miranda* (2013), *Tropical Travels: Brazilian Popular Performance, Transnational Encounters, and the Construction of Race* (2018), and *The Social History of the Brazilian Samba* (1999) and coauthor (with Stephanie Dennison) of the books *Popular Cinema in Brazil* (2004) and *Brazilian National Cinema* (2007). She leads the Cinema, Memory and Wellbeing (CMW) project, co-founded with Julia Hallam (Professor Emeritus, Department of Communication and Media, University of Liverpool), for which she was nominated for an AHRC-Wellcome Trust Medical Humanities Award. Together Lisa and Julia produced a CMW toolkit for carers, now used across the UK and Brazil, and edited the book *Movies, Music and Memory: Tools for Wellbeing in Later Life* (2020).

Jacqueline Waldock is a researcher at the University of Liverpool, UK. She previously studied Music at Lancaster University, UK, and went on to complete a doctorate at the University of Liverpool in Musicology and Composition. Her research focuses on sounds of everyday life, listening cultures and soundscape composition as an ethnographic tool. Her publications include "Hearing Urban Change" in *Auditory Cultural Reader* (2016); "Crossing the Boundaries: Community Composition and Sensory Ethnography" in *Senses and Society Journal* (2016); "Home" in the *Bloomsbury Handbook of the Anthropology of Sound* (2020); and "The Conflicting Sounds of Urban Regeneration in Liverpool" in the *Bloomsbury Handbook of Sonic Methodology* (2020).

INDEX

Note: Figures are indicated by page number followed by "f". Tables are indicated by page number followed by "t". Endnotes are indicated by the page number followed by "n" and the endnote number e.g., 20n1 refers to endnote 1 on page 20.

ABBA 86, 88t, 92, 93, 97
Active Ageing Index 8
Aden, Roger C. 166
affect 12, 13, 20, 34, 36, 37, 94
   and aging with music 202–4
affective selves
   empathetic listeners 86, 89–96
   and political selves 86
Afro-Trinidadians 12, 104, 109, 121, 123n1
"After the Gold Rush" (Young, Neil) 2
Ageing + Communication +Technologies (ACT) 3, 31, 35, 132, 188n1
ageing, *see* aging
ageism 22, 148, 155n6, 209
aging 1, 2, 7–9, 39, 106
   active 8
   age and 105, 109–112, 132
   and aging self 141–4
   biological 106
   cultural 106, 109, 121, 123n7, 148
   cultures of 9
   healthy 8, 130, 148
   memory and 3, 7, 9, 10
   music and 10–11, 139
   and musical inheritances 30, 141–4, 145–152
   physiological 9
   and popular music 3, 134
   self 141
   successful 8
   tensions of 145–152

Ahmed, Sara 83, 94, 163, 186, 187
Alderman, Dereck H. 124n15
Allahar, Anton L. 123n1
Allor, Michael 163
Allore, Heather G. 8
de Almeida, Joel 150
Alvin 104, 109, 110, 112, 117, 125n23
"Am Thimisis to onirou mou" (Legas, Vasilis) 87t, 93
American Sign Language (ASL) 161, 165, 167, 179, 185, 189n7, n9, n10
Andrews, Gavin J. 34, 190n15
Anglican Church congregation of Westmount 163
Anka, Paul 72
Antze, Paul 132
Appadurai, Arjun 202
Arden, Jann 167
"art-sign" 166
Astaire, Fred 90
Astral Weeks (van Morrison) 87t, 92
Au, Agnes 191n20
audism 172–3
auditory discrimination skills 172
aural-based music 168, 179
Australia 4, 5, 37, 51, 52, 67, 94
Austria 32, 84, 85
autobiographical memory 54, 91, 112
autobiography 18
autoethnography 18, 36
"automobile sanctuary" 147
the Aztecs 58n2

INDEX

Baars, Jan 34
Bahan, Ben 167, 189n11
Balkmar, Dag 177
Ballarò 81
Banks, Jack 178
Barad, Karen 7
Bardini, Thierry 123n4
Barrett, Anne E. 23, 24
Barthes, Roland 95
Bartlett, David Ely 172
bass instruments 174, 191n23
BBC Radio 2
   Ken Bruce Show 3
BBC Radio 4 2, 3, 10, 22, 31
   Desert Island Discs 3, 10
   Inheritance Tracks segments 205n3
Beach Boys 201
Beatles 28, 29
Beaunoyer, Elisabeth 152
Becca R. Levy 8
Behar, Ruth 18
Belafonte, Harry 64t, 68, 72
Belfast 90, 92
Bell, Jonathan 177
Bellerive, Karine 6
Bellugi, Ursula 166, 189n12
belonging 47, 185
   and collective memory 53
   through memories of Finnish childhoods 61
"belonging-in-between" 12, 61
Bennett, Andy 12, 24, 28, 29, 34, 46, 47, 52, 54, 56, 109, 134, 141, 123n6, 125n16, 155n5, 204
Bennett, Tony 88t, 90
Best, Katelyn E. 168
Big Bopper 49
"Big Truck" (Montano, Machel) 117–19, 122, 126n30
Bigand, Emmanuel 8
Biggs, Simon 6
Bijsterveld, Karin 34
Birkin, Jane 38
Bissonnette, Joëlle 162
"The Black Hills of Dakota" (Day, Doris) 155
"Black Man Feeling to Party" (Stalin, Black) 108, 114–15, 122, 125n24

"Black Velvet Band" (the Dubliners) 33
"blast" 112, 114
Blat, Josep 151
Blaxx 117, 121, 122
Bob Hope 155
Bocchi, Gianluca 62
Bocelli, Andrea 147, 155
body, embodiment 9, 13
bordering 62
   musical inheritance 65–72
borderscapes 62
   borders and 12
Born, Georgina 10
Boston 92
Boswell, Eve 36
Bourdieu, Pierre 5, 6, 7, 174
Brabender, Virginia A. 54
Brake, Michael 44
Brambilla, Chiarra 62
Brazil 129, 143, 144, 150, 151, 153, 210
Brown, Barry 93, 95
Brown, Julie 10
Bugental, Daphne B. 8
Bujold, Geneviève 164
Bull, Michael 147
Bush, Kate 46
"Buttons and Bows" (Bob Hope) 155

Cabot, Heath 96
Caine, Michael Sir 2
calypso 103, 107, 119–120, 124n9, 125n24
Canada 2, 4, 5, 32, 163, 188
care centers, care 11, 13, 134, 135, 142, 149, 152
Carmi, Elinor 151
carnival music 125n21
cars and music 176, 177, 201
Casey, Edouard 124n15, 126n29
Cash, Johnny 33
Catherine Degnen 144
Cavicchi, Daniel 141
"CC Rider" (Thorpe, Billy and the Aztecs) 49, 51–2, 58n1
Centre for Women, Ageing and Media (WAM) 22

INDEX

CESIE (European Centre of Studies and Initiatives) 82, 85, 98
De Chaine, Robert 20, 34, 36, 39
"Chantilly Lace" (Big Bopper) 49
chantsigne 167, 181
Chaudhury, Habib 75, 149–150
Chen, Wenhong 151
"chip" 125n27
"Chorus of the Hebrew Slaves", *see* "Va, pensiero" (Verdi, Giuseppe)
Christine and the Queens song 33
Churchill, Warren N. 166
Clark, Margaret 8, 134
club 108, 130, 150, 151, 201
cochlear implants 190n19, 191n20
Cohen, Leonard 28, 29, 134
Cohen, Sara 13, 105, 123n5, 123n6, 125n20, 131, 132, 133, 135, 139, 141, 142, 143, 154n1
collective music listening 4, 10, 136, 129, 154
collective self-therapy 43, 56
and soothing sociality 53–6
Collins, Michelle 143
color music 189n13
"Comme d'habitude" (François, Claude) 2
commonalities and affinities 170
concert space 201
Conway, Martin A. 144
Cook, Nicholas 10
Cotton, Shelia R. 151
Cottrell, Stephen 10
counterculture 29, 30
Craven, Eric 163, 189n9
  Digital Literacy Program 163, 164
Creech, Andrea 8
Creedence Clearwater Revival 49, 52–3
Cripps, Jody H. 161, 166, 167, 181, 182, 189n10, 192n28
Crosby, Bing 155
Cruikshank, Margaret 24, 25
culture 3, 5, 19, 37, 46, 51, 70, 118
  car stereo 177
  Deaf 161, 180, 190n16
Czitrom, Daniel J. 201

Dan, Maximus 125n23
dance 11, 30, 32, 37, 107, 121, 124n13, 169, 180, 200, 204
  age and aging 109–110
"Dancing Queen" (ABBA) 86, 88t, 92, 93, 97
Darrow, Alice-Ann 172
Day, Doris 26, 29
"Day-O" ("The Banana Boat Song") (Belafonte, Harry) 64t, 68
"Dead Skunk" (Loudon Wainwright III, American) 87t, 90
Deaf communities
  ASL singers in US 185–6, 189n9
  experiences of music 179
  LSQ French 189n9
  in Montreal 11, 13
  and music 186
  music culture 180
  musicking in 161
  schooling 190n16
  singers 167, 182, 184, 190n19
  trajectories of 186
"Deaf music" 164, 167, 175, 179
Deaf musicking 163, 179
Deafhood 162, 186, 188n2
"deafness" 188n2
decline narrative 8, 146
Deferred Action for Childhood Arrivals (DACA) 119, 126n31
Degnen, Catherine 144, 148
dell'Agnese, Elena 62
Dennison, Stephanie 130
DeNora, Tia 46, 56, 83n 95, 141, 200, 204n1
  Music and Everyday Life 43, 45, 51
Derno, Maiken 204
Derrida, Jacques 6, 163
Desert Island Discs (BBC Radio 4 program) 3, 10
"Desi Girl" (Mahadevan, Shankar) 2
Despeyroux, Charly 167
"Differentology" (Garlin, Bunji) 120
van Dijck, José 34, 75, 83, 91, 104, 110, 115, 140, 201
  concept of human memory 115
Dion, Céline 167, 184
disorientation 186, 187

djouk 107, 124n13
"Doh Back Back" (Sparrow, Mighty) 111, 116, 122, 125n28
"doing signs" 164
"doing voice" 164
Dolci, Danilo 82
"Don't Fence Me In" (Crosby, Bing) 155
Donegan, Lonnie 2
Donen, Stanley 90
drums 172, 174
the Dubliners 33
"Duerme Negrito" (Sosa, Mercedes) 87t, 90
Duffett, Mark 176, 177

Eastern Orthodox Church 72
Edelman, Joshua 21
Edwards, Jane 8
Eidsheim, Nina 175
"Eight Days a Week" (Beatles) 28, 29
Electric Light Orchestra 46
Elliott, Richard 134
embodiment 13, 183, 200–2
emotion 12, 17, 18, 19, 20, 30, 34, 44–6, 86, 89, 93, 97, 106, 131, 144, 149, 150, 200, 202, 204
emotional investment 92
empathetic listeners 86, 89–96
England 5, 38, 131, 135, 154n1
English-to-ASL songs 181
"ethereal hearth" 201
Evans, Peter 51
the Eurythmics 34

Facebook 62, 92, 112, 115, 116, 190n17
Fairley, Jan 149
Fallon, April E. 54
feelings 44, 47, 53, 56, 180, 203
  of belonging 53–4
  emotions 12, 19, 33, 44, 47, 53, 56, 180
  of isolation 56
  and memories 33
  and remembering 36
Ferreira, Susan M. 151
Ferreri, Laura 8

Finland 4, 11, 12, 63, 77n11, 77n4, 78n16
  "belongingness in-between" 61–2
  bordering and borderscapes 65–72
  relational technologies and memory objects 72–5
  workshop 62–5
Finnegan, Ruth 44
The Hidden Musicians 44
Finnish Broadcasting Company (FBC) 72, 78n15
"The First Time Ever I Saw Your Face" (Flack, Roberta) 2
Flack, Roberta 2
Fono 77n10
Forman, Murray 13, 98, 134, 141, 143, 146, 147, 148, 149, 177, 198, 98
France 32, 182, 184
François, Claude 2
Freedman, Jesse 20
French-to-LSF (*langue des signes française*) songs 181
Frennaux, Richard 56
Frith, Simon 43, 46, 47, 50, 51, 54, 155n5, 168, 179
"Funny Girl" (Streisand, Barbra) 155
the Fureys 33

Gainsbourg, Serge 38
Gallaudet University 180, 182, 191n27
Gardner, Abigail 12, 20, 24, 37, 38, 125n16, 125n18, 134
Garland-Thomson, Rosemarie 163, 183–4
Garlin, Bunji 120
Garofalo, Reebee 46
Garro, Diego 189n13
Gaucher, Charles 190n16
A Gay Festival of Light Classical Music 67f
Gaynor, Gloria 94
Geerts, Evelien 11
generation 5, 6, 12, 19, 25, 26, 33, 39, 46, 97, 140, 142
  of Deaf people 181
  exchange 47
  gap 26
  memory 46

multigeneration 28
postwar 28–9
time and 36
traits 46
Germany 32, 65, 77n11
Getz, Stan 49
Gibbs, Anna 83, 89, 94
Giebel, Clarissa 143, 149, 150
Gilberto, Astrud 49
"The Girl from Ipanema" (Gilberto, Astrud and Getz, Stan) 49
Given, Jock 151
Glennie, Dame Evelyn 175
"The Good, the Bad and the Ugly" (Ennio Morricone) 88t, 96
Goodall, Harry A., Jr 6
Goodman, Jordan 164
Gouk, Penelope 8
Graffition Via Roma, Palermo 82f
Gras, Dimanche 113, 126n30
Green, Ben 53, 54
"Green, Green Grass of Home" (Jones, Tom) 137, 142
Grenier, Amanda 34
Grenier, Line 3, 4, 7, 9, 13, 20, 34, 123n4, 125n16, 134, 148, 149, 162, 189–190n14, 198
Grist, Hannah 18, 22, 30, 32
grooving 175, 200
Groovy music 125n27
Groovy music 125n27
Grossberg, Lawrence 10, 105, 123n3, 192n29, 199, 202, 203
Growing Old Disgracefully 2, 3, 22, 23–4, 29, 30, 31, 32, 35, 37
Guilbault, Jocelyne 12, 123n1, 125n17, 126n33
guitar 52, 53, 114, 167, 173
Guitton, Matthieu J. 152
Gullette, Margaret Morganroth 7, 22, 146, 148, 152–3, 162
Guzman-Castillo, Maria 130

Haenfler, Ross 24
Halberstam, Jack 24, 26
Hale, Timothy M. 151
Hall, Stuart 188n3
Hallam, Julia 130, 131, 142, 148, 153

Hallam, Susan 8
Han, Min Wha 166
Hanson, Pauline 94
Haraway, Donna 7
"Have You Ever Seen the Rain" (Creedence Clearwater Revival) 49t, 52–3
"healthy aging" 8, 130, 145, 148, 149, 152, 153
hearing interpreters 167
Hebblethwaite, Sharon 56
Hehman, Jessica A. 8
Heidegger, Martin 106, 112
Hekkinen 144
Helismaa, Reino 64t
Heller, George N. 172
"Hello" (Kes) 115–16, 122
Hellwig, Otto 151
Helsinki 63, 70, 77n5
Hennion, Antoine 10, 11, 63, 83, 122, 123n4, 126n34, 188n4
Henson, Donna F 6
héritage 5
Herman, David 171
Hesmondhalgh, David 141
"Hey, That's No Way to Say Goodbye" (Cohen, Leonard) 28
Hill, Sarah 21
Hintzen, Percy 123n1
histories 6, 20, 89, 110, 131, 172–3
Hodkinson, Paul 47
Hoelscher, Steven 124n15
Holmes, Jessica A. 161, 175, 180, 186, 191n20
Homan, Shane 51
Horowitz, Jason 81
Houle, Sara 164
human aging, *see* aging
Humphries, Tom 161, 180, 185
Hunte, Angela 120
Huyssen, Andreas 105
Hyltén-Cavallius, Sverker 75, 170
Hytönen-Ng, Elina 5, 12, 62, 77n10

"I, Yi, Yi, Yi, Yi [I Like You Very Much]" (Miranda, Carmen) 137
"I Have Heard of a City Up Yonder" (Lvovich, Aleksandr) 71

"I'm Not in Love" (10cc) 46
"I've Got You under My Skin" (Sinatra, Frank) 155
"I Will Survive" (Gaynor, Gloria) 88t, 92, 94
identity 3, 22, 27, 28, 45, 122, 153, 188n3, 189n8
  cultural 28, 70
  Deaf 188n2
  professional 92
Inheritance Tracks 1, 4–5, 17, 44, 61
  bordering 65–72
  in challenging times 56–7
  choosing 19
  collective self-therapy 53–6
  feminist approaches 18
  Growing Old Disgracefully 21–3
  logistics and dynamics of 62–5
  as process 6–7
  reflexivity in 26–30
  as research method 2–4
  shared memories 46–50
  sharing 197
  WAM International Summer Schools 30
  women and 17
  workshops 9
Innes-Brown, Hamish 191n20
Intangible Cultural Heritage 154n3
Ireland 32, 42, 84, 85, 90, 142
"Isoisän olkihattu" ("Grandfather's Straw Hat") 64t, 68, 77n10
Istvandity, Lauren 10, 24, 92, 99
Italy 92, 143, 190n16
Itard, Jean-Marc Gaspard 172

Jaffe, Rivke 112
"Jamono" (Daara J Family) 88t, 92
Janata, Petr 104
Jankowski, Katherine 185
Jansen, Bas 47
"A Jardineira" (Silva, Orlando) 140
Järviluoma, Helmi 5, 12, 62, 64, 69, 70, 77n9, n10, 104, 125n20, 143
"Je t'aime, moi non plus" (Gainsbourg, Serge) 38
"Jean and Dinah" (Sparrow, Mighty) 113–14, 121, 122

Jennings, Ros 2, 3, 17, 18, 20, 22, 24, 28, 30, 32, 37, 38, 85, 125n16, n18, 134, 205n2
Jerusalem 77n7
Jouvè 107, 110, 115, 124n12
Julie-Élaine 189n14
"Just Because I'm a Woman" (Dolly Parton) 140, 155

Kaiser, Marc 179
Karelia 63, 77n4
Karelian Isthmus 68, 69, 71, 72
"Karjalan Kunnailla" ("On the Hills of Karelia") 69
Kassab, Sera 168, 171
Kassabian, Anahid 45, 83
Katz, Stephen 8, 34, 123n7, 125n16, 149, 199
Kaufman, Sharon 8, 134
Keenan, Elizabeth 24, 25
Keil, Charles 141
Ken Bruce Show (BBC Radio 2) 3
Kennaway, James G. 8
Kertzer, David I 28
Kes 115–16, 122
Keynes, Milton 44
Khabra, Gurdeep 154n1
Khaled, "Aïcha" 87t, 92
Khalili, Laleh 107, 124n8, n14
Killman 189n12
Kim, Christine Sun 180, 184
"King of the Road" (Miller, Roger) 49
Kirchgaessner, Stephanie 82
Klima, Edward S. 166, 189n12
Kontos, Pia 143
Kreutz, Gunter 8
Kriebernegg, Ulla 36
Krumhansl, Carol L. 18, 39
Kuhn, Annette 3, 24–5, 28, 29
Kuntz, Matthew 167
Kupari, Helena 71
Kurin, Richard 154n3
Kurki, Tuulikki 72

LaBelle, Brandon 97
Ladd, Paddy 185, 188n2, 190n16
Laforest, Suzanne 167, 168, 171
Laine, Jussi 62

INDEX 217

Lambek, Michael 132
Laroche, Julie 164
Lauantain toivotut levyt (*Saturday's Most Wanted Tracks*) 72, 73, 74, 76, 77n14
Leduc, Véro 13, 173, 185, 189n9, 190n16, 191n20, 192n28
Lefebvre, Henri 83, 98
Legas, Vasilis 87t, 93
"Leh Go" (Blaxx) 117, 121, 122
Lehman, Eric T 56
Levy, Becca R. 8
Lewis, J. Parrish 186
Lezotte, Chris 177
"Like Ah Boss" (Montano, Machel) 118, 122
listening 12, 34, 35, 38, 45, 47, 49
Liverpool 154n4
  community care centres 13
  Inheritance Tracks workshops 132, 149, 154n4
Lloyd, Rachel 151
Loaf, Meat 28
location 11, 13, 31, 39, 48, 200–2
Loeffler, Summer 169
Lumsden, Karen 177
Lupton, Deborah 21
Lutheran Church 71, 72
Lvovich, Aleksandr 71
Lyonblum, Ely 181, 182

MacDonald, Raymond 8
MacFarlane, Brian 117
Madonna 134
"Madureira Chorou" ("Madureira Cried") 150, 155n8
Maffesoli, Michel 55
Mahadevan, Shankar 2
Maierhofer, Roberta 36
Maija Alftan 74
Maler, Annabel 161
Malraux, André 123, 126n35
mandolin 73
marcha carnavalesca (carnival march) 155n8
Mardi Gras 125n22
Marley, Bob 201
Marozeau, Jeremy 191n20

Marschall, Sabine 75
Marsh, Charity 166
Marshall, Barbara A 8, 9, 155n6
Martin, Peter J 24
Martin, Wendy 8
Martyn, John 29
Marwick, Arthur 29
Massumi, Brian 202
Mastodons 120, 126n32
materiality 5, 73, 76, 141
"mattering maps" 105, 123n3
May, Jon 24, 39n1
McBurnie, David 114
McDonald, Raymond 155n5
McHugh, Kevin E. 155n6
McQueen, Helena 8
McRobbie, Angela 168
mediations 3, 4, 10, 46, 123n4, 177, 191n22
Mehdi 179
"Meksikon pikajuna" ("Mexico Express") 64t, 73
memory 1, 3, 9, 105, 108–9, 132
  and aging 4, 11, 105, 148
  autobiographical 54
  collective 53
  cultural 131
  and emotion 17
  generational 46
  making 3, 9, 18, 170, 186
  music and 8, 105, 197
  objects 72–5, 91
  vernacular 140, 144
memoryscaping 4, 170, 173, 185
Men Explain Things to Me: And Other Essays (Solnit, Rebecca) 89
Mesch, Gustavo 151
methodology 1, 7, 10, 11, 84, 143, 150, 154
"Mexico Express" (Mohr, Gerhard) 77n13
Miell, Dorothy 155n5
Milestone, Katie 177
Miller, Roger 49
Miranda, Carmen 131
(mis)fitting 185
  fitting and 183
Mitchell, Joni 8, 29

Mitchell, Laura 8
"mix tapes" 47, 134
Moglen, Helene 35, 39
Mohr, Gerhard 77n13
Monarch, Soca 106, 107
"Monia vuosia" ("Many Merciful Years", Bortnjanski, Dimitri) 71
Monin, Joan K. 8
Montano, Machel 117–19, 120, 122, 126n30
Montreal Oral School for the Deaf (MOSD) 171, 172, 190n8
Montreal 163, 191n25
  Atwater Library and Computer Centre 163, 189n6
  Deaf adults in 13
  Deaf communities, musicking in 161
  Inheritance Tracks workshop 163
Moore, Allan F 46
Moore, Butch 36
Morricone, Ennio 83
van Morrison 92
Moulin, Chris J. A. 144
Mouskouri, Nana 38
Moussard, Aline 8
Movies, Music and Memory (Hallam and Shaw) 142
"Mr. Blue Sky" (Electric Light Orchestra) 46
MuchMusic 179, 184, 191n24
Muggleton, David 44
"multi-modal connectivities" 198, 205n2
music 1, 10–11, 44, 76, 103, 105, 106–7
  autobiographical memories and 18
  carnival 125n21
  and cinema 130–1
  contagion 12, 34
  and cultural identity 28
  cultural transmission 18
  culture 118
  emotion 44–6
  experience 54
  feeling and remembering 36–8
  gender 29
  generation gap 26–30
  and genre 29, 200

groovy 115, 125n27
inheritance 20, 61, 133, 134–5, 141–2
listening 130–4
media 2
memory 18, 24, 34, 39, 43, 56, 82, 83
multitemporal interconnectivity of 28
plural forms 200
taste, interconnectedness of 27
therapeutic qualities 44
therapy 43
women and 30
music inheritance 61, 134–5
  bordering, in workshop 65–72
  Inheritance Tracks Workshops 135–8
"musical occasioning" 93
musicking 10, 132, 162, 188, 200
  in Deaf Communities 161–3
  diversified acts of 165–170
  significant moments of 170–1
Musiikkiraita (music track) 5
Musique Plus 178, 179, 191n24
Mussolini, Benito 81
"My Mammy" (Jolson, Al) 140, 155, 146
"My Old Man's a Dustman" (Donegan, Lonnie) 2
"My Own Dear Galway Bay" (Gary, John) 140, 142, 155
Myerhoff, Barbara 8, 134

Nabucco (Verdi, Giuseppe) 64t, 75
narratives 3, 6, 24, 46, 86, 91, 94, 95, 106, 131, 132, 141, 143, 145, 148, 197, 199, 202, 204
neoliberal "active society" 8, 124n11, 149
neuroprosthetic devices 191n20
Ng, Reuben 5, 8
Nielsen, Harriet B 20
"Nightmare" (Shaw, Artie) 2
nongovernmental organizations (NGOs) 12, 81, 85
Norander, Stephanie 166
Nowak, Raphaël 45

INDEX

"O Leãozinho" (Veloso, Caetano) 87t, 92
"O Mio Bambino Caro" (Puccini, Giacomo) 143, 155
Obama, Barack 126n31
"Odnozvutjno gremit kolono" (Lvovich, Aleksandr) 71
O'Hara, Kenton 93, 95
"Oh! Sweet Nuthin " (Velvet Underground) 87t, 92, 93
"Olen kuullut on kaupunki tuolla" ("Song about Heaven") 71
Olick, Jeffrey K. 162
"the Only Living Boy in New York" (Simon and Garfunkel) 87t
"Only the Lonely" (Orbison, Roy) 155
Ono, Hiroshi 151
"Ooh Poo Pa Doo" (Thorpe, Billy and the Aztecs) 58n2
Oppedisano, Suzanna 164
Oralism 172–4, 188, 190n16
"Orient Express" (Mohr, Gerhard) 77n13
Orlando, Leoluca 82

Padden, Carol 180, 185
Pai, Manacy 23, 24
Palermo 81
  workshop 81, 82, 84–6, 87–8t, 93
  Inheritance Tracks in 84–6
Paquette 190n17
"Party Done" 120
party music 12, 106, 108, 112, 123n4, 125n21
"party songs" 125n24
Passeron, Jean-Claude 6, 174
Patrimoine 5
"peak music experience" 53
Peel, John 86, 93
Le people de l'oeil (*The People of the Eye*) 191n26
percussion instruments 172
performance 10, 37, 46, 47, 56, 106, 107, 117, 132, 146, 149, 153, 166, 180, 181, 187
Perityt musiikkiraidat 76
"personhood" 150
Pfahl, Michael E. 166

Piaf, Édith 38
place 12, 17, 29, 65, 71, 93, 97, 108, 144, 165
Playboyz panyard 117
Plessow, Eric(h) 77n13
Pöllänen, Sonja 5, 12, 62
Pollock, Timothy P. Jr. 166
Popular Music Heritage, Cultural Memory and Cultural Identity (POPID) 131, 154n1
Powell, Jane 90
power relations 8, 9
"power soca" 118, 125n27
Presley, Elvis 147, 155
Prins, Jacomien 8
Priyanka Chopra, Jonas 2
Puccini, Giacomo 140

Quan-Haase, Anabel 151
"Que Sera Sera" (Day, Doris) 26, 29
Quebec sign language (LSQ) 161, 165, 189n7

radio 2, 3, 10, 28, 31, 201
Radstone, Susannah 83, 97
Rakowski, Sonja K. 104
Rathbone, Clare J. 144
Ratzenböck, Barbara 36
Rautavaara, Tapio 64t, 68, 70, 77n10
"Rave On" (Buddy Holly) 155
Ray, Charles 58n1
recollection 74, 95, 97, 98, 144, 162, 166, 170, 171, 178–9, 185, 199
Reddock, Rhoda 124n11
Redmond, Rebecca 23, 24
Regev, Motti 84
reminiscence 17–18, 35–8, 86, 90, 130, 131, 134, 145, 149, 152, 153, 154n4, 201, 202
"reminiscence bumps" 18
Renan, Ernest 141
Rholehr, Gordon 124n9
Ribière, Mireille 95
Ricoeur theory 94
Rio de Janeiro 150
Robbins, Joyce 162
Roberts, Les 133, 154n1
Robinson, Laura. 151

Rogers, Ian 46, 54
Roivainen, Irene 77n9
Romania 32
Romo, Vanessa 126n31
Rosenblum, Ely 161, 166, 167, 181, 182, 189n10, 192n28
Roudinesco, Elisabeth 6, 163
Rowles, Graham D. 75
Royal Wedding (film) 90
Rubio, Tristana Martin 8, 24, 56
Rudder, David 119
Russian Orthodox Church 72
Ruud, Even 97

Sabat, Steven 143
Sacks, Harvey, 77n9
Salvini, Matteo 82
"sans humanité" calypso 124n9
Saturday Live (BBC Radio) 2
Saunders, Daz 165, 167, 171, 192n28
Sawchuk, Kim 3, 7, 9, 13, 20, 34, 149
Sayago, Sergio 151
Schlagers, Finnish 69, 72, 73, 77n11
Schmitt, Pierre 172, 182, 184, 187, 189n9
Schubert, Emery 191n20
Schulz, Jeremy 151
Scott, James W. 62
Scully, Liz 164
Second World War 76
Seepersad, Randy 125n17
Seigworth, Greg 36
A Senior Moment (Grenier, Line and Valois-Nadeau, Fannie) 4, 7, 9
Shank, Barry 44
shared memories 43
sharing 1–2, 9, 12, 13, 20, 30, 31, 34, 37, 44, 46, 51, 197–200
Shaw, Artie 2
Shaw, Lisa 13, 130, 131, 135, 143, 148, 149, 150, 153
"She's a Rainbow" (Rolling Stones) 87t, 89
Sheller, Mimi 177
Shields, Rob 55
Sicilian Workshop 81
Sicily 4, 81
sign-based musicking 167

signed language (*chantsignes*) 181, 189n10
"signed music" 164, 167, 180–2
"signed song" 164, 189n11
"Siipirikkoinen" (Trio, Cuulas) 64t
Silva, Orlando 140
Sílvio Caldas 140
Skjoldager-Nielsen, Kim 21
Small, Anita 161, 166, 167, 181, 182, 189n10, 192n28
Small, Christopher 10, 132, 162, 166, 167, 182, 200
Smith, Kimberly 146
Smith, Nicola 47
Smith, Patti 2
Smolar, Andrew I. 54
Social Sciences and Humanities Research Council (SSHRC) of Canada 188n1
Sohn, Christopher 62
Solera, Temistocle 77n7
Solnit, Rebecca 89, 98
Solomon 172
song worlds 12, 83
"soothing sociality" 12, 44
Sophie Dupéré 152
Sosa, Mercedes 87t, 90
"sound souvenirs" 34
soundtrack 5, 10, 43, 96, 99, 107, 119, 142, 170, 176, 182, 203
Soviet Union 77n4
space 6, 10, 12, 18, 21, 24, 26, 34, 35, 37, 48
"A Spaceman Came Travelling" (Chris de Burgh) 140, 142, 149, 155
Spanu, Michael 179
Sparrow, Mighty 111, 113–14, 116, 121
Spotify 31, 32, 36, 133, 135, 143, 150
Stalin, Black 108, 114, 125n24
"Stand by Your Man" (Wynette, Tammy) 140, 155
Stern, Michael J. 151
Stevens, Catherine J. 191n20
Stevenson, Andrew 124n15
Stoffelen, Arie 62
stories 6, 10, 13, 32, 34, 36, 45, 48, 50, 54

storytelling 4, 12, 113–120
  and disrupting borders 81
  "doing of memory" 112–13
Straus, Joseph N. 191n26
Streisand, Barbra 155
"Sugar Bush" (Boswell, Eve) 36
"Summer Holiday" (Richard, Cliff) 155
"Sunrise" (Simply Red) 88t, 89
Surr, Claire Alice 143, 144
Susan Crafts 141
"Suspicious Minds" (Elvis Presley) 147, 155
Sutton, Julie P. 43
Suutari, Pekka 70
Sweden 170
"Sweet Dreams Are Made of This" (the Eurythmics) 34
Szary, Amilhat 62

"Talkin' Bout a Revolution" (Chapman, Tracy) 88t, 92
"technologies of self" 43
temporality 24
10cc (rock band) 46
testimonies 4
Theater of Music Optics (Zorn, John) 189n13
therapy 20, 34
  soft 54
  group 54
Thormahlen, Wiebke 8
Thorpe, Billy 49, 51–2, 58n1
Thrift, Nigel 24
Tickell, Kathryn 37
Tillmann, Barbara 8
"Tilted" (Christine and the Queens song) 33
time 4, 10, 21, 24, 26, 30, 31, 34, 36, 39, 43, 44, 50, 52, 55, 56
  and space 12, 18, 37, 48
"Time to Say Goodnight" (Bocelli, Andrea) 147, 155
TimeSpace 18, 24, 28
Toivelauluja ("wished songs") 69
Tom Jones 142
Tomic, Stefan T. 104
Tondo, Lorenzo 82

"Too Young to Soca" (Montano, Machel) 126n30
"Top of the World" (Carpenters) 88t, 94, 95
Townsley, Eleanor 106, 124n14
Trentalange, Mark 8
"Trini to De Bone" (Rudder, David) 119
Trinidad and Tobago 12, 103
Trio, Cuulas 64t
Tropics of Discourse : Essays in Cultural Criticism (White, Hayden) 124n10
Trotta, Felipe 204
Trouillot, Michel-Rolph 105
Trump, Donald 119, 126n31
Tubular Bells / War of the Worlds Mike Oldfield/Jeff Wayne 49, 52
van der Tuin, Iris 11
Turkle, Sherry 75
Turner, Victor 21
Turner, William Wolcott 172
Twigg, Julia 8

UK 4, 22, 32, 83, 129, 138, 149, 153, 165
  care settings 152
  music performances 153
UNECE/European Commission 8
UNESCO 154n3
United States 4, 103–4, 172, 176, 177, 182
  ASL signers in 185
  signed songs 181
Urbania 190n17
Urry 176

"Va, pensiero" (Verdi, Giuseppe) 65, 73, 74, 77n14
Vakimo, Sinikka 61, 62
Valois-Nadeau, Fannie 3, 7, 9, 13, 20, 34, 123n4, 125n16, 134, 148, 149, 162, 198
Vameste, Dominique 62
Varvarigou, Maria 8
Veditz, George 191n26
Véro Leduc 164, 184
Vesijärvi Library Hall 62, 77n6

violin 73
visual music 189n13
Vroomen, Laura 47

Wachtel 124n15
Wadleigh, Michael 46
Wainwright, Loudon III 90
Waldock, Jacqueline 131, 136, 137, 142, 143, 147, 148, 153
"Walking the Streets in the Rain" (Moore, Butch) 36
Walsh, Margaret 177
Washburne, Christopher 204
watching music (videos) 178
"The Water of Tyne" (Tickell, Kathryn) 37
"We Ready for De Road" (Garlin, Bunji) 120, 121
"West Side Story: Act 1: America" (Bernstein, Leonard) 155
Western 96, 97
WhatsApp 112
"When You Were Sweet Sixteen" (the Fureys) 33
White, Daniel 202
White, Hayden 124n10
Williams, Dianne 125n17

Wilson, Graeme 155n5
Wilson, Viv 190n15
"wine" 124n13
Wintour, Patrick 82
Witcher, Pamela 182, 192n28
women 3, 12, 17
  and musical inheritances 30, 31–5
Woodward, Kathleen 18
World Health Organization (WHO) 8
"Wuthering Heights" (Bush, Kate) 46

Yates, Simeon J. 151
"You Are My Sunshine," (Cash, Johnny) 33
"You're All the World to Me" (Bennett, Tony) 88t, 90
Young, Iris Marion 170, 173
Young, Laurel 56
Young, Neil 2, 56
Young, Stephanie L. 166
Youssouf, Hodan 192n28
YouTube 64, 75, 92, 112, 133, 135, 137, 143, 150, 151, 178

Zelizer 166
Zournazi 202
Zupnik, Justin A. 18, 39

www.ingramcontent.com/pod-product-compliance
Lightning Source LLC
Chambersburg PA
CBHW062219300426
44115CB00012BA/2140